Sylvia Patterson is one of pop journalism's best-known voices. Born in Scotland, she moved to London aged twenty to join *Smash Hits* as Staff Writer, going on to freelance for *NME*, *The Face*, *Glamour*, *Q*, the *Guardian*, *Sunday Times* and many other publications across the UK and US. Her 2016 debut memoir *I'm Not with the Band* was shortlisted for the Costa Biography Award and won BBC Radio 1's Annie Nightingale's Book of the Year. Her 2023 follow-up *Same Old Girl* documented her tragic-comic mid-life misadventures through the lens of a cancer diagnosis. With Tyler James, she co-wrote his best-selling 2021 Amy Winehouse memoir *My Amy: The Life We Shared* (a *Sunday Times* Book of the Year).

Also by Sylvia Patterson

I'm Not with the Band
Same Old Girl

With Tyler James

My Amy: The Life We Shared

I'M NOT WITH THE ~~BAND~~ MAN

Sylvia Patterson

FLEET

First published in Great Britain in 2026 by Fleet

3 5 7 9 10 8 6 4

A CIP catalogue record for this book
is available from the British Library.

Hardback ISBN 978-0-3497-2807-0
Trade paperback ISBN 9780349728087

Typeset in Caslon by M Rules
Printed and bound in Great Britain by
Clays Ltd, Elcograf S.p.A.

Papers used by Fleet are from well-managed forests
and other responsible sources.

Fleet
An imprint of
Little, Brown Book Group
Carmelite House
50 Victoria Embankment
London EC4Y 0DZ

The authorised representative
in the EEA is
Hachette Ireland
8 Castlecourt Centre
Dublin 15, D15 XTP3, Ireland
(email: info@hbgi.ie)

An Hachette UK Company
www.hachette.co.uk

www.littlebrown.co.uk

CONTENTS

'Yeah, I'll tell you what you can do with
your eye teeth and your job ... you can
take that mail and that franking machine
and all that other rubbish I have to go
about with, and you can stuff 'em right up
your arse!'

Jimmy, *Quadrophenia* (1979)

PROLOGUE

THIS IS THE MODERN WORLD

Up on stage in an Amsterdam arena, the million-album-selling, No. 1 troubadour Dermot Kennedy is doing everything in his power to not appear to be a million-selling, No. 1 troubadour. Wearing a tie-dyed denim jacket and paint-splatter-effect jogging pants, he could be the cap-doffing busker he once was on the streets of Dublin, acoustic guitar dangling on a strap by his hips. His hands are busy, held in a prayer sign of gratitude as four thousand glitter-eyed fans swoon, sob and cheer at the close of each of his mournful, melancholy ballads. Teenage girls fill the front rows, offering up sacramental gifts to the Bambi-eyed, shaven-headed Irishman: huge origami hearts in white, pink and yellow. It's late 2019 and pop culture is now dominated by the lonesome troubadour, a phenomenon risen in the wake of the almighty Ed Sheeran, with the evidently central requirements of relatability, sincerity and authenticity. They are, they're ultimately saying, not pop stars at all, they're ordinary, *just like you*. Dermot, though, unlike the also then-rising Lewis Capaldi (the comedy Scotsman self-described as 'the male Adele'), doesn't do jokes. Instead, as the audience listens in silence, he gives each of his powerfully sung, emotive songs a grave explanatory backstory.

'This is a song about trying to retain your hope and your love of love,' he weeps, soon declaring 'darkness won't endure' and imploring before each new number, 'if you know it, please sing with me!' Amsterdam sings with him, mass sing-alongs you might hear at an *actual* Mass, giving Chris Martin a run for his communion money as today's Vicar of Mindful Pop.

Earlier that day we'd spoken in a hotel foyer, the measured twenty-seven-year-old proving unexpectedly withering over the culture he'd newly arrived in. 'There's a lot of bullshit out there, a lot of fake, vacuous silliness,' he declared, seeing the rise of the earnest singer/songwriter as the antidote to often-soulless contemporary culture. He despaired over a music industry prone to 'shortcuts', to labels following the money, who sign new artists 'who don't even have music yet, just viable products with a marketing team.' The middle-class son of a banker dad specialising in IT, he was wearing huge headphones tuned to *New York Times* podcast 'The Daily', keen for updates on 'Trump's impeachment – I listen to podcasts all the time.' Podcasts, for Dermot, like so many of his generation, had overtaken music's once vital function, as a prism to an alternative world, to enlightening voices throughout culture, art, history, comedy, politics. 'Long-form podcasts, two, three-hour conversations, people aren't stupid,' he confirmed. 'A friend of mine reckons there's gonna be a real cultural awakening.'

Dermot, like everyone, was a product of his time. He arrived via the Spotify algorithm Discover Weekly (effectively today's A&R scout), which compiles playlists on the 'if you like that, you'll like this' basis (his self-uploaded music being a bit like Ed Sheeran's). Ambitious and dedicated, his pre-show routine eschewed the traditional temptations of a booze-berserk rider for a performance-enhancing regime: rigorous vocal warm-up exercises (his professional opera-singing vocal coach was with him on the road) and a blood-thinning aspirin as relaxant. His girlfriend also travelled with him, offering her services as a professional yoga/Pilates instructor and physiotherapist. It was all *incredibly sensible*. 'It is,' he agreed. 'Because living on a bus for months isn't beneficial for your mind, or body.'

Dermot Kennedy's mission, it turned out, was to be beneficial in every way, as he reminded us once more from the stage in Amsterdam. Towards the end of this relentlessly sombre show, this handsome young man we would once have called a pop star urged the devoted to close their eyes, as if in prayer. 'This song captures a place that to me represents home and comfort and safety,' he beseeched. 'Join me in that, even close your eyes, go to wherever is for you warmth and home . . .' Throughout the crowd, blind young people were now clutching onto each other like refugees on a storm-tossed lifeboat. As nights out go, it was emotional. What it wasn't was anything whatsoever to do with rock'n'roll . . .

Late November 2019 and it finally felt undeniable: this thing we'd always known as the rock'n'roll spirit was truly, this time, *finished*. It wasn't so much the sound – there will always be loud, incendiary, euphorically anthemic music – as the kind of singular character who dominated pop culture for decades. It's nothing to do with politics – today we're *bombarded* by politics, by earnest on-and-off-stage pronouncements, by constant, furious flag-waving at the ills of our volatile, polarised, horrifically violent world. No, it's the disappearance of the kind of maverick personality I'd been consistently thrilled, boggled and amused by, both growing up through the seventies and eighties and through the japes of a lifetime's music journalism, an evolving lineage of eccentric, outré, often wayward creative characters, many fronting bands, many so huge they redefined the nature of pop itself. Today, they've been fully eclipsed by the solo, strident, in-control female pop star (impressive and often dazzling as they are, none are what we might call mentalists), the high-glam hip-hop/R&B star and the searingly driven, introspective singer/songwriter.

As I write, in the summer of 2025, seemingly enormous American singer/songwriter/influencer Alex Warren has been No. 1 in the UK for *twelve consecutive weeks* with the blubsome ballad 'Ordinary' (a US Billboard No. 1 for nine non-consecutive weeks), a TikTok, YouTube and Netflix reality TV star turned troubadour who, at twenty-three, is married, attends AA meetings to stay permanently sober (his mother was an alcoholic) and is a practising, Catholic-raised Christian whose music is inspired by what he calls 'worship-music'. Dermot Kennedy would definitely approve. (His twelve-week triumph broke records, as the US solo artist with the longest-running No. 1 single in UK chart history, after which he was ousted, for one week, by coquettish kitsch-pop temptress Sabrina Carpenter, and then *returned* to No. 1.)

Taylor Swift, meanwhile, remains the planet's foremost singer/songwriter colossus and while my admiration is enormous for the gifted pop giraffe, having spent an afternoon with her on her 2013 *Red* tour, I know the kind of visionary Tay Tay is: an exceptional talent, dressed as a glitteringly silhouetted cartoon, with the profit-led brain of a Chief Marketing Officer who defers only to her ultimate role as CEO of Taylor Swift Inc. She is acutely smart, coolly in control and when it comes to the numbers, as her equally business-brained buddy Ed Sheeran told me in 2014, 'Taylor Swift knows everything about everything.' She even brought me a cake, which she'd baked herself, a 'pumpkin loaf' which was gingery, moist and delicious, nestled inside a linen pouch-bag, which she'd also made herself, embroidered with a cartoon wooden spoon and a cow jumping over the moon. I was charmed, of course, even as I knew I was being played like an antique lute. This level of stratospherically high achiever, however, could never be my kind of pop star, an alien in ways I could never relate to, as opposed to the aliens I always could: the amateurs, dreamers and DIY schemers, the ones whose lives crackled with chaotic energy, often on the verge of falling apart, who skittered around the edge of reality, who were *funny*, who embraced bedlam and rejected control, who were the definition of the rock'n'roll spirit. Even if the term rock'n'roll itself is now a laughable anachronism, one which not only doesn't belong in the current decade, it belongs in the *previous century*: yesterday's cultural movement, as all cultural movements become – a twentieth century artform.

At age fifteen, waaaaay back in 1980, I didn't know much but I knew I wasn't sensible, pleasant, healthy or ambitious for anything except never having a 'proper' job. And I didn't want to be. I wanted excitement, weirdness and the Revolution, forever seeking out heroes who'd stick it to the Man in a class-warring culture dominated by mass unemployment, the miners' strike and global nuclear threat. In the early years of Margaret Thatcher's premiership I saw the Man v the Little People everywhere, and the Man always won, a worldview emerging where all forms of authority were not to be trusted, hierarchy and institution rejected, as was capitalism, monarchy and religion. I didn't care about money, or security, or the future, refusing the life 'choices' already mapped out for an early eighties schoolgirl at my average comprehensive in Scotland, where a 'careers' officer offered a lifetime's toil in banking, nursing, secretarial admin or the police force. Help!

There was scant thought involved, because it was simply unthinkable: I was the kind of person who would run away with the circus, escape what I saw as the trap of smalltown life, of forty years in monotonous work, of sudsy domesticity, of conventional thinking, of genuflecting compliance, of walking the same streets, seeing the same faces, thinking the same thoughts, every day, forever, until the inevitable degenerative disease and hideous death, unfulfilled on every level, at the age of seventy-one (at best).

There was, I always felt, *more* out there. Adventure. Travel. Romance. Magic. So many people to meet, so many striking characters in interesting shirts telling me unimaginably intriguing things. And music journalism brought me all of that, as an evangelical pop culture believer entrenched in the music industry from the mid-eighties onwards, through the nineties and into the noughties, when, at the turn of the millennium, everything changed as the Man upped his game. Pop culture was now the Global Entertainment Industry, incorporating Celebrity Culture (and its offshoots, talent shows and Reality TV), everything became a brand, marketing and sales teams ruled, 'the needs of the market' ran every show in town and language began 'pivoting' to ever-more corporate 'agile ninja leverage deliverables' baloney-speak.

From the early noughties onwards, as the digital age and free music emerged, pop culture began chasing its own tail, chasing the last hit, the last fleeting phenomenon, becoming a homogenous algorithmic flatline seeking not the new and risky but the bankable and dependable, the very opposite of the wayward outsider. From the mid-2010s onwards, my conversations with musicians and artists began alighting, often unprompted, on the sterilisation of culture, on the disappearance of the bonkers, reckless, free-wheelin' character and the rise of the shiny, focused, committee-bolstered pop star, accusations levelled (occasionally unfairly) at the titans of the day (all of whom remain titans today) – Ed Sheeran, Calvin Harris, Adele, Sam Smith, Katy Perry, Drake, Taylor Swift,

Rihanna – while the only guitar-ish band anywhere in the soaraway hit parade were weedy synth-pop yodellers Bastille.

Back in 2018, one day after the death of the Fall's Mark E. Smith, the Manic Street Preachers' feather-boa and frock-wearing bass player Nicky Wire leaned back in an armchair inside London's gilded Landmark Hotel. His mood was one of cultural alienation, boredom and despair. 'The chasm in British culture just gets wider and wider,' he lamented, absent-mindedly taking off and replacing his outsize rock star's shades. The Fall had been central heroes to the teenage Manics, who saw a kindred radical purpose in Mark E. Smith's self-proclaimed prole art threat.

'A lot of lights are going out,' he carried on. 'It does amalgamate into a torrent of anxiety and self-doubt. Which we used to thrive on!' Today's music gave him 'brain paralysation', the only contemporary musician he admired was America's 'fearless' art-rock stylist St Vincent, while the earnest troubadour phenomenon he ascribed to 'a generational soppy malaise'. Beneath his grey-and-white-striped jacket, a Bowie 'Heroes' T-shirt was visible, an image serving as a memento mori from the reign of the alien pop star. 'I think the best songs have been written,' he declared. 'There'll never be anything as good as "A Day in the Life". Technology just has changed everything. I'm not a Luddite, I just can't keep up. It's not about nostalgia, it's just what's fucking disappeared, it's about loss, more … a *thud*. With Bowie in particular. Fuck me we were lucky, to have that.'

At then-forty-nine years of age it wasn't just his generation: his fifteen-year-old daughter, behind her bedroom door, was playing Oasis, Abba and her dad's Sonic Youth CD collection. Seven years before the Oasis Live '25 tour was strikingly and ecstatically attended by the Young People, reminding millions worldwide what rock'n'roll used to sound, look and feel like (an introduction to millions more), she loved the forty-five-year-old Liam Gallagher.

'She loves Liam's interviews, the humour, the irreverence, the relating to a character,' he mused. 'There's a longing for something which is not available. Fucking hell, what's happened?'

Back in the nineties, an iconic Manics T-shirt featured a masked woman wielding a tommy-gun and the words, 'This Is the Only Answer to Rape'. Nicky Wire now had a new slogan: 'Do No Harm.' It was a startling evolution for the man who once wished death on his contemporaries, for a band whose early lyrics sneered over 'laughing' when John Lennon was shot, who were preoccupied with nihilism, depression, self-harm, alcoholism and suicide – with the tragedy at their core of the disappeared, self-mutilating talisman Richey Edwards (who infamously sliced '4REAL' into his forearm with a razor blade in '91). I contemplated how, in today's victim-centric, offence-seeking, post-joke world, there could never be a new Manics, they'd be cancelled by every student union in the country, banned from safe spaces and draped in screaming trigger warnings amid demands for 'heartfelt' apologies and attendance of awareness workshops.

'We would be shut down straight away, yes,' nodded Wire. 'Everything is of its time.'

In 2015, lifelong renegade and relentless Pope-botherer Sinéad O'Connor also despaired, over the contemporary female stars especially. 'People's reasons for making music have changed,' she was sure. 'It used to be people wanted to make music because we're all fucked up and degenerate and maniacs and there was no other way of expressing ourselves. Nowadays, they don't really care about the music, they want to be famous, it's about how they look. If you get your tits out, you're a maverick. Female musicians have been hoodwinked.'

In 2014, I spent the afternoon inside Noel Fielding's kaleidoscopic art studio in North London. Back then, Noel was the nation's beloved rock'n'roll captain on *Never Mind the Buzzcocks*, three years before he became the nation's surreal-jumpered sweetheart on *The Great British Bake Off*. He was perched on a stool beside his best mate, guitarist/songwriter and rock'n'roll vibesman Serge from Kasabian. The pair were newly returned from a 'supplies' expedition to a nearby Costcutters, where a five-year-old girl had stood in the booze aisle, mouth agape, transfixed by the two arrestingly dressed grown-up men: a billowing turquoise smock etched with silver stars and moons, a scarlet medieval jester's bonnet and sparkly golden boots (Noel); a billowing black bat-winged cape with scarlet lining, a hood and matching bonnet (Serge). It was the year Kasabian headlined Glastonbury, with a guest appearance from Noel, flapping onto the stage in a swish-around cloak dressed as Vlad the Impaler. They had much to say about the era they were living in.

'My mum and dad,' announced Noel, 'when they saw the Faces, Frank Zappa and Hawkwind at the same gig, the first band didn't come on 'til one in the morning. The headline was at five! Everyone steaming. Now, you can't get a fucking drink past one o'clock in this country. Even in London. We *have* become really conservative.'

Talent shows, he added, had also changed the landscape.

'The more you're exposed to the mechanics of the whole business the more the romance disappears,' he noted. 'The more you know what you have to do to *make it*, whatever that means: have a stylist, a manager, not drink. That wasn't what it was about! Bands used to be a gang, bands used to be the nutters.'

'I won't expose any bands,' added Serge. 'But going to festivals you meet a lot of people and there's nothing more depressing than going backstage, seeing a band come off stage and just flip their laptop open. At online shopping. And having – no shit, I've seen it – chicken and broccoli after a gig. I'm thinking, "Are you not gonna have a drink now? Cause some carnage?" And they're [pats slender stomach] "Naw mate I've gotta watch . . ." Pffff! You don't deserve to be doing this job! We see it so much it winds us up into being even *more* ridiculous and living up to it *too* much, "I don't wanna be *you*, mate".'

Soon they were foaming over the disappearance of new musical ideas generally, Serge eulogising over the days 'before the accountants got involved, just making stuff up, ideas, get in an ice cream van, play in forests, be free.' Why was it, I wondered, that the internet hadn't given us the most creatively free generation of all time?

'There's too much choice,' decided Noel. 'The stuff that gets a hundred million hits is "Gangnam Style". Or a squirrel singing an Elvis song.'

The pair knew, simultaneously, that they sounded like old men, even if Serge that year was a spry thirty-three years of age.

'I'm ancient now, I'm forty-one,' asserted Noel. 'I was brought up in the seventies and eighties, my parents were brought up in the sixties and everything was insane. The children's programmes were insane, the music was insane, the clothes were insane, the colours were insane. It does make you sound like an old man when you rant like this but there's a generation of people who've not had any links to psychedelic anything.'

In late 2019, Anglo-Asian-pop pioneer Tjinder Singh from Cornershop was already declaring 'bread' and 'coffee' more culturally central than music, musing over how 'the algorithm is already dumbed down, automatic commercialism, from

Tokyo to California to Huddersfield, they're using the same technology so they're all the bloody same.' The digital democracy, once seen as an infinite opportunity, had now led, he scoffed, to 'everyone having a good word to say about everything – that can't bring about great things, you've got to get your hate right!'

By 2024, forty-two-year-old Jon McClure from mid-level indie hobos Reverend & the Makers was now convinced he and his ilk – a sometime drug-skewed, swaggering polemicist – had passed into ancient folklore.

'I feel like we're the last of summat,' he told me, in his profoundly Sheffield accent, frontman of a band which emerged in the post-Libertines, mid-noughties 'indie sleaze' era alongside Arctic Monkeys. 'We've got young fans and they look at me like I come from a bygone era,' he carried on, having an afternoon pint in a London Kings Cross pub. 'Like, "You never sold out? You did drugs!?"'

In his early purist years he turned down product ads for £250,000 – 'It were, "No, I'm for real, I've got a message"' – and £1 million from a record label if they could, somehow, replicate the sound of the Arctic Monkeys' stratospherically successful debut album.

'Told 'em to fook off,' he chirped. '"No, we have synthesisers." Do I regret it? Fucking hell yeah! You know when Richey Manic did the 4REAL thing? I think we're the last generation who ever cared like that. No one cares anymore, right?'

In recent years his acquaintance Richard Russell, boss of independent label XL Recordings (who signed the Prodigy, Adele and later-years Radiohead), posited a metaphor for music's position in youth culture today. 'Richard said, "Music used to be the shoe. It's the laces now. Technology is the shoe. You're just an adornment."' Jon was no Luddite either, was creating music with AI at Sheffield University, listened to 'loads of new music, there's some great artists around, but everything just floats around in some weird, atomised world.'

The night before we met, his nine-year-old son had a sleepover with three other nine-year-old boys. 'All on YouTube, watching some balls being flung around,' he blinked. 'I'm like, imagine if the Beatles were sat indoors watching this shite? They'd never have written "Love Me Do"!'

We finished up the last of our three afternoon pints.

'I sometimes feel like we've all been involved in some fucking mad cult,' he concluded, ruefully. 'And it's proved to be bollocks!'

Where all these observations were passionate, true and even funny, we old timers have long accepted it: we're now simply somewhere else. Today, culture moves at cosmic speed, increasingly accelerating away from everything to do with 'rock'n'roll,' the spiralling galaxies of the Entertainment Industry whooshing past those renegade olden days like an unstoppable, ever-expanding universe. Guitar music was surpassed in dominance by the spectrum of hip-hop as far back as the early 2000s even if, here in the mid-2020s, there's an ongoing resurgence in guitar-led, grooved up, alt-rock bands, some of whom are thrilling, many female-fronted, few of whom anyone's heard of beyond their fragmented fanbase, our atomised era turning all-comers into a cult.

New artists flood into culture daily like a globe-circling tsunami *every single second*, mostly via TikTok and YouTube, whether quirky DIY indie, politicised punk and post-punk, experimental alt-pop, visually disturbing anti-pop, gender-queer electro-pop, dayglo 2D K-Pop, all-kinds-of-everything-remind-me-of-you pop, all vying to become the latest billion-streamed 'phenomenon' in a world where artists, now, can be giants in their own world with zero impact on the outside world. I'm constantly emailed by PRs fan-faring 'global superstars' with 'billions' of streams, who've released 'platinum-selling' singles and received multiple Brit and Grammy nominations, all of whom I've never heard of. There's simply no measure of reach, no central TV or radio show, no one cares about charts anymore, the only numbers which count are streaming figures and social media followers. What we now call 'legacy' mass media is over. Culture is now sourced by individuals through algorithmic pockets on either social media or streaming platforms, universal fame replaced by infinite pixels of micro-fame, rendering music no longer a predominantly communal experience. It's surely one reason why mega-gigs are so feverishly craved: so little in contemporary culture – sport aside – offers a truly mass, communal experience. And where Taylor Swift might be the most universally famous pop star on Earth, I know plenty people across the generations who know none of her songs beyond 'Shake It Off'.

Everyone, meanwhile, appears to be some kind of activist. From teenage social justice warriors and righteous Gen-Zedders, to furious millennials and endless celebrity campaigners, it's not only been fashionable for years to have Something to Say, but mandatory. Often, though, it's the obvious stance, the easy stance: a risk-free progressive opinion ricocheting around the generational echo chamber, with zero jokes. They're a serious lot, the young, because we live in serious times. From traumatising social media to environmental collapse to geo-political chaos, horror, division, violence and genocidal war – no wonder the dominant headspace of the young is pan-dimensional pain. No wonder they're permanently fraught with self-consciousness, fear, cynicism and apocalyptic thought, forever seeking out their 'safe space'.

There's talent everywhere, of course, there's *always* talent and today's best-loved left-field pop star, Billie Eilish, is doing exactly as she should be, representing her generation – specifically their neuroses, fluid sexuality, body dysmorphia and multi-fold mental health issues. In 2024, aged twenty-two, she told *Rolling Stone* magazine she was 'a depressed person', who'd had no fun in seven years and barely been out in public in five, spooked by the public attention (and had taken, instead, to extensive bouts of home-alone masturbation, with a mirror). Then, in summer 2024, she guested on the spirited No. 1 remix of 'Guess' from the UK's self-appointed rave-pop 'brat' Charlie XCX, a song about having your type of underwear guessed, its visual featuring much writhing on a mountain of underwear alongside multi-personnel, snog-heavy, hands-down-pants action. Its release came with additional info from their PRs: 'All bras and underwear used in the music video have been donated to "I Support the Girls." ISTG collects and distributes essential items, including bras, underwear, and menstrual hygiene products, allowing people experiencing homelessness, impoverishment, or distress to stand tall with dignity.' Commendable, of course. But this kind of thing was not expected of Madonna. Or Prince.

In late 2023, I asked spiralling flame-haired pop champ Jess Glynne if she felt fame might not be as much fun as it once was. Back in 2021 she'd been abused on social media for using, unbeknownst to her, a transphobic slur on a podcast, for which she apologised, before deleting all her social media accounts.

'It's different,' she considered, then aged thirty-four. 'I love my journey, but I've also been incredibly bruised and battered and put in a fragile state. As a woman you're analysed for everything you do, everything you say, everything you wear, how you look, and it's worse now because of social media. It's definitely not as fun as it used to be. I wish I was in the seventies and eighties. If I could be in any era, it's then. My mum was in the music industry in the seventies and eighties, and she had it the best! It's just ever evolving, isn't it? I've seen a lot of casualties.'

She'd been profoundly traumatised by the fate of her teenage hero, fellow North Londoner Amy Winehouse. No wonder, for Jess and her millennial contemporaries, they sought to control their own narratives, uninterested in the risk of living-on-the-edge, where so many before them have perished. The age of naïve, carefree innocence is gone; simply, and fatally, the so-called rock'n'roll lifestyle just isn't cool anymore.

'It definitely had an impact, when Amy passed,' she affirmed. 'When you idolise someone ... I was devastated. What upset me the most was the way it happened, I was like, "The media have just taken her from us." I never want that to be me. It's a wild world.'

Jess was just the latest young person to voice a worldview I'd been hearing, by then, for a decade: 'Things,' the young have told me, time and again, 'were so much better in *your* day.' This is not the natural order of things. And has never happened before.

There used to be another way. A freer, funnier, ultimately more life-affirming way. The way of the weirdos and outsiders, the shameless and the lawless, the maladjusted and the maniacs who came to inspire, shock, bewilder, provoke and guide us towards thrilling new cultural frontiers. As were all the characters, one way or another, in this compendium of encounters. Some were carousing chieftains celebrating the euphoria of life. Some were heroic escapees from a life of no hope. Some were cautionary tales in how to throw it all away and, in the end, somehow survive.

Today's cultural heroes, naturally, will mean just as much to their own generation as mine did to me. Even if they're nothing like my lot, and I doubt would ever want to be. My lot may have been, in many ways, damaged, awkward, fragile, erratic and often self-destructive, but they were my kind of heroes: freedom-fighting forces-of-nature who instinctively knew the game is rigged, who stuck a gleeful two fingers to the rules, to polite society and the eternal tyranny of the Man. Many of whom, alongside doing our madness for us, as all proper artists must, were irresistibly charming. Including the one who walked away from unimaginable privilege into a life of peril, preferring a drug addict's life in bombed-out Soho, living on an actual wall . . .

1

SISTER MORPHINE

1965, Marianne Faithfull, ethereal beauty and Swinging 60s siren, has her biggest hit (No. 4) with 'Come and Stay With Me'

March 1965. From my vantage point, as a mewling newborn placed in an apparently enviable Silver Cross pram, I knew nothing of the shifting cultural plates beneath my wheels, distant rumblings forging the mountainous new terrain of an imminently fabled decade. There was no Swinging Sixties in my war-generation parents' home, their stone-built cottage in the Scottish village of Luncarty more usually swinging to the jaunty sounds of Jimmy Shand's accordion, but the decade's impact was already acute, forming the elemental foundations of the person I, and so many of Generation X, would become.

Nineteen sixty-five was a staggering year for pop music, a year so rich in songs, sounds and visions, so steeped in the musical visionaries we call the Greats to this day, the roll call now seems laughable, an abundance of enormous hit singles beginning their immortal ring through history: the Beatles' 'Help', 'Ticket To Ride', 'I Feel Fine', 'Day Tripper/We Can Work It Out'; the

Rolling Stones' 'The Last Time', '(I Can't Get No) Satisfaction', 'Get Off of My Cloud'; the Supremes' 'Come See About Me', 'Stop! In the Name of Love'; the Beach Boys' 'California Girls'; the Temptations' 'My Girl'; Tom Jones' 'It's Not Unusual'; the Byrds' 'Mr Tambourine Man'; the Kinks' 'Tired of Waiting for You'; Nina Simone's 'I Put a Spell on You'; the Righteous Brothers' 'You've Lost that Lovin' Feelin''; the Walker Brothers' 'Make It Easy on Yourself'; the Shangri-Las' 'Leader of the Pack'; the Yardbirds' 'For Your Love'; James Brown's 'Papa's Got a Brand New Bag'; Sonny & Cher's 'I Got You Babe'; the Who's 'My Generation'; Bob Dylan's 'Like a Rolling Stone' . . . These were the songs, voices, haircuts and deathless fashions which defined the still-emerging counterculture, unprecedented sixties characters who formed the indelible blueprint for the romantics, misfits and dreamers of the decades to come through the seventies, eighties and nineties (and a handful in the digital age thereafter). They themselves, naturally, had grasped the pulsating baton from their own immortal forebears, often the extreme, chaotic, unpredictable iconoclasts who birthed rock'n'roll in the mid-fifties through blues, jazz, gospel, country, R&B and soul – alongside booze, drugs, sex, religion, death, transcendence and multifold forms of madness.

In March 1965 – as I wriggled, obliviously, in my Silver Cross pram – Marianne Faithfull was No. 4 in the soaraway hit parade with the wistfully merrie 'Come and Stay With Me', the first single ever bought by a boy in Manchester called Steven Patrick Morrissey, two months shy of his sixth birthday. I knew nothing of Marianne then, of course, the tremulously voiced artiste and imminent 'muse' to peak-sixties Mick Jagger. But forty-four years later here she was in Luxembourg, telling me a story she wasn't supposed to tell a pesky reporter, and being loudly interrupted . . .

'Aw, Mah-rianne! That should not be in ze paper!'

So blurted the distinctively accented Frenchman François Ravard, then manager/boyfriend of the aristocratically accented, sixty-two-year-old Marianne Faithfull. She was telling a story with fabulous indiscretion about a sometime Rolling Stones 'tech assistant' she and François named Steve. It was 2009 and one of Steve's jobs for years had been to look after Keith Richards' well-appointed Jamaican homestead, where Keith barely ever stayed. Through the winter months, however, there was a visiting resident, the model/actress/artist Anita Pallenberg, Keith's long-term girlfriend throughout the late sixties/seventies, who remained close to both Keith and Marianne.

'But she couldn't go this winter,' observed Marianne, 'because Steve got shot in the crotch.'

It was this statement which caused François' outburst, his hands buried in his face. Steve, it turned out, was so thrilled with his glamorous domestic situation he'd taken the opportunity to fully live the rock star dream.

'He usually drives Anita about,' chortled Marianne, ignoring the protesting Frenchman, 'but now he can't do anything because the house is like a hospital. He was shot in the crotch by a jealous husband. But he [the husband] missed. So, Steve will get better and be able to shag more wives. Oh well. Life is one big risk, isn't it?'

Risk. If there's one word which connects the lineage of characters we've come to call the mavericks, it's surely that one. In the late sixties/early seventies it wasn't Mick Jagger *or* Keith Richards who embodied the uncompromising spirit of the risky non-conformist, it was Marianne Faithfull, the luminously blonde, aristo-blooded ingénue. Nineteen years old when she ran off with Mick Jagger in 1966, she inspired several Rolling Stones songs, including 'Sympathy for the Devil', which Jagger wrote after she'd gifted him novelist Mikhail Bulgakov's devilish masterpiece, *The Master and Margarita*. In 1970 she then stunned her own groovy generation with her counterculture move on the counterculture itself, wafting away from Jagger to live on a wall in bombed-out Soho, homeless, on heroin, preferring that to a life of boundless privilege with the celebrated popinjay superstar.

I'd no idea what to expect when sent to meet her in the charming European enclave of Luxembourg, though a reputation had built up through one infamous interview. In 2001, the *Observer*'s Lynn Barber, arguably the UK broadsheets' leading celebrity interviewer at the time, subjected Marianne, then fifty-five, to one of her famed demolition jobs. We were strolling through cobbly streets when Marianne recalled the supposedly definitive portrait, of a late, rude, diva-esque megalomaniac with delusions of grandeur, and the similarly rude François, who bawled Barber out about her 'fucking tabloid paper'.

'It was *hysterical*,' announced Marianne, throatily, that day. 'It was when I was still drinking and François was still drinking, *a lot*. The ghastly Lynn Barber is famous for being a (crisply enunciated curse), but I didn't know that yet. François was sitting just behind us listening and she told me she used to work for *Penthouse* and suddenly she asked me if I'd ever had sex with a dog. Of course, that wasn't in *the thing*. A provocative question. I didn't react, I said, "No, have you?" Why would you ask that? At that moment François jumped up, blind drunk, and started yelling at her and she just ran away. She is a *piece of work*. She was talking to me not as a human being or an artist but as a sex object and I don't like that, ever. *Dreadful* woman.'

Marianne brought this story up unprompted, not as some long-delayed reprisal but as an illustration of how people, as she'd experienced, always judged her.

'So I've always held myself in a guard position. Defend, defend, defend!' she explained. 'I've been frightened of meeting people who just wanted to meet "The Legend". Frightened of not being interesting enough.'

She referred to herself several times that day as 'The Legend', and just the once, 'incredible legend'.

So, I wondered, the Legend is a burden?

'No, it's also very useful,' she smiled. 'It's helped me position myself very well, actually. I can kind of do what I like.'

We were having lunch in a fine-dine bistro, Marianne ordering 'beef filet, au poivre' in her exquisitely scorched timbre and seeking 'all the news from London!' She was a punctual, warm, lavishly theatrical comedy-megalomaniac with high-camp delusions of grandeur and why would anyone expect, or want, Marianne Faithfull to be anywhere *near* down-to-Earth anyway? She admitted, back in those drinking years, 'I didn't like myself either' but talk of the Legend today (by which she meant 'everything that's happened') came with a self-mocking luvvie's flourish. And no true diva, certainly, would be seen before her public in the coat she was wearing that day. A calf-length, black, woollen Christian Dior, it was daubed in streaks of milky white from 'an accident' on the train: when she opened her 'beautiful Balenciaga bag' it was full of water from a leaky bottle, which had melted the peppermints inside, 'and the water went all over my coat, so that's why it's covered in shite.' The permanently present François Ravard was a wry, retro-bespectacled fifty-one-year-old with the look of Serge Gainsbourg and the accent of the cast of *'Allo 'Allo!*

'Miss Facefull,' he'd fret, many times, now contemplating her coat, 'how do you *do* zees sings?'

'Maybe I drowned in another dimension,' she surmised. 'I actually think we *do* have many alternative lives. Don't you?'

Marianne Faithfull had lived an alternative life here in this dimension, had spent her forty-four years since the quavering 'Come and Stay With Me' in a self-made folk-art vortex. Her eventful life had comprised pop stardom, film stardom, Mick Jagger, miscarriage, cataclysmic drug psychosis, three marriages, three divorces, a suicide attempt, Hepatitis C, breast cancer, depression, sometime status as the Most Beautiful Girl in the World and ongoing status as profoundly eccentric Godmother of Goth, beloved of generations of alt-pop greats from Jarvis Cocker to Nick Cave.

With many years squandered in narcotic oblivion, the mythological cartoon of her Decadently Doomed Aristocrat had eclipsed her creative contribution, but she was, undeniably, a seriously tested life survivor. For six years she'd lived in Paris, been teetotal and clean for five – 'even a little alcohol is too much, it's just being an addict' – permanently living in the curious, sober world of the once catastrophically addicted. Her nose told some of the story, a thin scar running from the top and forking down one side, from an incident where she took a blade to her face trying to release the imaginary insects crawling under her skin. 'Coke psychosis,' she shrugged, 'but hey, it happens to people a *lot*.'

Last summer she had a breakdown – 'depression, sometimes my whole life just catches up with me, you know?' – after which she embraced a series of treatments including 'therapy, acupuncture, exercise, massage, a chiropractor, I go to meetings, I use everything I can to help me.' Ever since, her lifelong paranoia had subsided ('I don't wake up anymore with nameless, rambling fear'), she was now 'much calmer' and able to cope with the Straight Life. 'It can be boring,' she noted, cheerfully. 'But you have to get used to it. Anita is the same.'

The biggest risk Marianne Faithfull ever took, surely, was to deliberately become a heroin junkie living on the streets of Soho ('inspired' by William Burroughs' novel *Naked Lunch*), spending two years in the early seventies among the bombed-out rubble of World War II, famously 'on a wall', publicly rejecting Mick Jagger at the height of his iconic fabulousness. 'Which is very, *very* insulting to Mick,' she now felt, back in the swish European bistro.

This, surely, was sheer punk rock? A cry of 'I reject everything'?

'Mmn, yes, it *was*,' agreed Marianne. 'Because I actually saw through the whole pop business. At twenty-one. It was bullshit. It was just business. A formula that keeps making money. There was also that thing of "two stars in one house", my own little ego fighting for a chance. I did love Mick, but the life was difficult, living with such a very famous person. And such an *incredibly* promiscuous person. I could see it very clearly. "I'm not required for this, I'm gonna fuck off."'

Marianne was looking for 'truth' on her wall. 'I really *was*, my life had been overwhelmed,' bewildered by Mick's behaviour, 'a boyfriend who screws around makes you feel like shit, and he *adored* me. It was all so peculiar.'

She already had one child, Nicholas, from her short-lived marriage to artist John Dunbar in 1965 and knew she didn't want more.

'I did not like childbirth,' she shivered. 'And [with Mick] I would've had to conform, you see? I would've had to have lots of children, the Alpha male thing. I couldn't have *done* Jerry's job [model Jerry Hall, Mick's former wife and mother of four of his eight children]. Poor Jerry was good at it.'

When Marianne rejected everything, she also rejected her status as an iconic beauty – 'I never liked the objectification' – though was 'delighted!' to hear fellow sixties minstrel Graham Nash had recently confessed to an 'unrequited schoolboy love' for her, swooning 'everyone wanted Marianne, she was a fantasy girl.' The Hollies' 'Carrie Anne', he confirmed, was written about her.

'It was slightly requited,' she twinkled, before a heavy sigh. 'I was much too young for all this. I should have just been having little boyfriends at school. Instead of being thrown into this sexual maelstrom. Which of course I succumbed to completely. By the time I was nineteen, I'd run away with Mick and I thought he was wonderful, I just didn't mean to get into all that big . . . *stuff*. And now I *must* have a *fag*.'

We strolled through Luxembourg's picturesque centre looking for a chemist. Marianne needed 'bronchial tea', medicinal teabags infused with expectorant which eased the lot of the smoker. 'I can't give *everything* up, even if I do have a permanent bronchial situation.' She then coughed fulsomely and spat onto the pavement. 'Excuse me; very lady-like, I know.' With her beautiful Balenciaga bag currently drying out, her handbag was now a chemist's plastic bag carrying a box of bronchial tea and two packs of Marlboro Lights, while closer inspection of her coat revealed not only the milky streaks but a broken front button and fraying cuffs.

'It's supposed to be frayed!' she insisted. 'Oh God, I'm meant to look like "Marianne Faithfull". This isn't what Marianne Fai . . . actually, it's *exactly* what Marianne Faithfull looks like.'

You look, I told her, like you're back living on the wall.

'Maybe in a way I never got *off* the wall.'

Four years later . . .

In 2013, the now sixty-six-year-old Marianne Faithfull was sipping green tea and watching, horrified, as she somehow spilt the leafy liquid down the front of her black mohair jumper.

'Oh it's just *me*,' she sighed, as theatrical as ever. 'I'm always covering myself in *shite*.'

Covered in shite once again, she was now in a suite of London's new, artfully refined Belgravia Hotel where a wall boasted a Tracey Emin nude etching titled 'SHE LAY DOWN DEEP BENEATH THE SEA', a fitting artwork for Marianne Faithfull's uniquely precarious life. She was in London that week primarily for her granddaughter's christening, daughter of the son she lost custody of in the heroin years, Nicholas, marvelling today at his success as a high finance journalist; 'I must've done *something* right.'

Today her lone addiction remained the Marlboro Lights she 'must' give up by May when serious dental treatment began: 'I'm having to choose between teeth and fags, and I choose teeth.' It was possibly her hardest battle yet: after nipping outdoors for *a fag*, she returned and applied a nicotine patch to see her through a snout-free forty minutes, with a pack of Nicorette chewing gum on standby. Much to her disdain that day, she was taking questions from readers of *Q* magazine. 'Bloody punters asking questions? Oh, I *can't wait.*' Truth is, the questions from punters were minimal and mostly made up by me, a necessary intervention from all *Q* writers for this particular Q&A format, otherwise the questions would be, primarily, about the possibility of a personal appearance in, say, Tunbridge Wells. It also provided an excellent opportunity to put into the mouths of fictional readers the boldest of prying questions.

Her 1979 'comeback' album *Broken English* had been a huge creative triumph, a lyrically salacious album which included the song 'Why D'You Do It?' featuring lyrics about blowjobs and 'barbed-wire pussies'. A reader's question was invented: would she let her grandchildren listen to it and did she still like to be provocative?

'I don't try to be provocative *anymore*,' she demurred. 'I wouldn't stop my grandchildren, but they actually are not interested. Bits of the song I still think are fantastic. Being tied to the mast of the ship of fools. I loved the barbed-wire pussy. With *Broken English* I had nothing to lose, at all. I'd no fear because I didn't care anymore. I thought I'd *die* after that, actually.'

I'd heard an intriguing story: that the Velvet Underground's John Cale claimed he came to London in '65 with the first Velvet Underground demo tape, which he tried to give to Marianne to pass on to then-Stones manager/producer Andrew Loog Oldham, but she slammed the door in his face. How did she feel about that now? She could've been credited with discovering the Velvet Underground?

'I don't remember *anything* about that, bullshit,' she dismissed. 'Don't tell me John Cale couldn't get another line to Andrew. At the time I probably thought John was weird. Until I left John [Dunbar] and ran off with Mick, I was a very straight little girl. Life with John was hard enough, he was taking acid, smoking dope, he'd never give me any and I didn't want anything to do with it. When I got to Mick, I decided I wanted to smoke pot. And slowly I had a trip. Descending. And then I hated being so famous with Mick. A lot of people can't take fame and I'm one of them. I've learned to live with it.'

Seeing as she'd told me, back in Luxembourg, how very famous 'and very promiscuous' Mick Jagger was, I wondered how living with such a man had actually felt?

'I just pretended not to notice, it was much too painful,' she confessed. 'When I went off with him, I was nineteen and when I was busted with the Stones, I was nineteen. [The infamous Redlands Drug Bust, when Keith Richards' home was raided by twenty police officers on a tip-off from the *News of the World*, and where Marianne was found naked wearing a fur rug.] That really damaged me, it damaged our relationship and by twenty-two I was living on the street as a heroin addict.

Do I blame anyone for that? For the Redlands thing, yes. I blame the police. I blame the *News of the World*. When the *News of the World* closed, I danced a *jig*. MI5 were involved. And the FBI. They were trying to destroy the Rolling Stones and they couldn't, but me? They nearly did.'

I wondered about the logistics, specifically, of living on a wall. How big was the wall?

'It was a bombed building on St Anne's Court, so the wall was the length of a building, with a back to it, which I could lean against,' she explained. 'Inside the crater there were the meths drinkers round a fire, and they were always very sweet to me. On heroin you don't feel the cold, so I sat on the wall, literally, day and night, for a year, maybe more. I even slept sitting up. And somehow, I was OK. People did look after me, even the cops. I never got raped or assaulted. But I was such a hopeless junkie, I couldn't even shoot myself up and had to go to my drug guru [the novelist/anarchist/junkie] Alex Trocchi in the daytime. I could've stayed with Mick, and he did love me, but I couldn't bear it, that world. I just felt . . . not good enough. Low self-esteem. All the things a drug addict feels. But I don't think I would've felt like that if the bust hadn't happened. I think we would've been fine.'

The best-known moment in Keith Richards' autobiography *Life* (2010) had been his assertion that Mick Jagger has 'enormous balls' and a 'tiny todger'. Could Marianne verify this, or not, once and for all?

'Oh *please*,' she responded, eyes heavenwards. 'I never even told *Keith* that. He had a nerve putting my name there. It was Anita, I think. But I actually think it was the publisher who wanted that in. Because it was the same publisher who printed my book [her 1994 memoir, *Faithfull*]. He got in touch and said if I would say something about that he would give me a lot more money. *Eighty thousand pounds* more. I said no. I didn't want it, although I needed it. But that's the history of my whole life! The money for Keith must've been an extra two million and Keith would think it was a laugh. But that's a very envious man, deeply envious, wanting to put Mick Jagger down. It was a great mistake, I think.'

I wondered about William Burroughs, who she met. How did that go?

'When I was clean and sober, I used to go to Naropa, Jack Kerouac's School of Disembodied Poetics run by Allen Ginsberg [in Boulder, Colorado] and I asked to see William, who I didn't know very well yet,' she began, enthusiastically. 'He was having his breakfast, two hard boiled eggs with soldiers. I was so influenced by William. I'd read *Junkie* and *Naked Lunch* and they affected me deeply. I was *so* young and *so* stupid I thought I could do it [become a junkie]. I said, "How could you do this to me?" and he just looked at me pityingly and said, "You were never meant to take that literally, that was a *novel*." I felt really stupid and left.'

For years she'd been dubbed the Godmother of Goth but here in 2013 goths were *Twilight* fans who fancied One Direction. What did she think the characteristics of a proper goth were today?

'Oh, nonsense, I was never a goth, I'm not like that!' came her firm response. 'I'm actually nothing like people thought. I was never very sexual, *at all*. I liked being loved and loving, but sex wasn't a big deal. I've now retired sexually. I'm sixty-six! And I'm very relieved I don't have to be a sex object anymore. It was a lot of pressure. People expected me to be this super decadent sex person. And I never was. I never gave anyone a blowjob *in my life*. It *disgusts* me and I want to be *sick*. So there!'

Over in a corner of the hotel suite, her PR representative now had his head buried in his hands. Which only made the mischievous Marianne warm further to her theme.

'Sorry, that's *true*,' she carried on, now chuckling uncontrollably. 'I was always aware I was not the right girlfriend for a rock star. Who could get a blowjob anywhere. I felt inferior. I was a prude! Mick was very nice about it. But I think he missed it. I also wouldn't let anybody touch me on that level. Never have. I've missed a lot of good stuff, I expect, but *too bad*.'

How, I wondered finally, as her PR motioned towards us, the expression on his face blaring 'Enough!', would she like to be remembered?

'As a nice person,' she concluded, with a smile, and an absent-minded brush of her still-damp mohair jumper. 'There's a lot more to life than fame and fortune and the sixties. I'm very proud of my letter from my dad: he read my book and said he's so pleased I grew up to be such a nice person.'

*

On 30 January 2025, news emerged of the death of Marianne Faithfull, peacefully at home with her family, aged seventy-eight. Amongst the many tributes, BBC 2's 'Whispering' Bob Harris, her lifelong friend, described her as 'an encapsulation of the sixties'. There has never been, and never will be, a 'new' Marianne Faithfull.

2

ANGER IS AN ENERGY

1978, from the Sex Pistols' collapse, Johnny Rotten is reborn as John Lydon with PiL's debut single 'Public Image'

In '76 I'd been way too young for punk, the only pogo thrills I'd known through both '76 and '77 via the comically sprung rod of iron we knew as the bouncy pogo stick. By September '78 I was still a child, one for whom the newly released *Grease*, the movie, was not only *the word* but the most all-consuming, all dance-floor flailing, all culture-dominating phenomenon my thirteen-year-old self had ever known. Well, since *Abba: The Movie*, a lengthy seven months previously and the *Saturday Night Fever* soundtrack a pop epoch earlier in November '77. These were the preoccupations of the weedy, romantic, musically fanatical kid I was, long blonde hair still in a white hairband, a bit like *Grease*'s sappy Sandy even if my eyes were now twitching towards the day when I could become, somehow, Bad Sandy, with the liquid leggings and the fag.

I'd not yet discovered John Peel and Annie Nightingale, still blubbing under the candlewick bedspread to the Commodores' 'Three Times a Lady' on Radio Luxembourg (the first single

I ever bought) but by '78 was a charts rundown devotee every Sunday night on Radio 1. Then, towards the end of '78, reality began to shapeshift via alien new visions. Alongside 'Sandy', 'Danny', glitterball disco and Showaddywaddy's comedy doo-wop, the charts, overnight, were full of curious characters, the line-up for *Top of the Pops* on 19 October 1978 a snapshot of a mainstream now fully reconfigured by a rabble of hyper-frenetic weirdos: the Boomtown Rats with 'Rat Trap', Buzzcocks with 'Ever Fallen in Love (With Someone You Shouldn't've)', Sham 69 with 'Hurry Up Harry', the Jam with 'Down in the Tube Station at Midnight', while the closing song over the end credits came from something called Public Image Ltd, with a striking photo of the russet spikes of now former Sex Pistol John Lydon.

One month on from the release of *Grease* and PiL's debut single 'Public Image' detonated into the UK Top Ten at No. 9, its pulverising opening bassline and caterwauling vocals plugging my very molecular being into the bedroom wall socket, sending a synapse-sizzling message which rearranged my atomic makeup forever. Not that I knew this at the time. The response could only be instinctive: with little clue what this man was singing, I fully heard the *way* he sang it. Fuck you, he was definitely saying, I won't do what you tell me. Even as the song caused a delirious outbreak of wrong-words shrieking and bouncing-off-walls, John Lydon was, to my thirteen-year-old self, a fantastically frightening madman, a uniquely caustic creature whom esteemed cultural critic Greil Marcus described in 1989 as 'perhaps the only truly terrifying singer rock'n'roll has ever known'. The idea of having a conversation with this person, at that age, wearing that hairband, would've been less likely than singlehandedly pogo-sticking all the way to Pluto.

Twenty-four years later . . .

'I'm not doing that, oh no, that's *terrible . . .*'

In a central London hotel room in 2002 John Lydon's message remained exactly the same: fuck you, I won't do what you tell me.

'Here's news for you,' he carried on, addressing both myself and an *NME* photographer, 'I'm not even on your fucking library site. On the web, y'know? It's like music did not exist before 1994. Well, *fuck that.*'

On a Monday morning at 11 a.m., John Lydon was careering around the hotel suite with a bottle of beer, the then forty-four-year-old doing everything in his considerable power to remain the only truly terrifying singer rock'n'roll has ever known. He was as sneering a punk rock forcefield as he had been a quarter of a century previously in 1977, the year of the Queen's Silver Jubilee, the year the Sex Pistols' 'God Save the Queen' was banned from its No. 1 status by the BBC and stayed defiantly audible at No. 2 anyway. Today, he'd been asked to be photographed with an old 'classic' copy of the music paper I was representing that day, the *NME*, from its seventies Glory Years, to celebrate its fiftieth anniversary. His unimpressed reaction could've evaporated a nuclear warhead at one billion paces.

'Your paper's done me no favours over the years, nothing personal, right?' he carried on, fixing me with his 'comedy' starey eyes, his hair that day a multi-coloured, multi-tram shocker. 'I'm not holding up copies of that shit rag. Who do they think I am? When did I turn into a calendar girl? I have no relationship with *NME. At all.* They are "the enemy".'

Gulp.

That year I'd been dispatched on a jousting expedition, the *NME* now his music press nemesis, decades on from its honorary mention in 'Anarchy in the UK'. If apprehension was understandable, it was made unbearably so by the instructions of the *NME*: to ask a succession of namby-pamby, Lydon-unrelated questions which would, they spelled out, 'be very useful for us,' including 'what did he think of the Strokes?' That way, should he loathe the New York upstarts, that year's *NME* darlings, a guaranteed blaring headline would ensue. Such was the nature of the once crucial music press in 2002, as the clickbait era emerged. *How embarrassing.*

By then, the history of punk and the Sex Pistols was as familiar to cultural historians as the pivotal events of World War II: nineteen-year-old, neon-orange-haired John Lydon discovered loitering in Malcolm McLaren and Vivienne Westwood's SEX shop on the King's Road, joined the fledgling Pistols, released debut single 'Anarchy in the UK' in late November 1976 and blew up British society a month later by swearing, live, on Bill Grundy's otherwise nationally invisible London teatime TV show. By second single, 'God Save the Queen' in 1977, the Sex Pistols were at the epicentre of the most volcanic youthquake uprising the planet had known since the birth of rock'n'roll itself.

By 2002, John had been an American citizen for decades, living in Malibu with his beloved wife Nora, after he'd been, as he told me that day, 'ramrodded out of this country many moons ago, *continual* police harassment, I thought, "I'm gonna get set up here, and I ain't going to jail for that nonsense", so I buggered off out of it.' That year he was reforming the Pistols for a supposedly last, glorious, twenty-fifth anniversary jamboree, including a show at Crystal Palace. For twenty minutes, however, he was significantly more interested in blow-torching the publication I was working for, my inward cringes made all the more intense by the fact I, too, was appalled by the 2002 version of the *NME*. The paper was consistently run, he intoned, by 'condescending, upper-class fuck wits, who love to look down on us oiks. I have to be either a conman or a thicko. They all came across to me as the kind of lonely kids who were bullied at school and here was their big vendetta, very much like policemen, when you think about it.'

He was irked, even back then, at the erosion of alternative culture – 'everything's been categorised, neatly boxed' – his beloved football also co-opted into a money-making opportunity infiltrated by the middle classes. 'Football once meant something, working class community, now it's like bowls, it's ballet for the boring, with big business moves and no loyalty.' Furthermore, culture was now run by 'advertising calling the shots', in a 'surveillance society' which the public passively accepted. 'There's no outrage, I don't hear boo or squeak, you all just take it up the jacksy, dans le chuff, *rear gear only*.' Here, he guffawed out loud before declaring the UK 'one big Ikea-land, nothing but shopping malls, American-stylee.' All his life, he carried on, he'd been ripped off.

'Mr Rotten 'ere, everything I've done in music, has been ripped off me royally and I haven't seen respect once for it,' he insisted. 'Right from fucking hairdos to clothes, nonsense like that which are just trimmings on a gorgeous cake. Every style of music, fucking endless arsehole copies. *Endless*.'

There were still, I ventured, bands out there who considered themselves 'punk'.

'How sad for them,' he balked. 'That was my time, right? I don't like the term punk, I never have. I despised it, it's a category. You should be standing up, proud, that you've got your own situation sorted out. Then you can be the equal of punk. But you cannot, *cannot* imitate it. The *Q* Awards. [*Q* magazine's then annual awards ceremony in a swish London hotel.] Wonderful. Yes, I saw punk at its finest there. Those fucking fin hairdos. Fucking national health spectacles and anoraks. Ooh I was *terrified*. Matching anoraks? *Will you fuck off.* Was it a joke? I thought *Q* had put this up as some elaborate fiasco to amuse me. Pathetic. *Blue Peter* runs the roost here.'

Did he think, then, that true originality was dead?

'You've forgotten history, so quickly!' he instructed. 'There's just an on-and-on repetition of what somebody else has done. Come up with your own shit. Don't tell me the Sex Pistols sounded like anybody else. Don't tell me Public Image ever did. Don't tell me any of my solo stuff sounds like anything you've ever heard. Now, how is that not so fucking difficult for me, but hard for you lot? And *I'm* a con man? *Fucking 'ell.*'

Here, I thought I'd give that Strokes question a go after all.

Why d'you think people love the Strokes as much as they do?

'Strokes?' he replied, genuinely confused. 'What's that?'

Young Americans, sound exactly like a post-punk/new-wave band from 1979.

'I don't know 'em. They might be big here, but they're not there. Neheheh! You've been sent someone else's trash.'

You must know them, New York indie-pop garage, skinny school ties . . .

'Oh, I know! Why, the singer looks like a junkie. That's unacceptable, see? It's so static and reverse.'

I wondered if he'd ever truly believed in the Revolution?

'Well, I've always been revolting,' he replied cartoonishly, with an inevitable guffaw. 'I was brought up told I'm trash. Right? So, it's a natural instinct for me to fight that back. That will *not stop.* I'm hardly power mad or money hungry, whatever I have is shared. When you're born in shit and filth and squalor and council flats, believe me, you don't see anything glorious about that at all, do ya? The Clash could waffle on ad infinitum about the glorious working class – that's something they see through the car window as they zoom to the luxury arena they're about to play at. "I want a riot." Well, how camp is that?

[Here, he adopted a nursery rhyme voice and roundly mocked the lyrics.] " . . .a riot of my own." I mean, really, it's limp wrists akimbo, innit? The Tiller Girls' cocked legs.'

I wondered what he saw when he looked at David Beckham, our most celebrated icon, indeed England captain, in 2002?

'Oh dear,' came his response. 'Talk about an empty vessel. They say an empty vessel makes the most noise, not this one. He's the empty vessel, her what stands next to him makes all the noise. I'm sorry, that's one of the silliest, most cowardly attempts at hairdos I've ever seen [the famed 2002 Beckham Mohican]. He's a bit of a sniveller. He wants to be young and daring but still have a side parting. The perfect role model for Blair's Britain.'

Public image, we got what we wanted, eh?

'Oh, people have gotta stop rooting in my old fucking cast-offs,' he withered one final time. 'Hello, Prodigy. I've no problems with them at all but they should fess up where that look came from. Essex boys, what d'you expect? Get out of my dustbins. Come up with your own shit. *I'm still here.*'

We rose from our seats and John Lydon wandered away, with a final message as I reached the door. It was the chorus from PiL's 'Rise', a song I'd loved since its release in 1986, the year I turned twenty-one in London, taking up what I imagined would be permanent residency on the road to the Revolution.

'May the road rise with you.'

Twenty-two years later . . .

'By Jingo, this one's for Blighty!'

It was a discernibly more agreeable John Lydon who talked to me on Zoom from his home in Malibu in 2024, the year after he lost both his beloved Nora (to Alzheimer's, John her full-time carer since 2021), and his best friend and lifelong manager John 'Rambo' Stevens (to an aortic heart dissection). His first exclamation post-'Jingo!' was a rumination on the dyed white uprising of hair in the middle of his head. 'At my age it's supposed to go grey, and I can't get it to go grey.' Even his hair wouldn't behave? 'I'm sixty-eight and it won't have it!'

At sixty-eight there was much John Lydon still wasn't having. I told him not a day went by, here in the mid-2020s, when I wasn't bombarded by PRs alerting me to the latest artist/band/creative concept declaring themselves 'punk' or 'post-punk', terms which were now almost fifty years old.

'Well once you accept a category you're finished really,' he mused, seated in an artwork-festooned room in his home, one of his own impressionistic paintings behind him of a dynamic, frothy ocean. 'I've got no real contempt for the bands but please don't be calling yourselves punk, you're *not*. You're fully backed and supported by a very industrious system, coming at life from an accountant's perspective. I don't view success in terms of money reaped in for record companies. Sales figures are actually a liability you should try to avoid.'

Even the original punk bands, he added, didn't operate the way the Pistols did.

'Punk bands really wanted to emulate whatever they thought the corporate deeds were going on behind the Sex Pistols and of course there were none!' he chuckled, now puffing on a perpetual gasper. 'It was *chaos*. And you can't imitate chaos, you're either chaotic or you're not. It *can't* be structured. And that's why I made a distinct move away from the punk movement. It was allowing the clichés of standardisation. I remember the *Sun* and the *Mirror* did a "How to dress like a punk" article.'

A 'punk wigs in Woolworths' situation?

'Marks and Spencer's woolly socks for the skinheads!' he jeered. 'Then, with record companies, it's, "Oh, write another

Never Mind the Bollocks." No! I won't be pigeonholed. I won't allow myself to be *guided*. No board of directors has ever dictated to me. That's made my life rather uncomfortable at times. *And I love it that way.* I do what I do and I don't give a *damn* if it makes me popular or unpopular. In fact, I prefer *unpopular*.'

Over forty-five years ago, when the world was considerably less corporate than it is today, John Lydon was already satirising the corporate world, with the 1979 release of PiL's second album *Metal Box*. A dubby avant-garde art-rock opus, it came housed in a circular metallic canister, embossed with the band's logo, containing three 12-inch 45 rpm vinyl records and costing little more than a standard LP.

'Packaging was something we'd already worked out, with the metal box, before we even wrote a song,' he pointed out. 'We were having a laugh with the institutions, "Let's turn that upside down inside itself." The name Public Image Limited was *very* corporate, PiL, and the logo, it was all a parody, and the songs inside absolutely bore no relationship to *the norm*. Without the use of calculators. Which drove the record company insane. They don't know how to cope with that. Or allow for self-mockery.'

We contemplated how everyone, today, is some sort of Activist.

'Because it's easy!' he hollered. 'They're *pretend* warriors.'

I mentioned Irish rap trio Kneecap, who'd been called 'the most controversial band since the Sex Pistols', the Belfast renegades who rap in Irish Gaelic. (We were talking the year before the now definitively pro-Palestine Kneecap saw a member charged on a terror offence for allegedly waving a Hezbollah flag on stage: soon afterwards, they defiantly announced their biggest-ever show for autumn 2025 at Wembley Arena, the same month the case would be thrown out of court.) At the 2024 Reading Festival, I remarked to John, they had the predominantly English crowd chanting 'Brits out!' while flailing in a mosh pit led by their tricolour balaclava-wearing DJ.

'Sounds like they've slightly missed the boat on this one!' cackled John. 'I was rather impressed with one of the demonstrations in Northern Ireland recently where a Union Jack and a tricolour were waved right next to each other. Over an outlandish situation. That coming together was superb, to my way of thinking. Because I'm not ever, *ever* seeking division. I want unity.'

I mentioned my year zero of '79 and how people like him had formed the adolescent foundations of post-punk people like me.

'I think accidentally!' he hooted. 'There was never any manifesto. I raised myself and educated myself with a sense of values. I tell the truth.'

John Lydon came from what he called 'the dustbin', his young life blighted by Dickensian poverty, a child of Irish immigrants brought up in fifties/sixties North London, an eventual family of four kids and two parents sharing one bedroom and an outside toilet, where John would famously flush, via the bucket he carried, the clotted results of his mother's many miscarriages. Aged seven he contracted meningitis (from rats), was lost to a coma for seven months, emerged with spinal curvature, starey eyes and no recollection of who he was, or who his parents were, or how to read. Self-education in a local library followed, alongside a questioning spirit, with an unquenchable need to express himself, a seventies glam-rock-obsessed adolescent who dyed his hair green. His father was so appalled he then kicked him out with the memorable declaration, 'You look like a Brussels sprout!' Adversity, instructed John, gave him his lifelong drive to walk through the fire of animosity, without fear.

'Meningitis almost killed me, it took nearly four years really to fully recover who I was,' he reminded me. 'But in that period, I re-learned to read and write, my mother taught me well. And that was a *brilliant* insight into what I was and what I could be. From there on I viewed the world quite differently. You do need those four years of being called dummy-dumb-dumb in order to figure out that you're not. My mum and dad were very strong influences in my life. *No self-pity allowed.*'

It's for this reason he'd seen the rise of contemporary academia-led cancel culture as not only anathema to a provocateur like him, but disastrous for mankind.

'It's not reality,' he intoned. 'You can't live on the planet that way! You need intense inner struggles *and* outer struggles in order to really find yourself. You have to fight these battles. You have to deal with playground bullies. It's the nature of survival. They're taking away your weapons here. They're leaving you defenceless. And frankly mindless. This *obsession*. To *join everybody else*. And *blend in*. There's no real threat in them, yelling and screaming the second they don't have their garnered opinion agreed to. The intolerance of it all is amazing, it's humourless, and ultimately, it's self-inflicted danger. How you gonna get on with anyone? Me, I *love* both sides of an argument.'

Such outbursts, naturally, had led to his own sporadic cancellation.

'The animosity towards me can be ferocious,' he nodded. 'But not from working class kids, y'see. It's those that have become institutionalised. The left-wing way of thinking is to stop us thinking. I've had the right-wing lot try that on me, and now this lot are at it. You need knowledge, of everything from everywhere. I've never *dreamt* of telling anyone what to think or what to eat or what to wear.'

Ultimately, he continued, absolute equality was a naïve pipe dream.

'If you really want a wonderful utopian future where everybody's gonna be equal and dress silly and it's all super fun, well then you're not living in the real world,' he assured. 'Who's going to pick up the trash, boys and girls? Some of us are just smarter than others. As a society we cannot exist if we're all exactly equal, nothing will be created. And that is the end of us all. Idiocrity.'

He aligned himself with no particular kind of politics and had developed a theory 'that the most perfect form of societal government is one that's in perfect confusion'. He cited as an example a trip to Italy back in '82, where he made crime thriller *Copkiller* (released as *Order of Death* in the UK) with Harvey Keitel, Italy governed at the time by a broad right/left coalition. He arrived in Rome to find a luggage strike, had to haul his own luggage everywhere, stepped outside to find a taxi strike, knew no one in Italy, officials eventually helping him blag a lift.

'I thought, my God how can they actually run a country like this,' he shuddered. 'And then, in the city, it's Ferraris whizzing by and *serious* culture and a love of really great food outside of the fish and chips I was used to. I admired that. I realised, it's like a Fellini movie for the Italians. Life is, "let the politicians say what they like, *this* is how we live". I liked the four-hour lunch in the middle of the working day and yet they get things done. It made sense to me.'

John Lydon was a far warmer character than he'd often been caricatured as, our conversation veering away from having-a-go to appreciating-what-we-have, his pronouncements more those of a one-world hippie than any agit-punk provocateur. He was a lifelong scholar of anthropology, a world traveller who'd never forgotten, while on a trip to Africa documenting sharks and gorillas for Channel 4, meeting villages of African kids, 'crying out for pens because they don't get educated if they don't have pens.' John and the crew bought biros and paper wherever they went, 'and the kids were so grateful, they wanted to be *educated*, not institutionalised, "Just give us a chance", and I don't see that gratitude and use of the tools provided today.' He was also a wildlife evangelist who called himself 'a koala hunter; I go hunting for cuddles in furry things!' He remembered the day he met the gorillas and was told by guides to avoid looking them in the eye, because they might see it as aggressive, competitive.

'And they were absolutely *insisting* they looked in my eyes,' he remembered. 'I got the distinct feeling they were trying to communicate, but they get angry because we don't understand what they're trying to tell us. Chimpanzees as well. We are *all* related. Although I've felt a chimpanzee's bottom, and I've never felt anything so waxy on a human. It feels like one of them incense candles! Oh, I *despise* zoos so much, I just see the cruelty in encaging something for our own amusement.'

For survival through the travails of human existence, his best advice was 'gallows humour – it's the Irish in me, we cry at weddings and laugh at funerals', a palpably 'up' man in an increasingly negative world, still grieving for his wife of over forty years.

'*No self-pity allowed here*,' he emphasised once again. 'I would let down those I've loved by turning into an old sour puss.'

Why was it, at sixty-eight, he'd not yet run out of energy?

'Well, I've been given great gifts. I'm a free thinker!'

The most terrifying singer rock'n'roll had ever known, then, would never be encaged for our amusement. He remained the original artwork, in a world of mass market prints.

'Originality doesn't begin by co-opting into a system,' he concluded. 'It has to be about your *own* way of thinking. You can fine-tune that with experience, but it might actually be in your DNA to just be an awkward fucker. Heheheheh!'

3

A NEW ROYAL FAMILY

1979, Adam and The Ants emerge from the shadows to redefine pop forever

Nineteen seventy-nine. My year zero. At fourteen, only one year on from naïve life as a limp-haired, white-socked, schoolgirl sap blubbing along to Olivia Newton John's 'Hopelessly Devoted to You', post-punk shattered into my life like a meteor from infinity straight through my teenage bedroom window. This was the year my mother despaired I'd become, overnight, 'a monster from outer space', sporting a short, bleached-blonde, vertical fright-wig in direct response to this suddenly unfolding new era. The late seventies/early eighties would prove a rush of dynamic energy arguably unmatched in musical history, a crackle of creative lightning illuminating overhead a newly born starburst galaxy.

The names on the post-punk roll call still astound today, platoons of singular eccentrics, posturing peacocks and firebrand characters newly defining the landscape, sprouting like exotic toadstools on visionary independent labels in Britain alone: Rough Trade, Stiff, Cherry Red, Beggars

Banquet, Postcard, Zoo, Factory, Mute, 4AD, 2 Tone. The best-known are still ringing throughout history today, via enormous-selling Top 10 singles, many at No. 1 (the Jam, Blondie, the Specials, the Police, Gary Numan's Tubeway Army) while John Peel and Annie Nightingale on Radio 1 (joined by Janice Long in '82) constantly blared the art-rock titans – Killing Joke, the Cramps, the Cure, Psychedelic Furs, Siouxsie and the Banshees, *thousands more*, including post-punk founding father and Bowie buddy Iggy Pop. It was '79 when I discovered Iggy via his post-Stooges *New Values* album, on cassette, this captivating, beautiful, flaxen-haired alien outlaw who paraded on stage his memorably handsome penis. In 1980 the Indie Charts were invented while, simultaneously, the billion-selling New Romantics turned up alongside the fabulously ghoulish Goths. Alternative music was now the New Pop Music, the term 'alternative comedy' emerged and by '82, on the BBC, *The Young Ones*' anarchic capers were a generational TV phenomenon. One dazzling figure, though, would briefly eclipse all others in his era-defining reach: Adam Ant.

He emerged from the avant-garde shadows in '79, the year I bought their stark, art-rock album *Dirk Wears White Sox* on cassette (no video ever seen), its artwork mostly ink-black, featuring a blurry grey image of a be-gowned woman's sinewy back. Adam and the Ants came to me, therefore, as a non-visual curiosity, their debut played obsessively through the permanently pounding ghetto blaster on my chiffon scarf-draped bedside table, the song 'Cartrouble', with its saucy lyrics about licking and polishing, causing outbursts of cackling mirth.

Imagine my adolescent shock and broiling passion, then, when Adam Ant suddenly beamed into view, in November 1980, as the Most Beautiful Man in the World. The video for Adam and the Ants' signature single, 'Antmusic', from their second album *Kings of the Wild Frontier* both changed Adam's life and bewitched a generation, unleashing the newly visualised concept of the leather-trousered, lip-glossed, pirouetting pirate, a white stripe daubed across his eye-linered face, frills on his cuffs and bows in his hair, thrashing out from the indie-rock cul-de-sac into kaleidoscopic global view. A No. 1 album in January '81, it featured three hit singles, became the UK's biggest selling album that year and won Best British album at the Brit Awards '82. No wonder, from '81 onwards, I'd equate all the best pop music not only with some kind of insurrectionary attitude, but enormous success: the greatest artists, clearly, also became the biggest.

Fourteen years later...

Nineteen ninety-five, and Adam Ant was sitting in a Camden boozer swearing his still exceptionally attractive head off as I attempted to ignore the still-wibbling adolescent within. It was the height of the Britpop palaver, he was here with his portly creative cohort Marco Pirroni and proving himself a gifted exponent of the well-placed curse. Adam hadn't been this revered since the Ants' early eighties apex, releasing a new album *Wonderful* in the year the Britpop upstarts were lauding their brilliance – *Kings of the Wild Frontier* had been the first-ever album purchase for both Damon Albarn and Alex James from Blur. Most vocal in her fandom had been Elastica's Justine Frischmann, who the 'news'-papers assumed fancied Adam, which Adam now responded to with fulsome disdain: 'Justine doesn't fancy me for fuck's sake, she was a fan of the band, end of fucking bollocks story.' That year Nine Inch Nails were also eulogising over the Ants, who'd recently supported the US terror-rock ghouls at Madison Square Garden.

'Scary shit,' thrilled Adam. 'Normal kids in 30,000-seater stadiums freaking out to stuff like "I'm Gonna Fuck You Like an Animal". Who says you've gotta kiss arse to sell?'

He contemplated *Dirk Wears White Sox* in heroically dismissive fashion.

'My arty independent rip-off album,' denounced Adam, who invented the Ants in London in 1977, year of the Sex Pistols' 'God Save the Queen'. 'Then,' Adam carried on, 'me and him [Marco] said "Right! Now we make some three-minute fucking pop *classics*, like T. Rex." The essence of pop is, one, brilliant fucking songs, and the rest is sex, subversion, style and humour, and that was us. We're responsible for knocking on the head looking like a piece of scruffy punk shit and bringing back the pure pop idea of dressing up, going mad and screaming your head off.'

Adam didn't think much of punk's foamingly venerated musical legacy and had some footnotes to add to the gilt-bound record.

'Punk was a laugh, but it weren't *that* good,' he assured. 'Most of the music was shit apart from two Pistols singles, the Buzzcocks and [Siouxsie and the Banshees] "Hong Kong Garden". After that you had twerps like Sham 69 shouting "skinheads are back!" which fucked the whole thing up cos the violence took over and we were all singing to a bunch of thugs. I used to whack the fuckers over the head with a mic stand.'

He was appalled by the reverence afforded Mr Sidney Vicious, Deceased.

'Last time I saw Sid he had his face beaten in and him and Nancy – and you could smell 'em before you saw 'em – were running away in a fucking beaten-up Morris Minor. It was pathetic. I'm not into perpetuating myths when *that* was the reality.'

Instead, Adam and the Ants embodied the kaleidoscopic

Pop Dream, one central aspect Adam's masterful dress-up directive, including the gold-braided military jacket from the *Charge of the Light Brigade* movie. The legend then emerged that it was all former manager Malcolm McLaren's idea, that he invented the Ants for a £1,000 'image consultancy' fee.

'Fucking liar,' spouted Adam, breezily. 'McLaren didn't write the songs, Adam and the Ants is sitting right here. As for the looks, I drew 'em out before we did 'em, like a storyboard, and same with the videos. McLaren sits there in his jerk-off Melvyn Bragg world of Paris-is-so-wonderful living out his existential dreams from nineteen-sixty-fucking-eight when he wasn't even *there* and he discovered *fuck* all. Eat my fucking *shorts.*'

Three original members of Adam and the Ants had been poached, it turned out, by Malcolm McLaren for the self-acclaimed Svengali's teen-punk upstarts Bow Wow Wow, specifically for their Burundi-beat-led single 'C-30 C-60 C-90 Go!'. Adam Ant, buoyed by incandescent indignation, then reinvented not only himself and his band but the actual era, pirate-pinching the Burundi beats his departed drummer had premiered on Bow Wow Wow's novelty song about cassettes. The sound became central to *Kings of the Wild Frontier*, a stylistic snatch which would see, today, both bands cancelled before they'd even begun for cultural appropriation.

This pioneering, thumpering sound, via two drummers, sounded exactly as it was built to sound, like a charging tribe of invincible warriors thundering over the horizon, its tantalisingly scarf-wafting chieftain out to kidnap a willing generation into his 'new royal family', as the *Kings of the Wild Frontier* anthem so audaciously declared. Before he'd even invented the phrase 'ridicule is nothing to be scared of' (from 1981's No. 1 'Prince Charming') here was a high-camp cacophony of canine yelps, yodelling, voodoo incantations, spaghetti western guitar pings, cartoon gunshots, salty sea dog whistling and dastardly panto-rock hollering. And my sixteen-year-old self in '81 was forever charging around dance floors in Perth pretending to *be* Adam Ant, twirling and flouncing with cascades of pink and green wool dangling from bare upper arms while wielding an imaginary cane. I wasn't the only one: throughout the Ants' dominant year of '81 the nation was entranced, adolescents everywhere affixing laces around their kneecaps in an approximation of the next-look Dandy Highwayman in 'Stand and Deliver', the most glamorous fantasy pop sensation since Bowie's Ziggy Stardust. Adam Ant now became, officially, the most beautiful man on 'Earth'.

'It was beyond our control,' noted Adam, still a vision of black hair/glimmering blue-eyed extra-terrestrial majesty at what seemed to me at the time a fossilised forty years old, and minus a few hairs. 'We went from selling 30,000 copies to – boom! Hysteria. Didn't see it coming.'

Marco: 'We only did the two-drummer Burundi thing to fuck Bow Wow Wow off. Heheheh!'

Chaos, overnight, became their day-to-day reality.

Adam: 'Unbelievable pressure. Writing songs was something you were supposed to do on your day off.'

Marco: 'I used to have to *sneak* into the studio, they'd find us and go, "Well, what the hell are you doing?" I'd be, "Er, nothing. Writing lyrics." And they'd be, "We need you for a photo shoot." For *fuck's* sake.'

More chaos ensued. Adam became Prince Charming, posturing pompadour with love hearts on his cheek, the band then had three managers, inevitably fell out and split up. With the similarly frilly-cuffed New Romantics suddenly sailing atop the airwaves, Adam Ant went solo, became the very staples in *Smash Hits* pop gazette, now a cartoon superhero for eight-year-olds whom the old folks loved for his seemingly harmless, campy hilarity. Meanwhile the nation's dance floors were forever filled with ecstatic teenagers with strips of white make-up slashed across their noses. Did he notice?

'You'd have to be *dead* not to,' he snorted. 'When your audience starts to look like you, you've got to move the fuck *on*.'

Naturally, he moved the fuck on to pretending to be an astronaut (1984's 'Apollo 9' single, which peaked at No. 13) by which time, 'I just didn't fucking fit in anymore.' He relinquished, with grace, his pop crown to Culture Club and disappeared to America where he studied his other craft as a bit-part thespian in movies and TV. He remained, though, that mid-nineties day, a pop fan and began eulogising over the Britpop phenomenon. 'What's happening now is like punk without the stupid violence and to me that makes it a lot cooler.' He was also, simultaneously, a bloody-minded, deadpan, sarcasm-deep raconteur of blusterous mirth who talked like a twenty-one-year-old East End spiv on crystal meth. So, to those who judged him in 1995 as some dodgy 1980s-revival peddler he countered, unsurprisingly, 'Fuck you! The Rolling Stones are the biggest band in the world, and they've survived from the seventies so why can't I from the eighties?'

As for those who mocked his drink'n'drug-free mind-control philosophy ...

'Media rock stars on drugs?' he jeered. 'Total fucking embarrassment, rich fucking idiot starlets. All that "I'm so lonely so I'm gonna fuck myself up and you've all gotta worship me"– *very* dated. I'd have dismissed Nirvana totally if it wasn't for the music. They should all do more fucking and less sitting around talking a load of bollocks.'

Adam Ant, born Stuart Goddard in Marylebone, central London, in 1954, was a considerably more intriguing (and alarmingly unstable) character than this brief, Britpop-fixated interview could ever have let you know. Some of this I blame on his then unwillingness to disclose any lifelong psychological struggles, the rest on myself and the distracting bedlam of the fabled 1990s. A disruptive only child, at infant school he threw a brick through his head teacher's office window two days in a row, and was then placed under supervision where an empathic teacher nurtured his emerging artistic talent. Soon an art student (and drop-out), at twenty-one he attempted suicide and was briefly sectioned under the mental health act for the first time. Seeing the Sex Pistols live changed his life – 'I wanted to do something different, *be* someone else' – eventually forming Adam and the Ants and becoming the biggest pop star in Britain: twenty-two hits between 1980 and 1985, seven singles lodged simultaneously in the Top 40 in 1981, 16 million records sold worldwide.

Simultaneously, through his twenties, unbeknownst to planet pop, he was treated not only for bipolar disorder but for depression and anorexia and by the 2010s was as famous for his mental breakdowns as his peerless pop persona, having been sectioned three times. In 2012 he was arrested on firearms charges after wielding a gun in the Prince of Wales pub in London's Kentish Town before assaulting a fellow drinker. Talking to the *Telegraph* in 2010, he was reflective.

'If you look at the symptoms of bipolar disorder,' he said, 'in all seriousness, the actual alarm signals are practically my job description: promiscuity, spending money lavishly, wearing weird clothes. It's very hard to get that across to a psychiatrist, who'll say, "Why are you wearing a leather jacket with studs on?"' He then shook his head. 'I don't know. I'm a rocker!'

Fifteen years before that, as our all-too-brief summit ended, he rose to leave and I took an autograph opportunity:

proffering a promotional photo, I told him about my chum Leesa, who'd told me that without the music of Adam and the Ants she would 'never have got through my parents' divorce'. He wielded a marker pen and signed, immediately, with a poker face: 'To Leesa, to see you through the next divorce.'

4

THE PEOPLE'S POET

*1979, John Cooper Clarke's 'Gimmix! (Play Loud)' becomes
a top forty hit (No.39) and brings poetry to the masses*

Nineteen seventy-nine brought another new cultural concept to my permanently boggled mind: the Punk Poet. At fourteen, my lifelong exposure to poetry had been minimal. School brought Keats' 1819 thriller 'Ode on a Grecian Urn', its opening line alone, 'Thou still unravish'd bride of quietness' surely the bedrock of the baroque, swoonsome stylings to come of Morrissey in the Smiths (despite his Keats dismissal in their '86 jangler 'Cemetry Gates' – Oscar Wilde, he pouted, was on *his* side). Keats, then, a nineteenth-century Romantic – and Pam Ayres off the telly. The rurally accented Ayres I'd loved since 1975, a memorable contender on then-essential Saturday night talent show *Opportunity Knocks* who bestrode the mid-late seventies as a one-woman comedy recital colossus, whose own most famed ode, 'Oh, I Wish I'd Looked After Me Teeth', would become a sentiment I ruefully identify with today. Only years later did I learn Pam Ayres' localised, kitchen-sink observations were a blueprint influence on this new poet

I loved, John Cooper Clarke, a scarecrow from Salford who would become Britain's foremost Punk Poet and dazzling verbal sorcerer.

He first strode into view through his greatest hit (a non-single) 'Daily Express (You Never See a Nipple In)', first released on his '78 debut album *Où Est La Maison De Fromage*, a bawdy paean to sexually squeamish middle England often heard on John Peel's nightly show. Consequently, he became ubiquitous support act to the punk and post-punk giants – Sex Pistols, the Fall, Joy Division, Buzzcocks, Siouxsie and the Banshees, Elvis Costello, New Order. Because of John Cooper Clarke alone, funny, smart, dextrously delivered poetry became a celebrated working-class artform. And in that adolescent year of '79, unbeknownst to me at the time, he laid down a crucial paving stone on the yellow-brick-road of my rapidly building belief system: without jokes, we are nothing.

Thirty-seven years later...

John Cooper Clarke was waving at me, with some enthusiasm, from a small, square table in the fashionable Hix restaurant in Soho, central London. I couldn't miss him anyway: at sixty-seven he remained a uniquely distinctive figure, with blackest bird's-nest hair, meticulously dressed in a neat mid-blue, three-button woollen suit jacket with matching tie.

'There's people in excess of a hundred years old with all their marbles, with a library card, having a pint and the odd cig,' he began, the kind of man who rejoiced in his own jokes with both infectious gusto and a filthy, dastardly laugh. 'Hundred used to be very rare. You were on the national news. Telegram from the Queen. By now, the Queen must have writer's cramp!'

In 2016, John Cooper Clarke was of pensionable age and

may well have been the happiest person I had ever met. He was hoping, he chortled, to live at least another forty years. 'I wouldn't mind pushing it to the early teens!' A regular in this crowded eatery, an artwork glimmered overhead of a pink flamingo flying through a blue and yellow neon hoop.

'I'm a bit peckish,' he announced, eagerly perusing the menu, a man famed for his spindlesome physique as if etched from a Tim Burton storyboard. He then ate like a king (Henry VIII), ordering a parade of the finest dining: brill (the most expensive fish on the menu), alongside three sides comprising 'double chips' (for two), creamed spinach and a whole giant baked celeriac, a lettuce salad and a bottle of exquisite wine – 'It's got to be French, hasn't it?' (his wife was both a wine connoisseur and French).

John Cooper Clarke was known for many things: his world-class wit, the heroin addiction that robbed his eighties, his resurrection in the noughties, which saw his poetry included on the GCSE English syllabus studied by the young Alex Turner from Arctic Monkeys – 'these days I'm compulsory at school!' – and his DJ stints on BBC 6 Music, sitting in for fellow niche-pop enthusiasts Iggy Pop and Jarvis Cocker. What he was never known for was a hearty, gourmet appetite.

'I don't get any exercise whatsoever, it's just quality food, so it's not necessarily that fattening,' he suggested, of his permanently whittled frame, folding away the prescription glasses he'd placed over his prescription shades to read the menu. 'I'm dead fussy. I've never been on a diet in me life and every time I weigh meself I'm the same as I was fifteen years ago. My body is a temple. A temple of fookin' *doom*. Heheheheh!'

That dastardly laugh rippled throughout our afternoon together, his speaking voice the slow, measured, beautifully enunciated Mancunian timbre which made everything he said sound like a line from a poem, or a stand-up comedy routine. Hix was a lunchtime sell-out, so loud with packed-in punters we had to lean in to hear each other, hair touching, all the better to witness several of his glinting, golden teeth. 'I'm worth more dead than alive,' he twinkled. He'd had his 'shite' teeth fixed twenty years ago.

'Before that,' he added, as another giggling episode approached, 'I used to describe Shane MacGowan as the guy with the Hollywood smile. Heheheheh!'

John was an unhurried, magnificently genial fellow with an honorary doctorate from Salford University, whose conversation ranged across sixty years of cultural intrigue. Always synonymous with the post-punk era, he was acutely 'from the sixties', a born raconteur who'd witnessed the birth of rock'n'roll.

'I'm old enough to remember before Elvis,' he chirped, tucking into his exquisite brill. 'And everybody thought rock'n'roll was a flash in the pan. "It's collapsed, it's all about calypso now." I was sentimental about Frank Sinatra in 1965. Ella Fitzgerald. Doris Day. Fantastic!'

His life had been informed by myriad freedoms.

'I lived in a time where you were thrown out of the house in the morning and they didn't expect to see you, as long as you came back for your tea,' he beamed. 'There wasn't a nonce around every corner. We used to make our own daggers. You'd buy a nine-inch nail for a penny from the iron mongers, go down the railroad track, a train'd come along and flatten it and you'd put a wooden handle on it and you had a perfect dagger. Everyone had one.'

Kids today he found woefully namby-pamby.

'Oh they *are*, they need to be kicked out the house, the sun's out, gerrout!'

Son of a communist engineer, he was a sickly kid expected

to die through tuberculosis, was routinely off school and self-educated via books.

'I've never been a liberal,' he intoned, cheerily. 'My dad was a communist, and engineers were treated like the new aristocracy in Stalin's Russia, so he thought this was the garden of Eden! He was in the Communist Party, I went to a Catholic school, I was half Jewish, half Catholic with a bit of Marxist-Leninism thrown in, which meant whatever company I found myself in, I was always in an argumentative, oppositional position, y'know? So, at school, if they were having a go at Jews, which they did, I had a go back, and when they were rabidly anti-communist, I was railing against them with my communist pals. From a very early age I was always in the world of ideas.'

Which clearly made him an excellent orator?

'It did,' he nodded. 'Good at taking positions I actually didn't believe in, like a lawyer. I can argue one way or another about anything.'

A beatnik mod in the sixties, he was obsessed with words, music and American culture. 'Dean Martin, Jerry Lewis, the old poets, H. W. Longfellow, "I shot an arrow into the air!"' he marvelled. 'Victorian morals *and* Patti Smith, a lot of those people in the New York punk scene began with literary ambitions.'

Arriving onto the cultural map as punk arrived, he was already, as he put it, 'ridiculously old for punk, about twenty-six, although I've since found out everybody but me was lying about their age.' He recalled a non-glamorous seventies. 'It's been beautified,' he proclaimed. 'It was the ugliest period ever, sweaty polyester and godawful food. Even the hippies had some kind of glam and in the forties and fifties people really took care of their clothes.' As the post-punk uprising was eclipsed by synth-pop and the New Romantics pirouetting on

MTV, he succumbed to the eighties scourge of heroin, lived with the Velvet Underground's Nico, a fellow addict, a period of tragic unproductivity for the once prolific poet.

'Life wasn't that poetic,' he noted, rumly. 'The getting off stuff, going to the doctor's, I was always ill. I never thought I'd get my mojo back. I don't know how I *did* get it back. And I think what I'm writing *now* is better than I did then.'

I hoped that one-offs like him, John Lydon and Iggy Pop were finally being paid properly?

'We've been broke most of our lives,' he acknowledged, forkful of fish in mid-air, 'but I've never been more financially well off than I am now. It's a good trajectory!'

His mojo had returned, slowly, through his recovery in the nineties, even as he witnessed, appalled, the cultural dominance of dance music.

'Dance music for blokes and blokes can't dance,' he insisted, although he'd appreciated Oasis. 'It was like I hadn't heard a guitar band in ten years.' The clothes, however, he definitely didn't appreciate. 'I didn't fit in,' he pointed out, of the nineties' ubiquitous binman chic. 'I couldn't wear a *tracksuit*.'

In 2015 the good Doctor had appeared on a BBC 4 panel show, *What Ever Happened to Rock'n'Roll?*, contemplating what rock'n'roll meant, if anything, here in the twenty-first century. As a force, he believed even then, it had surely had its innings.

'It does seem to have lost its nous,' he still believed, sipping his delicious wine. 'People blame *X Factor* but those shows have always been around. *Opportunity Knocks*.'

He cared much more about the arrival of his celeriac, which caused a bellow of 'fabulous!', followed by a serenade to his favourite punk band.

'Every day I play a Ramones record, the core values of rock'n'roll!' he elevated. 'I was their No. 1 fan, saw every show when they came over, they never made a bad tune, every damn one a single.'

They had the best legs too, similar to his own: drainpipe seventies spindles.

'I went to Johnny's grave in Hollywood, you can't read it for lipstick kisses,' he thrilled. 'For years they were the only band I liked, my default band. Which song? Any! Who can you say that about? Not even the Beatles and the Stones. They never hit a wrong note, terrific, fabulous, totally pop. The Beach Boys without a beach.'

Here, a reverie consumed him, eulogising over his youthful days as 'a total mod, a mohair mod, a soul boy', his nights out as a lad at the Twisted Wheel in Manchester.

'Amphetamines and Coca-Cola,' he remembered, dreamily, 'all-nighters, Ben E. King, the beginning of the northern soul phenomenon, rare groove, soul, R&B, purple hearts … They were issued to the American Air Force on a weekly basis as part of their kit, they'd dish 'em out to the amphetamine-fuelled masses, that's how that started.'

The hippies, meanwhile, were not his people.

'A middle-class thing,' he dismissed. 'They were bourgeois rich kids, students. We had core working-class values, we wanted a job, money. Just before hippies I was fascinated with the sixties writers, I belonged to that world, with its links to modern jazz. That's where they got the look from, Miles Davis, three-button jackets, Jimmy Griffin, Chet Baker, Sam Cooke, those are the people we were trying to look like, sharp, clean, a working-class elitist thing, exclusive!'

His golden teeth glimmered some more. Those 'shite' teeth were fixed, it turned out, through a deal: his dentist came to him with a request, to do a benefit for Greenpeace, of which he was a member.

'I've never been that convinced about the death of the

planet,' opined John, nonchalantly. 'He said, "I'll do what I do for you, if you do what you do for me." So, he sorted me teeth out really cheap. But I've got to say I did that benefit for the benefit of my teeth rather than the planet . . .'

Pam Ayres, at least, would've approved.

The People's Poet was to prove himself heroically un-PC, bereft of a liberal bone, often engaged in 'generational warfare' with his then-twenty-two-year-old daughter. He wasn't having *The Great British Bake Off*, because men can't bake. 'I'm not having baked goods from a man!' he roared. 'They'd just cut corners. It requires a lot of manual effort and I'm not confident on the hygiene.' On climate change he blared, 'I smell a rat!' (he suspected the science was, ultimately, in the scientists' financial interests) and celebrated the thrills of consumerism. 'I would consider myself a materialistic person.' From here, he applauded the dollar-based boasting of long-mainstream hip-hop. 'I used to love *Cribs*, fantastic, that's the way to live, solid gold muscle cars, gerrit now while you're young and fresh, dudes!' Furthermore, he was appalled by the then-emerging student practice of 'no platforming' in academic institutions, as had recently happened to Germaine Greer and Peter Tatchell over transgender issues. 'Stalin could only *dream* of such restrictions!' he boomed. 'Now, if you're wrong, it's not enough that you're wrong, you have to be *evil* and you must be *closed down*.'

There was no point, he added, in believing you could change the world.

'Nobody can save the world. Have you seen the size of the fucker!?' he cackled uproariously. 'If the world *is* doomed, all the fucking cycling and switching off lightbulbs and vegetarianism in the world won't stop it. I think maybe the world *is* coming to an end, but I don't think it's my fault.'

Yes it is, you were a post-war baby boomer!

'I do come from that privileged generation!' he hooted, unperturbed. 'I had tuberculosis as a child and if I'd been born eighteen months earlier, I would've been dead. They discovered [TB antibiotic] streptomycin. I've got every reason for thinking things have got better. We no longer die at thirty-five. Food's nicer. People can afford stuff now. Even poor people. It's not Dickens. People moan as much but they're moaning in front of a plasma screen television in a centrally heated apartment. Women don't die in childbirth. I *am* talking about the developed world! We can drink the water out of a tap. People drank beer, even children, it was safer than water. That gin was your friend in ancient times! There's never been a better time to be alive.'

The way he saw it, as an irrepressible life enthusiast, we should spend far more time appreciating our own good fortune.

'Oh, every *day* I thank God I was born English,' he erupted. 'The best language in the world that everyone wants to speak. You never run out of poetry! We might moan but it's what we do. I love moaning. Sixty per cent of my act is moaning!'

Two hours in, with a car waiting to whisk him back to Essex, he wondered if we should 'have another bottle?' We settle for another glass of wine and pudding instead.

'I'll try that steamed bergamot *sponge* pudding,' he boggled, savouring even the word, seemingly happy to stay here all afternoon. He'd lived his whole life 'in the moment, an existential life', admitted he'd been 'reckless' but remained a spectacularly upbeat spirit.

'Unless it was compulsory, I've never taken out any insurance, ever,' he confessed, happily. 'I've never bought anything I couldn't afford. I don't have a computer, or a mobile phone. Things couldn't have gone better for somebody like me, than it has. I never had a career path. I've never had a career! It's been instinctive. Maybe it was something to do with growing up with the idea of not having a life expectancy. I've never got a mortgage, the fact I've got anywhere to live is down to my wife, totally. Somebody up there likes me. I've done all the wrong things. I've got a guardian angel. If you look at what I've done, even my job as a poet, I never got the encouragement. I've always flown in the face of advice. I've always done what I want.'

He'd watched 2016 unfold as a death knell to so many true greats: David Bowie, Prince, Muhammad Ali, Sir George Martin, Victoria Wood ... Did it affect him, in any way?

'I just thank God it ain't me!' he elevated. 'Death, my constant companion. All my life people have been telling me I ain't got long for this world. For one reason or another! Whatever doesn't kill you makes you stronger, right? I'm a lot stronger than I look. I've always avoided stress. I'm quite instinctive in what would *bring* stress, it's part of being paranoid, you can see it all. I've never regretted not doing stuff, I've more regretted *doing* stuff.'

The thing that bothered him most about death, in fact, was that he'd miss his own obituaries.

'The lights went out over Europe,' he guffawed, now making one up himself. '*Boo-hoo-hoo*. There'll never be another. A certain flinty integrity, had the former John Cooper Clarke. The hearse couldn't get in, there were more people there than at Woodstock. Heheheheh! Several women threw themselves onto me coffin. "We don't wanna live in a world without him!"'

Like an Ayatollah?

'The Ayatollah of punk! And then the day after the *Daily Mail* says, "But was he really *that* good?" That's when you *know* you've arrived.'

Suddenly, he mentioned he'd had 'an ear worm all day', the theme tune to high-glam eighties TV drama *Dallas*.

'Dur, *dur*, DUUUR ...'

Maybe, I ventured, it's because he was now living, unfeasibly, the life of Texan oil magnate J. R. Ewing?

'Things,' he exploded, 'have gone that well!'

The car outside had now been waiting for over an hour. He signed for something but didn't, it turned out, pay for anything: he was friends with one of the chefs, did a show for him once in the downstairs bar, 'and on the strength of that I haven't paid for a meal here since … I've got the keys to the city!' He teetered towards the door on those spindle legs, stronger than they look, approximately one ounce heavier than he was when he came in, now magnificently nourished and agreeably refreshed. With a final wave and a hollering 'cheers!' he disappeared into his chauffeur-driven car, not only an invincible survivor but a gentleman, a scholar and officially a doctor. English poetry's one-off Dr Vibes.

5

2,000 MILES

1980, The Pretenders' 'Brass in Pocket' becomes the decade's first No.1, while Chrissie Hynde popularises fingerless black lace gloves years before Madonna

For small-town adolescent girls like me in 1980, possessed by globally incoming new wave, there were few women to align your calamitously chaotic soul with. Debbie Harry was the alien-beautiful unicorn beamed from Valhalla, Siouxsie Sioux was a haughty, cruel-eyed terror-ghoul, Kim Wilde was the one the little brothers fancied and Toyah, of course, was a loony-tune Woolworth's fright-wig. Chrissie Hynde, though, in the best possible way, was a *dude*. With legs. And fingerless black lace gloves. And invincible eff-off attitude.

It was all there, on glorious display, on the sleeve of the debut *Pretenders* album alongside her shiny, zipped, pillar-box-red leather jacket. Chrissie Hynde's look, and the look on her face, were now as thrilling to me as the beguiling music within ('Kid', to this day, brings a swell of moist-eyed emotion). Now a year into obsessively reading the 'inkie' music press, first *Sounds*, then *NME*, her sudden presence as frontwoman and principal songwriter was made all the more vital in my expanding musical universe dominated by young men. Across the inkies, only Blondie's Debbie Harry was a regular female presence but by January 1980 the Pretenders were everywhere, now *unavoidably* No. 1. The album's third single, 'Brass in Pocket', was not only the band's No. 1 breakthrough but the first new No. 1 single of the 1980s, while the album itself was also No. 1, for four consecutive weeks. All in the month my school friend Sandra, the most dedicated Pretenders fan of us all, turned fifteen.

Sandra was the coolest one at our school, with legs good enough to pretend she *was* Chrissie Hynde: all skinny jeans, Cuban-heeled boots, paisley neck-scarf, heavy eyeliner and enigmatic two-tonne fringe. The lyrics to the irrepressible 'Brass in Pocket' were both funny and swaggering, about the nerve it took to front a band, which few women then ever did. This, however, was never Chrissie Hynde's intention – she always hated what she called 'the girl in rock thing' – but for adolescents like us she was living proof that girls could not only be guitar-totin' rock'n'roll stars but, in her case, *harder than the rest.*

Twenty-eight years later…

Chrissie Hynde was shouting, near a garden of meditation. We were in the exquisitely landscaped Regent's Park in London, perched in the leafy café garden where all was serene until Big Mouth here arrived. She'd been asked to sign an autograph for Sandra, for whom Chrissie Hynde had remained an all-time inspirational hero. She'd listened to the story of Sandra, furled her lips into a furious pout, silently signed the vinyl sleeve of my very own copy of the eponymous debut album, literally narrowed her still heavily-linered eyes and let me have it.

'Why d'you have to *tell* me that?!' she blared. 'Why do I have to know that? I mean, I'm *glad*. Just let me sign it, great, but saying that can only make me feel uncomfortable. I've had many years now of feeling like an absolute *cunt* because I don't respond right, I don't go "Oh, thank you!" Then I agonise about it for weeks. *Weeks*. I don't wanna be mainstream and I never did because I don't wanna lose my freedom. I made a girl cry once. I was backstage trying to talk to friends I hadn't seen for *years* and all of a sudden someone's going [theatrical giddiness] "Your voice!" [Here, she rolled her eyes heavenwards.] I said, "You know what? Don't be so impressed with *talents*, the only thing that means anything is if someone's *kind* to someone else, the rest isn't that important, don't *make* it that important." I looked over and she was crying. And I was, "Oh God, hand me a *gun*. Let's put *one* of us out of our misery."'

She picked up the last square of her vegan pecan cake, threw it past those legendarily equine teeth, slewed a black coffee, whipped out a lilac lipstick and rolled it around her lips without the use of a mirror.

'So,' she announced. 'Wanna walk?'

Here in Regent's Park in early spring 2008, almost three decades on from my own adolescent worship, and Chrissie Hynde's legs, and attitude, remained identical. Everything else, however, was a Hawkwind roadie in 1974 whose Harley had possibly been stolen. Now fifty-seven, her iconic bob was grown-out, wispy and lightly flecked with grey, her functional black hoodie bearing skull and crossbones and the slogan, 'Akron, Ohio, 1825: Where the Weak Are Killed and Eaten'. Her skinny blue jeans had holes in the thighs and the traditional totem of the trusty roadie poked out from her jeans front pocket: a hefty metal keychain. Today, we'd been scheduled for a drive in her eco-immaculate Smart Car, but she couldn't find her car keys – 'and I *never* do that' – so we were walking in the park instead. And a walk in the park with Chrissie Hynde was definitely no walk in the park, more a military-paced three-hour obstacle course where you ducked underneath, swerved around and took a direct hit from a volley of verbal bullets. A woman who remained, after thirty years as a rock'n'roll freedom fighter, as the Pretenders' founding drummer Martin Chambers described her in 2007, 'as subtle as napalm'.

The story of Chrissie Hynde's early London years was, to any girl who became a music journalist in London in the eighties, beyond intriguing into the realm of intoxicating tableau. 'Well, it *was* interesting,' she conceded, now striding purposefully across open parkland. Her arrival from Ohio in May 1973, aged twenty-one, had been an actual rock'n'roll pilgrimage: a fledgling rock singer 'from the age of five', she had Iggy Pop tacked on her bedroom wall alongside an article written by the *NME*'s renegade writer Nick Kent and so believed London was the city 'where they'll know who Iggy Pop is'. She sold handbags, worked in offices and within a few months met Nick Kent accidentally at a party in glam-free Acton.

'Incredible,' she nodded. 'I wasn't disappointed with London, but Marc Bolan was not playing in the local pub like I thought he would be. So, I started talking to this guy and he said, "Can I stay at yours tonight, I've nowhere to stay?" I said, "I guess" and he arrived with a U-Haul van with about three thousand records covered in yoghurt and wax, dumped them in the middle of my room and stayed for a year.'

A relationship began, her friends became the central punk rock characters, she attempted to marry Sid Vicious to stay in the country (they were thwarted by a closed register office), played in bands with Mick Jones from the Clash, worked in Vivienne Westwood and Malcolm McLaren's clothes shop

SEX until another *NME* scribe, the late Ian MacDonald, suggested she try writing because she was always 'mouthing off'. Her first review, of a Neil Diamond album, saw her 'slagging everything off' and the hate mail, alongside a reputation, duly arrived.

'It was a blast. If a record was coming out there was a *reception* for it in the pub in the afternoon with all this free booze and the *NME* crowd would be sitting there and then you'd go and slag the record off.'

Her first interview was with a porn-fixated Brian Eno – 'I think I bigged that up' – and she continued for a year, 'blagging it, happy to just not go to work but they were making me into a personality and I thought, "I don't wanna be negative about music anymore."' Chrissie moved on, in search of a band, but not before she'd passed on her metaphorical baton.

'I sold Julie Burchill her first typewriter,' she revealed. 'A plastic portable, I offered it to her for seventeen pounds and she gave me twenty, a generous girl. But by then Nick and I were having a war anyway. A scabies war. Started with scabies and then some other sexually transmitted diseases. So I went to all the record companies, "Chrissie Hynde, *NME*", got some records, took 'em to Cheapo Cheapos, sold 'em . . .'

Suddenly, she stopped.

'I hope I don't have to keep talking about this for the rest of my *life*,' she balked. 'Is there anything else we can talk about, or do you have to do this? I wanna put a bullet in my head if you want the truth. Yes I do!'

She pouted, again, in silence.

'Wanna see the meditation garden?'

Biography abandoned, we decided to 'hang out' instead.

We strode, still purposefully, into the park's meditation garden, which was meditative indeed, even with Chrissie Hynde now in it, its circular enclave something of a soothing balm to her evidently brittle psyche. 'Ah, this is better,' she sighed, stepping into a tranquil idyll of flower beds, benches and a dark bronze statue of a girl with a lamb entitled, 'To All Protectors of the Defenceless' (unveiled in 1931 by the Animal Welfare Council). A lifelong animal rights activist known to have been arrested for civic disorder, she peered into a pastel-blue sky overhead. '*This* is rock'n'roll!' she yelped, now spiritually transforming into a benevolent hello-clouds hippie. 'As long as there's birds singing and there's a sky there's something worth living for,' she enthused. 'I'm glad I couldn't find my keys. We'll just keep walking, you can *feel* the spring, it's all getting ready to blow.'

The sap is rising, as they say.

'I *wish*.'

Since the Pretenders' 1979 debut single, a cover of the Kinks' 'Stop Your Sobbing', Chrissie Hynde had been one of the few female leaders of a rock'n'roll band, ever, and was certainly the first woman I'd ever met who was romantic about venue scaffolding. 'When I see the scaffolding and the rope ladders,' she swooned, of her continual on-tour life (today she was mere days back from America), 'it feels right to me, I always feel part of the road crew. You bet I even love vans? Gimme a *little* concession to glamour, *please*.' She had zero truck with any discussion on 'the gender bullshit – it's the androgyny I love about rock'n'roll.' She'd been asked, forever, about why there were so few women guitarists, or women fronting rock'n'roll bands.

'I can't go there with that,' she withered. 'Somehow, it's not in our DNA or something. I've seen all these pathetic feminists going [whiney voice] "We weren't encouraged." What, like Jeff Beck's mother was going [coaxing voice], "Now Jeffrey, you get upstairs, you haven't practised your guitar for five hours yet today." Bullshit! The only theory I've come up with in all these years why women don't play guitar is cos men use it as a tool to pull chicks. And in my personal experience I haven't pulled one bloke in thirty years because I'm on stage. It just doesn't work that way with us. We're trying [here, she mimed an 'arm's length' manoeuvre]. The truth is, any girl can get fucked. It's harder for a guy. I hear all this from feminists, "We have to be strong, we have to prove ourselves." Bullshit! Just do your thing! It's like the word luck. Luck is the word poor people use to describe rich people. I got where I am today because that's how bad I didn't wanna be a waitress. That's the secret to *my* success."

With men, did she have a type?

'Warm and of this planet,' she replied. 'I have no standards, I'll have anyone that wants *me*. Come one, come all. Just *come*, somebody.'

She swore she had no idea how men responded to this attitude.

'How do *I* fucking know?' she jeered. 'I have to spend two months on a tour bus, overnighters, with five blokes, I'm not thinking about it too much am I?'

She likened her bawdy sense of humour to Roy Chubby Brown and continually referred to moody Scottish actor Robert Carlyle – she had 'a Robert Carlyle Film festival at home last year, I'm a fan' – so I surmised she had a gigantic artistic crush on him.

'I don't know if there's anything artistic about it.'

I wondered how she felt about mainstream pop being dominated, as it was at the time, by the women of perv-pop, from Lady Gaga's pop-art provocations to the Pussycat Dolls' full-on prozzie-pop, all PVC pants and lap-dancing poles.

'Well, if you think being a prostitute is exotic, try it and find out for yourself,' she snorted, with some disdain. 'I guess those girls like it. What I want is for no one to look at my ass or my tits. You know in *Spinal Tap*, when he has the new guitar and he says, "Don't touch it, don't even *look* at it"? I'm that guitar. I spent so many years perfecting my don't-fuck-with-me hateful look that I never learned how to flirt. When I get on stage, I'm there to set up the guitar player. And the bass player and drummer. That's my thrill and my forte, like a conductor. I'm a team player, I've got a football player mentality. I'm Kenny Dalglish setting up Joe Jordan. That's who I am. I'm Gordon McQueen. But you're right. Old birds who dress like blokes, there's not that many left, I guess. Come and get it, boys.'

No wonder, perhaps, in 2008, she'd been Morrissey's friend for almost twenty years – 'he's a riot' – a man who called Maida Vale, close to her London home, 'Made Available'. Strolling alongside the shrubbery, she offered an impersonation, jutting out her lower jaw as far as it could go. 'Uh, Chriss*eeeeee* …' She also remained friends with Johnny Marr, who joined the Pretenders for one year in late '87. The pair became stoner buddies who once went to Jamaica, were picked up in a van at the airport, were 'gagging for it', found a miniscule roach left by a Neville Brother on the floor and duly smoked it. 'And I have never been so high in my *fucking life*,' she chortled, 'we had a *riot*.'

An official Regent's Park gardener trundled into view. Possibly in his sixties, he was dressed in grey waterproof trousers, green jacket and floppy green hat while wheeling a large light brown bin, as if in full garden camouflage. Chrissie was impressed and wandered over.

Chrissie: 'Hiya! We were admiring your brown bin and how you were camouflaged to fit in.'

Parkie: 'Thank you, I'm glad you appreciate something in the garden.'

Chrissie: 'Oh it's *gorgeous* here, I'll be here every day . . .'

Parkie, contemplating bin: 'Not many people coming here admire this!'

Chrissie: 'We appreciate the discretion. It's all about to kick off in here, isn't it?'

Parkie: '. . .'

Chrissie: 'The flowers.'

Parkie: 'Oh, I thought you meant the Revolution.'

Chrissie: 'They're gonna have their *own* revolution!'

Parkie smiled and quietly wheeled his bin away.

The violently private Chrissie Hynde had always found interviews 'skin-squirmingly embarrassing'. She endured them primarily to promote vegetarianism (she owned an award-winning vegan restaurant, VegiTerranean, in her native Akron), 'but I also like the music, so you have to hawk your fish.'

By now she seemed unperturbed she had a pesky reporter following her around who evidently wouldn't go home, even as we wandered beyond the park, onto a main road, where she gestured to a bus stop in hope. 'So, are you gonna get a bus or what? Unless you need more [she rolled her eyes] information.'

We passed a café.

'Wanna tea?'

We sauntered inside and had tea, plus cauliflower soup, which she wolfed in three minutes by fully upending her bowl. 'I'm hungry, I can't get with the spoon.'

The one thing she rarely discussed was her extended family, from her two grown-up children – Natalie, her daughter with the Kinks' Ray Davies, then aged twenty-six, and Yasmin, her daughter with Simple Minds' Jim Kerr, then aged twenty-four – to her two ex-husbands (Kerr, artist Lucho Brieva), to close friends like the equally militantly vegetarian McCartneys (she became great friends with Linda).

'There are people I don't care to mention in public, for fear of attracting the wrong sort of attention,' she demurred. 'The things that I hold very dear to myself, I keep them dark. It's not for everybody, your own. You can't expose it to the light.'

I wondered if she was strict with her children in the way, say, Mick Jagger famously was?

'My friends thought I was strict because my kids weren't allowed to tell me to shut up like their kids were,' came her arch reply. 'They had manners.'

I wondered if it was true that she apparently always 'knew' she would have a child with Ray Davies.

'*No*,' she replied, appalled. 'I've never heard *that* one before. Oh *please*. That is *absurd*. I wasn't too baby-friendly when I was young. I'd never even held a baby until I had one. Although I took to it very well indeed and was, if I do say so myself, quite a good mother. Certainly, I always put them first. And I had so much fun with those kids, they were a *riot*.'

I told her I went for a cup of tea with Ray Davies two years previously and she was mildly intrigued.

'Was that unnerving?'

He was, I confessed, both unnerving and unexpectedly still attractive in his early sixties.

'He was thirty-eight *then*,' she cackled, saucily. 'There's not a great deal of interaction these days but we're aware the other one is still alive.'

Many people were convinced they were actually married.

'We weren't,' she confirmed. 'But whose business is it, after all? I mean, is Dionne Warwick married? [Here, she narrowed her eyes.] Do we have to know everything? There's only a few things you really have to know. Goodwill to your fellow man. Really, start there and work backwards.'

She lived alone with Sid, her Scottish terrier rescue dog who was currently staying with friends while she'd been on tour and she wasn't looking, particularly, for a boyfriend. 'I'm *eternally* single. I've made enough cups of tea in my life.' That September she would turn fifty-eight and found nothing bizarre in approaching her sixtieth year. 'If you don't die you keep getting older, how is *that* weird?'

Did Paul McCartney know she'd always been able to forge all the Beatles' signatures?

'Yes he does, actually,' she grinned. 'Because I was over there [at the McCartney family home] really early on, his little boy came to me one day and I scribbled it on a piece of paper thinking "Ha ha!" Next thing I knew he took it straight into his dad. I was mortified. I don't know what I was expecting, why wouldn't he have? It's funny, when my girls got old enough they said, "Is Uncle Paul Paul McCartney?" I told him that one day and he said his young daughter had said, "Dad, are you Paul McCartney?"'

Her daughters must've thought she was *very* cool.

'Hmph,' she harrumphed. 'My one daughter said to me the other day, cos I said, [whines] "Oh, I've gotta do some *press*," she said [exasperated] "Muuum, one of my friends said, 'your mum's pretty cool and everything but she's pretty miserable isn't she?'" Which makes me feel pretty miserable. Y'know, I'm doing what I love doing, everything's great, the band is *fucking* great, I probably love it all even more now because my kids can do their own thing so why do I come across as miserable? When I'm doing what every other mother*fucker* on the planet wishes they could do? They must think, "Fuck off, man." Cos *I* would. [Deep sarcasm] "Oh, you can play guitar in a rock band and travel around the world and get paid to do it for *your whole life*? Oh, boo hoo! Poor you, excuse me while I get some sleep cos I've got to go to the office at six thirty." *Please.* Don't let me be *that* guy. Anyway. Enough of my yackin'. Fucking *hell*, I'm gonna take you to a *flurry* of buses . . .'

*

Chrissie Hynde, for all her supposed misery, her bluff belligerence and wilfully disconcerting narrowing eyes manoeuvre, was a different kind of guy altogether, as fundamentally joyous a rock'n'roll spirit as a seventeen-year-old boy who'd newly found himself in the coolest rock band on the planet, all of his own invention.

'So,' she implored, now standing outside a bus stop, 'do any of *these* take your fancy?'

A bus route was duly selected.

'Thanks for today,' she announced, unfeasibly, 'because I have to tell you I've been missing walking my dog and this is the closest thing I've had to it for a while. I hope you take that in the best *possible* way.'

Off strode the dude called Chrissie Hynde, who didn't look back, keys ever-jingling on the end of her roadie's keychain. For one day only, as her (and my) hero Iggy Pop almost once said: who wouldn't wanna be her dog?

6

TOORA LOORA

1982, Dexys Midnight Runners' Celtic knees-up 'Come On Eileen' becomes a global No. 1

There was no escaping 'Geno', the first No. 1 single from Dexys Midnight Runners, in springtime 1980. Here was a song and a band I could not bear, deeming Kevin Rowland and his beanie-hatted pals trumpetingly over-earnest and void of an atom of humour. It was their second No. 1 single in '82, however, where I chose to rest my case, finding 'Come On Eileen' an irksome Irish jig-about (and ever after, throughout adulthood, the scourge of the nation's weddings). At seventeen I was peroxide blonde and plume-haired, far more beguiled by the goth-art glam of the similarly-plumed Gene Loves Jezebel than any drearily yelping troubadour and – even worse – Dexys were now enormous. 'Come On Eileen' was No. 1 for four weeks, selling 1.2 million copies (and No. 1 in the US), creating a household name in the unfathomably dressed frontman, whose outfit in '82 appeared to be shredded waistcoat, scarlet gypsy necktie, no shirt and decades-old denim dungarees more befitting an itinerant skip dweller. It was, perhaps, a reaction to the hyper-stylised pop star in the era of the New Romantics, who I loved for both their preposterous togs and masterful tunes, led by flouncing popinjays Duran Duran, Spandau Ballet and Culture Club.

That year we also endured far less agreeably dominant elements: radio-throttling, US TV/movie themes (Irene Cara's 'Fame', Survivor's Rocky III-helmed 'Eye of the Tiger') and ludicrously bothersome novelty songs (Tight Fit's 'The Lion Sleeps Tonight', Bucks Fizz's 'The Land of Make Believe' and the Goombay Dance Band's 'Seven Tears'). Dexys' 'Eileen', though, was the best-selling single of them all and Kevin Rowland remained, from then on, a foamingly revered musical hero, especially to the mods, especially the fellers, second only in their genuflecting worship to the Modfather himself, Paul Weller. But he always remained to me a self-reverential, shirtless gypsy madman who beat up a journalist pal in the mid-eighties for being, you know, a journalist. I'd always wondered, nonetheless, what burned at the core of this curious, dramatically volatile figure.

Thirty years later . . .

Sheer intrigue brought me to Kevin Rowland in 2012, newly reconvened with various members of his former Runners to create *One Day I'm Going to Soar*, an album of alarmingly theatrical am-dram lunacy and the first new Dexys album in twenty-seven years. I knew he'd lived a chaotic young life, mired in violence, arrests, drugs, isolation, poverty and fear-based inertia but nothing prepared me for his formidable intensity, a man penetrating my very DNA with the blinkless glare of his huge, canyon-deep brown eyes.

We were downstairs in the café of the Premises, the rehearsal rooms near his East End London home, a small space where we sat on adjacent seats, he with a bottle of still water, beneath signed prints of musical contemporaries, from Michael Kiwanuka to Laura Marling. His intensity included an almost compulsive need for light interrogation – whether I'd heard the new album, journalistic background, whether I saw the last tour – and, seemingly satisfied, he began by talking, unprompted, about age: he was about to turn fifty-nine.

'I think you know you're getting old when you start saying, "Not bad for fifty-odd" or whatever,' he brooded. 'You heard your parents talking like that and here we are. So . . . you like this album?'

Well, I ventured, you don't put a lot of yourself out there for scrutiny, do you? You're like a sprite. (The album's themes, mostly doomed romance, were couched in characterisation.)

'Like a sprite?' he responded, startled, evidently thinking about the fizzy drink. 'I've got water! What's a sprite? I'll go with the flow . . .'

That year a famed darts player had died, the one who'd been interlinked with Dexys since their '82 *Top of the Pops* appearance covering Van Morrison's 'Jackie Wilson Said'. Behind the frugging band beamed a backdrop not of Jackie the soul singer, but Jocky, the Scottish, jocular, gap-toothed arrowsmith, creating the instantaneous assumption of a howling BBC blooper (which persisted for decades).

'Jocky Wilson, I didn't really feel anything about that,' he shrugged, of his passing. 'I find all them little anecdotes that surround old Dexys a bit tedious really. I *do*. I'm interested in the music, and I think some of those things detracted from the music. I'll tell you the most interesting thing about that. We *asked* them [*Top of the Pops*] to put that picture up, for a laugh. Nothing really happened and then in the nineties it was on *Never Mind the Buzzcocks* and they showed it as a *Top of the Pops* gaffe. As a result, it did the rounds of those TV gaffe shows.

I think because Dexys had such an image of being miserable bastards [people in the media] couldn't accept it!'

He laughed, a hitherto unheard sound in pop history, a high-pitched trumpety hoot – 'Hah! Hah! Hah!' – much like the honks of Jimmy Carr. 'As if ten of us wouldn't have noticed a 20-foot picture of a darts player on the stage with us. They couldn't see that we had a sense of humour . . .'

One hour earlier I was being significantly more baffled by Kevin Rowland's erstwhile unknown sense of humour during full band rehearsals for the song 'I'm Always Going to Love You', a duet featuring guest vocalist Maddie Hyland, twenty-nine. Flirting extravagantly, the pair were beautifully dressed, she in towering heels and a flowing black coat, he in a fawn felt cap and crisp, wide-legged turned-up denims. The song, all perky strings, was partly spoken word, the story of a flourishing romance which suddenly, inexplicably dies. Within three minutes Kevin went from a declaration of love to announcing he was 'incapable of love', as a furious Maddie howled, 'Don't talk to me!' and plunged to the carpet, hands to her face. (She was, Kevin later told me, shedding real tears, 'she's a Shakespearean actress.')

The album could've been called, in fact, *Kevin Rowland Is Not Much Cop With Women: The Musical*, a bizarrely literal narrative detailing the life of Kevin, a man born 'lost inside', who becomes disillusioned with success, falls in love, decides he's using women 'as a challenge', believes he's 'incapable of love', discovers it's OK to be alone and is finally 'free'. With little sign of their signature brass parpings and fiddly Celtic soul, this was a woozy jazz night at the am dram society, Rowland's expressively rich vocals occasionally turning as croonsome as Vic Reeves' yodelling pub singer (he'd had singing lessons, he said, gravely, 'to help me convey my emotions'). This was an insanely melodramatic and occasionally (surely) comic departure for the mythologically intense Kevin Rowland, both a brooding presence and chipper cockney character who continually mentioned my name. Back in the downstairs café he told me, soberly, that this album was six years in the creating, many songs co-written with the reconvened musicians, and wasn't *necessarily* about himself.

Yes it is.

'It's a story.'

It's about you!

'It's a story! But obviously you're going to draw from your own experiences.'

Had he really felt incapable of love? Is that how things had been?

'For me? [Lengthy pause.] It's difficult to comment ... I don't talk about me life. Aw, you're a prober, you are, Sylvia.'

Had he always felt 'lost inside'?

'Naaaah. Character, innit?' (expansive wink)

Did he intend some of the lyrics to be funny?

'Course. People who know us well know there's humour there.'

So, he'd struggled with commitment, messed women around, wasn't even sure what love was ...?

'And all that malarkey. [Becoming aggrieved] Sylvia, I'll tell you something. If there's *one thing* I can't do it's talk about the lyrics. It's excruciating. They're pure, instinctive, there's nothing I can say about the lyrics that's not *in* the lyrics, d'you know what I mean?'

He drummed his fingers hard on the table, shifted in his seat and appeared to be about to scarper. Instead, he sighed, said, 'I can't believe it's finally happened' and mentioned false starts three years ago – 'studios were booked, but I wasn't ready.'

What was stopping him, I wondered?

'Massive fear, no doubt about it. Of? Doing a shit record.'
Fear of failure, then?

'Yeah-yeah-yeah. Perfectionism. Terrible. It's a curse. That stopped me doing anything for *years*. There were three Dexys albums in the eighties. And I didn't feel confident I could do anything as good as that.'

Kevin Rowland, at almost fifty-nine, was both, as he himself observed, a very private person and perhaps the most emotionally honest man in the history of rock'n'roll: very few were so willing to display in public a gourmet table of vulnerabilities, insecurities, crises of confidence and torturous bouts of performance-related anxiety. The first thing he did that day was clutch his neck and say, 'My throat's getting tight, I'm sure that's stress,' and begin puffing in and out on a drinking straw to alleviate the problem.

Wolverhampton raised, London schooled, of working-class Irish descent, he was the teenage petty criminal turned hairdresser who formed Dexys Midnight Runners in the post-punk creative combustion of 1978, whose sound evolved from trumpeting soul to jiggly Irish fiddles. They released three albums, *Searching for the Young Soul Rebels*, *Too-Rye-Ay* and acknowledged lost masterpiece *Don't Stand Me Down*, while Kevin wilfully alienated not only his own band (the members continually left) but the entire cultural landscape. He refused to conduct interviews with the 'hippie' press and beat up, in broad daylight, a *Melody Maker* journalist, the late and much-missed Barry McIlheney, who'd go on to edit *Smash Hits*. He also beat up his label boss and refused to engage with his peers, thus remaining creatively 'pure'. By 1986 it was all over, a brisk, brilliant, belligerent career inspiring in some ever since an unconditional devotion. He'd been disillusioned, with both success and what he felt was showbiz nonsense. Hadn't he?

'How d'you know that!?' he responded, oddly. 'Well, you're probably right. That was a lot of the problem in those days. I didn't hang out with my peers. I was very isolationist. It was all fear driven. I thought it was the right thing to do, "fuck them and der-der-der", all ridiculous, it led me into a corner. Quite a dark, lonely place, y'know?'

But, I pondered, he should've been having the biggest party of his life – 'I don't think it was *about* having a party,' he frowned – before asking whether he experienced any moments of achievement at all, even joy?

'I never felt that,' he replied, tragically, then thought again. 'I felt it for a few weeks. After "Geno", for a couple of weeks. Maybe a month after "Come On Eileen". But then I just felt the pressure, of what I've gotta do next and "I can't handle this". I'm a bit like that now to tell you the truth. I'm starting to get stressed out. I've been freaking out. I'm just a fucking stress bucket, d'youlknowhatImean? But I didn't know it when I was young, I thought it was everyone else's fault. It was *all* fear driven.'

Is that where the anger came from? He was very angry.

'I was. You should've been a fucking therapist, you, Sylvia. I bet you *are*. Have you had training?'

You beat up a pal of mine once, Barry McIlheney.

'What can I tell you? Barry's a nice feller. He's a mate of mine now. Well, I wasn't angry when we did the Jocky Wilson thing, that was funny. Listen, I was … Cor, you ask tough questions, probing, that's why they send you on these jobs, to people like me.'

But … but … you've been in therapy! You've gone through all this with proper psychological professionals, not the likes of me.

'My programme of recovery is where I've really sort of … seen the biggest change, I think. I was angry. Guilty as charged.'

Through therapy, then, I pressed on, maybe he discovered where the Fear originated from?

'I was expected to not do very well in life,' he now managed, admirably willing to help me out. 'Left school at fifteen. Didn't have an education. I'd been arrested and up in juvenile courts four times by the time I left school at fifteen. Very nearly went to approved school. Miraculously escaped borstal a few years later.'

His young life was then blighted by petty, and not so petty, crime.

'Miraculously escaped prison,' he confessed. 'I'd been to court about sixteen times. Violence, burglaries, assaults, stealing cars. I mean, not [he moulded his fingers into a gun shape]. Stupid things. I could *easily* have gone to prison. And probably wouldn't have been able to handle prison. Friends of mine who did a lot less went to prison. I was going nowhere, I thought I was a nobody.'

At twenty-three, twenty-four he finally began cutting hair, men and women's, finally joined a band, his brother's, finally wrote a song and then finally formed his own band.

'And then thinking I couldn't do that, those things are out of reach, for me,' he added, forlornly. 'And I was . . . saved in some way, blessed. So I had a massive determination to do music. It felt like life or death. If I can prove myself, have a hit record, do something, be on *Top of the Pops*, be *somebody*, no one can put me down. That's why I was so driven. I *must* do this. And when I got something, I was, "What the fuck am I gonna do now?" I just don't think I was very stable from a very young age. I *pretended* everything was alright. I was never easy-going, y'know? I'd love to find a way of being happy-go-lucky, Sylv.'

After phenomenal success through '80 to '85 came extreme wilderness years.

'I was a guy without a life,' he sighed. 'I had put everything into music, I was disillusioned, so where's the drugs?'

He crumbled into depression, booze and cocaine addiction (up to four grams daily).

'I used to get into fights when I was drunk, go crazy when I took cocaine, so . . . hah hah hah!' he honked, ruefully. 'It's better I leave everything alone. But drugs are alright you know? I'm just not someone who can use drugs socially. What about you? I've got an addictive personality, it's just in me. I think I always knew I could easily go that way. That's why I was so anti-drink and drugs in [the original] Dexys. In the seventies, I was a bit of a bugger for speed and whatever else I could get my hands on.'

Staggeringly, he was homeless for two years, squatting in a flat in North London's glam-free Willesden.

'I wasn't on the street,' he clarified, 'but I was in a place for two years where I didn't pay any rent. A flat. By myself. I said to the landlord, "I'm moving in," gave him the first month's rent and never paid him after that. That's life, innit? There's worse things.'

Where were his buddies?

'Me buddies?' he blinked. 'Well, people get out of your way, really, when you're on a path of self-destruction. I saw friends from time to time, but I was on a path, y'know? Nobody can do anything if you're on a path. But I'm alright now. And better without anything, better for everyone else as well hah hah hah!'

Why did he not want to engage with the world and basically destroy himself? What was that impulse?

'I *really* don't know why,' he insisted. 'I think it's just in me. For years Dexys was my addiction. '78 to '85. So, after that, y'know, I was burnt out, broke. And disillusioned. Misunderstood. I alienated the press. Alienated my record company. Alienated everybody. That was it. I dunno, Sylv, I don't look as deeply into stuff as you. I had a problem, got some help, sorted it out, I'm alright now.'

As a kid he'd thought he *could* handle stardom.

'I just wanted to be a fucking pop singer,' he sighed. 'I wanted to be like the Beatles and Rolling Stones and play music and have a good time and wear nice clothes and meet women ... what went wrong?'

It must've been testament to an inner strength, surely, that he was sitting here right now?

'Not really.'

Throughout the chaos of his young life his parents must've been worried about him. Did they ever try to help?

'Em,' he replied, after an extensive pause. And then a rueful laugh. 'I think they were probably bemused by me. "What's he doing now?!" A generational thing. I mean, look, I was getting into trouble with the police.'

Did his dad threaten to tan his hide, as that generation would've said?

'You're very probing, Sylvia!' he responded once again, with an extra-penetrative stare. 'You're a very naughty gel! I'm not gonna tell you *anything* about my family. Hah hah hah! I'm not gonna get into that!'

Kevin Rowland was, then, the personification of the rock'n'roll archetype who, if it wasn't for music, would definitely be in prison. But there was also, behind the formidable glower which persistently consumed his face, an occasional twinkling softness in his strikingly burnished brown eyes. His previously elusive 'Jimmy Carr' laugh, honking and high-pitched, became, if not constant, a regular. 'Wanna chocolate?' he wondered, proffering an Ombar – an acai & blueberry superfood vegan chocolate bar. Was this one of his things? 'One of my *things?* Well I like sweet things, don't like getting fat though.'

When Kevin Rowland musically reappeared in 1999 with his bizarre covers album *My Beauty* he'd been free of all booze and drugs since 1993, the year he entered and had since remained in a 'programme of recovery'. No substances were involved, then, in his decision to wear the much-mocked dress on its cover, silken folds bunched into his arms revealing bulging knickers below. It wasn't so much the dress that boggled, though, as the fact he had his knackers out.

'Well, I don't regret that for a moment,' he coolly replied. 'I was *completely* sound of mind. I don't see that as anything negative or anything to do with a fragile emotional state, as has been stated! I liked it.'

It was merely, he carried on, his then-latest sartorial experiment, always searching for 'new ideas', attempting to 'pioneer', a man who wore a sarong in 1995 (three years before David Beckham) and then a leather kilt. 'I *try*,' he lamented. For years he'd practised yoga, 'getting myself strong' and in January 2010 after a series of ailments refused to heal (shoulder, knee trouble) his yoga teacher suggested five weeks, 'to cleanse and all that', at an Indian ayurvedic retreat, a traditional Hindu treatment centre involving herbal medicines. He rose daily at 6 a.m., had one morning meal (a curry), 'tiny single bed, washed with a bucket and a tap, no shower, very basic, hardcore, very good for me' and mostly contemplated his life in the surrounding garden. 'And I thought OK, what do I really want to do now? I wanted to make this record. I was ready.'

Was he finally happy being himself, being 'alone' and 'free' like he sang on the new album?

'Well, I'm still struggling with everything,' he concluded, brightly. 'All the anxiety. But I'm doing alright. [He puffed his cheeks.] Oh, who knows! I can't talk too much about me life, I'm a private person, I really am. Okay? Cool.'

He drummed his fingers on the table one last time.

'Alright, surely you've got enough now?!' he implored. 'I'm going. Back to rehearse. You've got *loads*, darlin'.'

How did he feel about the fans who called him a genius?

'Well, I'm *not*,' he retorted. 'D'youknowhat? I don't hang around with *anybody* who is a Dexys fan.'

Just tortured, then?

'I've been tortured in the last hour!'

He honked once more with laughter, rose to leave, shook my hand, said, 'I'm alright, I'm better than I was,' and disappeared back to his beloved music.

Four days later, thirteen days before the start of Dexys' intensely awaited four-date theatre tour, their first shows in nine years, word arrived that Kevin Rowland's voice had now, albeit temporarily, 'totally gone'. I spared a merciful thought for rock's most fragile frontman: still no sign of any puncturing holes in his permanent bucket of stress. On the bus home from our encounter, I'd contemplated his chocolate gift, the health-food Ombar, and how it might be a bit like Kevin Rowland had been that day: rich in antioxidants, organic and, at nearly sixty, still intensely raw.

*

In 2025, Kevin Rowland, at age seventy-one, finally published his autobiography, *Bless Me Father*, detailing the beatings, bullying and abuse he endured from his father as a kid. This violence he came to 'enjoy' because it meant he wasn't just being ignored, 'it was this thing we shared together,' positing the relationship as the defining experience of his life.

7

THERE IS A LIGHT

1983, The Smiths' 'Hand In Glove' and 'This Charming Man' elevate 'indie' into a romantic literary artform

Morrissey's face loomed towards me as large and beautiful as the marbled creation of Michelangelo's David. The familiarity rendered me dumbstruck: the pronounced jut of the jaw, those cornflower-blue eyes, the dark, dramatic eyebrows an approximation of the rare, black-feathered Verreaux's eagle in flight, the softly toppling quiff forever unchanged, and no wonder: as Morrissey himself once quipped, 'why meddle with a masterpiece?' My inner voice, where no outer voice emerged, blared inside my head: 'JESUS CHRIST IT'S MORRISSEY.'

It was 1992, Morrissey was still Morrissey, *Morrissey from the Smiths*, the band which formed the contours of my sensibilities like no other before it in the early-to-mid eighties. *Morrissey*, whose lyrics shattered into my conscience like a heart-shaped brick through an intricately stained-glass window, shards of lyrical opulence scattering towards me on irresistibly sparkling melody, to pierce my skin and embed themselves, forever, inside my thumping teenage heart. And now we were being introduced, unexpectedly, accidently, in a pub in Camden through the mutual PR friend he was with. No hand outstretched, no words exchanged, just a brief acknowledgment, a tip of that head, but I knew what he was thinking.

'Oh puh-lease, *an apostle.*'

I felt sixteen, clumsy and shy all over again, cringing into the valves of my now twenty-seven-year-old heart, where those lyrical shards remained embedded. 'He can,' I thought, 'see right through me.' I made my excuses and left – i.e. *ran away.*

In 1983, the year Culture Club's inescapably chipper 'Karma Chameleon' was the UK's biggest-selling single (closely followed by Billy Joel's inescapably jolly 'Uptown Girl'), the year a major demonstration marched through London against nuclear weapons, as the word 'yuppie' emerged (young, urban professional, obsessed with cash and social status) and PM Margaret Thatcher continued privatising life itself, the Smiths bloomed out of the radio as if a fully formed gladioli had grown from seed to maturity in time-lapsed minutes.

I was eighteen years old, newly left home, lost and naïve, living in a squalid flat share in my hometown of Perth, single and yearning for connection, for love, for *something to save me.* Straight from school I had a job I loathed (sub-editor on grandma's magazine *Annabel*), commuting to a city I despised (Dundee), with a bleached-blonde, side-shaved eighties quiff I had to comb down in order to not be sacked, and a burgeoning reliance on Carlsberg Special to ease my inner torpor. I might as well have had a Morrissey quiff-shaped target on my back announcing a demographic misfit bullseye, the definition of what Morrissey always referred to as a Smiths 'apostle'. For years his interviews alone were the indie commandments chiselled on stone and arranged around my psyche like the trilithons of Stonehenge.

From '83 to '87 the music and lyrics of the Smiths, that glittering constellation of poetic insight into what it means to be young (in all its excitement, horror, loneliness, heartbreak, drama, kinetic energy and gallows hilarity), was my post-school education, the peerless soundtrack to four crucially formative years, eighteen to twenty-two, the years I might otherwise have spent at university. Like a sorcerer's key flying towards me on a magic pillow of mesmerising sound, the Smiths unlocked the library to the ancient poets and world class wits, to subtle subversion and sexual ambiguity, to ideologies that made me even more of an anti-monarchist than I was already, and when *Meat Is Murder* was released in February '85, a vegetarian overnight. Moving to Dundee that year, I floridly etched a scene from the hypnotising opus 'How Soon Is Now' around the bedroom cornice of the latest mouldering flat: 'You could meet somebody ...'

Twenty-nine years later ...

Manchester Central Library, 2014. Almost three decades on from the Apostle Years and I was feeling slightly jangly, waiting inside the Dickensian, book-lined Chief Librarian's Office, about to have an actual conversation with the *other* man responsible for all that character-forming music which saved my late-adolescent life. And this time I wasn't a punter in the pub, I was a 'professional' and could not run away.

'What's occurrin'?'

These were the first, unexpectedly northern words lifting from the lips of Johnny Marr, striding purposefully into this beautifully wood panelled and polished literary space. In his hand dangled a bag of green tea, looking more '1978' than he probably did in 1978: a Manchester Modernist Society badge pinned to his none-more-new-wave olive-green jacket, over a black-and-white-striped T-shirt, sporting chipped silver nail polish, hair by the Small Faces. 'It is,' he conceded, of his meticulously cultivated look, now aged fifty-one, 'a bit CBGB's.'

Manchester Central Library is where the fourteen-year-old Johnny Marr hid from the rain, which flattened his hair, bunking off school throughout 1978, his own year zero and for many of the glimmer-eyed dreamers of the post-punk generation. In the grand, circular reading room of this 1930s-built neoclassical structure, the obsessive teenage guitarist forensically studied the music press which fired his mind with the cultural thrills he could also find in this imposing, pillared room: Aldous Huxley, Oscar Wilde, avant-garde German philosophy. Above his head a biblical proverb circled the ceiling in golden lettering, 'WISDOM IS THE PRINCIPAL THING . . .' Shortly after his fifteenth birthday, Halloween 1978, he left school forever.

'I had other things to attend to,' he quipped, with a grin. 'And the reason I've such respect for pop culture is because it gave me an education. It gave me a *life*.'

Wow, I thought to myself, what happened to him, through music, is exactly what happened to me. He was after all – shockingly – only eighteen months older.

Thirty-six years on from his fifteenth birthday and Johnny Marr had returned to Manchester Central Library and would stride, later this afternoon, through its newly renovated corridors, asbestos-lined wood panelling now replaced by a contemporary gleam of white walls, chrome and glass. He was constantly approached by well-wishers, from students to middle-aged library staff, each announcing, 'I'm a big fan!' and each time he gifted them a plectrum from a seemingly bottomless magic plectrum pocket. 'eBay gold,' he grinned. '£2.75.' No one mentioned the Smiths. But they didn't look like Cribs fans to me.

*

One hour earlier, back in the Chief Librarian's Office, sipping his green tea, Johnny Marr had been attempting to avoid, as ever, having an interview dominated by the Smiths, the band he'd formed aged nineteen in 1982 with Morrissey, which redefined the very possibilities of popular music. Since their split in '87 (contractual wrangles, pressure, exhaustion), the further they've stepped into history, the more revered they've become. Noel Gallagher, an original eighties Smiths apostle back in Burnage, once described Morrissey as 'without a doubt the most literate man ever to make music'. Marr was his hero in both guitar – 'a fucking wizard' – and sartorial flair – 'I thought, "That's what I wanna look like."' Noel was also certain you can be inspired by Johnny Marr but never copy him. 'He's unique – no one can play what he plays.'

For over twenty-five years he'd played musical chairs in a hangar-sized Hall of Fame, either temporarily joining bands (The Pretenders, The The, US alt-rock heroes Modest Mouse, Yorkshire's indie yelpers the Cribs), inventing new ones (The Healers, Electronic with New Order's Bernard Sumner) or adding voodoo-fingered wizardry to diverse giants, from Talking Heads, Bryan Ferry and Oasis, to Girls Aloud and German soundtrack composer Hans Zimmer, the pair Oscar-nominated for *Inception* in 2010. In early 2013, he released debut solo album *The Messenger* (occasionally Smiths-esque) his imminent second, *Playland*, more a thundering post-punk adrenalin rush, made with his young band, echoing Generation X and Wire, lyrically contemplating twenty-first-century conflicts with technology, distraction and money. There was no nostalgia here, then, for those pesky retrograde apostles.

'I make music that excites me *now*; do people want me to be walking round with a quiff thirty years later?' he scoffed, cheerily. 'I don't want David Hockney doing splash paintings in 2014. Enough people like what I'm doing now, thank you very much! Fuck what other people think . . .'

Noel Gallagher called him, his now lifelong friend, 'a euphoric, "up" guy'. He persistently countered the negative with the positive. 'It's in my nature.' I'd always wondered, therefore, what lingered in Johnny Marr's upbeat soul that expressed itself so staggeringly eloquently in the exquisite sadness of so many of the Smiths' greatest songs. Days before we met, I listened at monumental volume, for the first time in years, to their baroque orchestral masterpiece 'Last Night I Dreamt That Somebody Loved Me', the Smiths' seventeenth and final single, and actually dropped to the floor, onto my knees, and wept. It was *all too much to bear.*

'Job done, job done!' thrilled Johnny Marr, clutching my arm with the very hand that created this frankly Shakespearean sonic tragedy (even before Morrissey's devastating lyric). 'That's my favourite. Of all those old songs. Kind of gothic. Well, that's the way I was feeling at the time. And I get those feelings to this day, which is an identification with melancholy, absolutely. But . . . but . . . this band now is not about that . . .'

I persevered. I'm not sure that song could be bettered anyway, I told him, so maybe why bother?

'I don't think it *is* better than what I'm doing now,' he replied, perturbed. 'It's just different.'

I'm not sure people will believe that. I think they might think 'he's in denial'.

'Well I don't care whether people think I'm in denial or not, because I'm not!'

He was definitely in denial . . .

Johnny Marr was a physically slight, psychologically robust, intensely creative man profoundly of his time, creatively born in the aftermath of the culturally explosive early eighties, all Fatcher-loathing and feminism, gay rights and boisterous alternative comedy. 'All those things going on when I started the Smiths seem like pretty good ideas to me *now*,' he pointed out. Like Morrissey's (and the Gallaghers'), his parents were young Irish immigrants into post-war Manchester, his mum seventeen when he was born, his extensive family musically possessed by the Everly Brothers, Johnny Cash and traditional Irish ballads. A guitarist at ten, a Neil Young badge on a fellow school kid's collar led him to future Smiths bassist Andy Rourke. Living on the sprawling new Wythenshawe council estate, he smoked marijuana and practised guitar in a night-time bedroom lit only by 'an orange streetlight coming through the window of this concrete box built in 1972.' In tough seventies Manchester the sensitive Marr was picked on by the hard lads. 'Directly singled out,' he nodded. 'For being different. What did they say? What, when they stopped throwing bricks at me, you mean? I got bricks rained down on me by a bunch of guys.' At fifteen, he met future wife Angie Brown, fourteen, the pair similar looking, soon skulking through Manchester's drizzly streets 'like Johnny Thunders and Siouxsie Sioux'. He played guitar ever more intensely.

'That sad emotion you're talking about has sometimes been really … uhm … close to the surface,' he suddenly faltered, eloquence deserting him. 'I had the positive outlook to balance it but my … environment didn't help it, to be honest. It was tough, for my family. Economically, culturally. There was intense Irish beauty and melancholy and an awful lot of drinking around. I came from a loving family but I wanted out, of my social situation. Music was escape. Nearly all my life has been about escape.'

In recent years he'd begun his autobiography, jesting 'there'll be musicians quaking in their boots, I'm talking about *you*, Bernard Sumner!' The pair's acid-fuelled escapades in the nineties had resulted in their boggle-eyed exertions down-ver-studio 'trying to make hi-hat sounds out of a sine wave'. Marr swore he hadn't read Morrissey's 2013 *Autobiography* – 'Nah' – and wasn't even curious. 'No, I'm beyond it, really.' I assured him there was nothing to worry about, which prompted an incredulous guffaw. 'I've got nothing to worry about anyway!'

Four days later . . .

It was a positively exuberant Johnny Marr who bounded into music producer Mickie Most's glass-fronted office in RAK Studios, West London. Since Most's death in 2003 his lair had been left as a time-capsule, walls of discs eulogising the mighty sixties/seventies pop single (The Animals, Lulu, Donovan, Suzi Quatro, Mud, Hot Chocolate) and one outsized four-seater brown leather couch. 'A lot of famous decisions were made on that couch,' beamed Johnny, 'and probably a lot of other stuff heheh! Let's sit on the famous couch . . .'

Today, in a buttoned-up crimson cardigan, he was prone to big-toothed laughs and manic eyes, almost *keen* to ponder the Smiths. Exactly twenty-nine years ago that very week the Smiths recorded sessions here for some of their best-loved songs: 'There Is a Light That Never Goes Out', 'Big Mouth Strikes Again', 'Rubber Ring', 'Asleep', 'Never Had No One Ever'. The Smiths' music was, he now acknowledged, 'magic, I'm very proud of my band', music which 'propelled us forwards, through catastrophe, every song was like a rocket we were clinging to.' Beyond the music, Marr's role was to counteract the chaos within this 'manager-less, dysfunctional group', constantly battling no radio plays, poor chart placings, unprofitable tours, no videos shown on suddenly almighty MTV because, being revolutionaries, they refused to make them. It was here in RAK where they eventually succumbed (appeasing their Rough Trade label) to a performance video for 1985's 'The Boy with the Thorn in his Side'.

'We said, if we're going to capitulate, we will, under duress, allow you to interrupt the space we're in but we refuse to move more than one foot away from where we are right now, and hurry up,' cackled Marr. 'We were punk rock in lots of ways. The video is utterly crap. We were young and wilful and unique and single-minded. Even when we were *wrong*.'

By '85 Morrissey was permanently quipping on the covers of the music press, the teenage apostle back in Burnage reading every word and, as Noel Gallagher once told me himself, 'pissing myself laughing, on the bus, *out loud*'. Morrissey's peerless propaganda inspired an illusion: that all four Smiths must be celibate librarians, high only on the scent of gladioli wafting above Morrissey's angelic head. In truth, Marr was a dope-smoking booze 'n' coke demon while Andy Rourke had succumbed to the eighties heroin scourge.

'It's much cooler that we were representative of that time,' decided Marr. 'I was and am a product of late seventies, early eighties Britain. We were bad ass.'

How Andy Rourke could function so deftly and prolifically seemed almost miraculous, Marr citing both his talent – 'Andy is an incredible musician' – and the band's regimented work ethic. 'Lifestyle never *ever* took priority over the music. The truth is, the label could hardly keep up with us,' he recalled, with some satisfaction. 'We'd stay up 'til dawn on exuberance, winging it. When you're creating, you're just *woooof!* It's freedom and inspiration.'

The end was 'horrible', the 1996 court case 'nasty' (drummer Mike Joyce sought, and won, 25 per cent recording/ performance royalties from Morrissey and Marr) but Johnny did not dwell. 'People have serious burdens to carry through life,' he reasoned, 'a lot worse than, y'know … a band falling out!' The Smiths, he'd been certain for years, would never reform. His and Morrissey's sporadic email correspondence, 'often cordial', was now over.

'There's only so many times you can be nice to somebody and not get it back, so you go, "OK then, fuck it",' he observed. 'We didn't know each other before the band and we don't ... y'know, we're not family. It's worse for the Gallaghers, the Davies [Kinks] brothers. It could always be worse. Even for the Smiths!'

Perhaps they would never reform because they had everything to lose?

'I wouldn't want to reform the Smiths, what would I be exchanging?' he wondered. 'What would I get from that? A ton of money?'

Abba turned down one billion pounds, apparently. Could he see himself doing that?

'D'you know what?' he spluttered, aghast. 'Fuck it, I'll join Abba, problem solved! No, I need to work for a living, keep my family going and I've never known it any other way. It's a decent motivation. It's good for you.'

(In 2023, any possibility of an original Smiths reunion died with their extraordinary bass player Andy Rourke, who we lost to pancreatic cancer at the age of fifty-nine.)

Johnny Marr's chosen lifestyle was good for anybody. A teetotal vegan who ran up to twenty miles a day, he was an *in-control* person: physically, musically, sartorially, seemingly emotionally.

'I can't handle *messy*,' he noted. 'But it really isn't about control. Everything I've ever done is just for the betterment of me as a musician and a man.'

Naturally, he dyed his precisely sculpted hair.

'Course I do, I'm in a fucking band!' he blared. 'You want ...

Nick Cave to look like Nick Cave. Young people ask me about dyeing my hair and I think, "Is this the fifties? Go'n ask David Bowie, you wanker!" All the new-wave bands I loved had dyed hair. I tried to dye Andy Rourke's hair once with household bleach and it all went in his eyes, could've blinded him. That was after I pierced his ear with two blocks of ice. Which I also did to Ryan Jarman [of the Cribs]. I'm *so* 1978 council estate, you can't ever shake it off ...'

He gave up booze and drugs not because he was an addict but because it wasn't a good look. 'Beyond mid-thirties, living a boozy, druggy rock-guitar-playing existence is a cliché.' Not that he minded messy in others. He would entertain at home till 4 a.m., 'if it's funny, I'm there,' until he heard 'the same story five times'. Then, he adopted a self-invented ruse. 'Carpet Bombing: a mixture of champagne, port and pot,' he grinned. 'It's like [he shouted] *tiiiimbuuur!* I set this shit out and call a cab.'

His lifelong romance had surely bolstered his equilibrium above all, young Angie the steadying moon around wobbling planet Smiths, their two grown kids then twenty-two (daughter Sonny) and nineteen (guitar-playing son Nile). He now had a message for Noel, with a grin: 'My son can play like me, quite easily.' Then married for twenty-eight years, the sometime post-punk spooks were both born on Halloween.

'It's uncanny,' he marvelled. 'And she's been anything but the dutiful Manc wife standing at the sink while hubby comes back from the Indie Wars. We're two sides of the same coin. Partners. My kids have an amazing mother. No wonder I'm such a happy guy!'

A big-toothed smile exploded.

'I'm sitting surrounded by all these records I used to actually *play*,' he suddenly levitated. 'What, twenty-nine years since the Smiths were here? Time goes by so quickly ... "He says, leaning back into Mickie Most's couch!" I've been called a workaholic, but I don't think I'm driven in any negative way. I'm just enthusiastic. I believe in bands, I believe in music, I believe it's art. I believe, still, there's nothing quite so powerful as an eighteen-year-old with nothing to lose.'

He leaped from the famous couch, shouted, 'It's a draw, it's a draw!' and, much to my astonishment, crunched my ribs in a bear-hug, a man who evidently saw these kinds of media summits as something of a duel.

There was one last photo to take, on the RAK Studio steps, where he spied an unacceptable crinkle in his immaculate crimson cardigan. 'Can you photoshop that out?' he beseeched the photographer. 'I don't give a shit about this [he pointed to his face] but I can't have that. What will the kids on the estate say? He's lost it! Ended up in London a scruffy bastard!'

No chance. Possibly even *less* chance than a Morrissey/Marr reunion.

Four years later …

Johnny Marr was in his ancestral homeland, sitting inside Maureen's Bar in the Olympia Theatre, Dublin's oldest, stunningly preserved Victorian musical hall. Still a slight figure with dyed black hair, he remained meticulous in his regulation post-punk dress code: leather-effect jacket, skinniest black jeans, immaculate black desert boots. He was in reflective mood, contemplating the lyrics of his latest solo album, *Call the Comet*, where he imagined 'alternative societies' to the fractious, divisive ones of 2018 and how intelligent life from outer space might visit Earth with urgent advice.

'To help us rebuild and reset,' he explained. 'Because religion isn't doing it. Capitalism isn't doing it. Politics isn't doing it. What the fuck's left?'

There were no specific mentions of that year's ongoing Trump/Brexit-led chaos – 'those fuckers don't deserve to be in my songs!' – although the song 'Bug' was, he added, 'a piss-take, a rockin' track that describes the evolution of the alt-right as a virus on the world's nervous system.' He sipped his tea and smiled. 'But it isn't totally a concept album otherwise I'd have to dress up as a wizard.'

Now fifty-four, he remained a romantic idealist and 'old school bohemian', his philosophical mood that day recalling his literary boyhood, immersed in J. G. Ballard and William Burroughs (often read back in Manchester Central Library).

'Their vision of the future was scary and imposing and bleak, but it was *interesting*,' he mused. 'Interesting young people in decaying tower blocks with paperbacks in a pocket, on their way to organise the resistance. Instead, today, it's become a different numbing dystopia: strip malls, huge flat screen televisions in tiny council houses, mobile phones, media control, the clever manipulation of information and people, this weird virtual existence. The impression of incredible wealth and opulence, where if you scratch under the surface, you see the effect, which is anger, frustration, abuse and we see that on social media. We walk around in these gentrified environments with this feeling of malaise and unease.'

In 2018, though, there was only one truly pressing question to be asked of Johnny Marr. In the year he lyrically despaired over the rise of the alt-right globally, Morrissey had done the opposite: endorsed alt-right party For Britain run by former UKIP leadership candidate Anne Marie Waters (who'd tweeted anti-Islamic propaganda to President Donald Trump's retweeting delight). How had Johnny Marr been, in his head, with all this?

'How am I in my head with it . . .' he said, slowly, and did everything in his power, as ever, to avoid both the word

Morrissey and any opportunity for a shrieking, Moz-related headline. 'Well, I think you're more interested in it than I am,' he swerved, deftly. 'I don't wanna say I don't give a shit, but . . . I don't care that much. Probably because . . . I'm really busy!'

What bothered me that year was whether this could damage the Smiths' legacy, a question met by sustained silence. In the hope of provoking a reaction I wondered: is Morrissey becoming the Donald Trump of pop?!

'Er!" he spluttered. "I think . . . journalists will probably make that decision.'

He sat back in his seat and finally offered up a meaningful response.

'See, the Smiths were about inclusion,' he reminded me. 'Expressing things about – and for – the outsider. The disaffected. The misfit. Whether that was because of your sexuality, your gender, your lifestyle, your place of birth or your race. That's what we *were*. And . . . nothing's gonna change that. For me. The Smiths were not about *hate*.'

Which is why, that year, there were T-shirts printed with the slogan 'Gutted about Morrissey'?

'Mmn . . . eheheh,' he responded, as a wry chuckle escaped. 'Yeah. But it sounds like I've moved on more than you have.'

Did he think the legacy, then, was bulletproof?

A lengthy pause ensued. 'I think the songs are bulletproof,' he eventually said. 'You can't ever take . . . you can't change . . . you can't change *history*. You can't change what those songs meant to people. And you can't change that I wrote the music. That Andy played the bass, Mike played the drums. Those things can't change. I just know what *I* know.'

He contemplated his lifelong 'obsessional' work ethic, how it comes with a cost, the instability, constant scrutiny, the body-warping, exhausting travel, the four hours' sleep on a tour bus overnight, for years, at his age.

'I've so many quote-unquote "straight" friends with proper jobs and they couldn't do it,' he mused. 'They go "fuck that, you're *mad*." But for all creative people, it's your life force. It's not just … a *lark*. And obsession can weigh heavy on you. Whether your relationships or your work or your future or past. When you see things poetically, being a sensitive person with this … storm inside yourself. There's a price to be paid for those beautiful glimpses around the curtain. There *is*. But I wouldn't change a thing.'

On the streets of central Dublin, Johnny Marr was witnessing a storm outside himself, surrounded by thrilled fans, mostly men aged twenty to fifty – 'Holy fockin' shit!' exclaimed one – accepting all requests for selfies. Standing on a River Liffey bridge for official photos, a teenager watched silently, clutching a reissue vinyl copy of 1986's *The Queen Is Dead*. He approached and Marr's face lit up. Marr asked him a stream of questions – 'What's your name?' (Conor), 'D'you play?' (guitar and bass), 'Who else d'you like?' (Oasis) – as he signed the album with Conor's specially brought silver marker pen, then reached into his pocket and handed him a plectrum from his ever-present stash. A quick, private word with Conor told me he was sixteen years old, discovered the Smiths via his forty-four-year-old dad (also an Oasis obsessive) and loved no contemporary music whatsoever. Conor, it turned out, had heard Marr was in Dublin today, so journeyed into town, album in hand, in the hope he'd simply bump into him. 'On the off chance,' he blinked. 'Amazing.' He knew, too, all about Morrissey's dubious recent pronouncements. 'Doesn't matter to me at all,' he said, boggling at his signed album. 'I just care about the music.'

The jury's in: the Smiths' legacy is, officially, *bulletproof*.

*

Today, I play Smiths songs sporadically, gingerly brought out like priceless parchments with metaphorical white gloves, susceptible to the degradation of too much light. And every time, I gasp out loud, or howl with laughter: they sound even *better* now, *bigger* now, more beautiful, smart and funny now, than they did all those decades ago. It doesn't matter to me, either, what Morrissey has become, *at all*: we cannot cling to the old dreams anymore, but nothing can tarnish these towering monuments to the possibilities of human art.

8

REBEL YELL

1984/1985, Billy Idol's 'Rebel Yell' and his preposterous lips are everywhere

Billy Idol was the most fantastically cartoony of all the punk cartoons. By late '84 he was never off MTV in America, youth culture's burgeoning conduit since '81 which made image, suddenly, pop's single most dominant force. This newly visual age was one skilfully exploited by my now all-time favourite magazine, *Smash Hits*, finding in its spirit of irreverence an anarchy of absurdism wholly absent in the ponderings and pretensions of the inkie music press. In '84 I was still working in Dundee, now the nineteen-year-old music ed on a 'style' magazine called *Etcetra* which positioned itself as a rival to *The Face* (and was so misguided, and misspelled, it lasted six months). *Smash Hits*, meanwhile, was the lawless bugle which brought us comedy nicknames for pop stars, with recent additions for Mark Unpronounceablename from Big Country (surname Brzezicki, no doubt a cancellable quip today) and Sir Billiam of Idol, the one who fully embraced the idiocy and potency of the primary-coloured, rock'n'roll caricature with a spectacularly shameless gusto.

He'd been a central figure to me since 'Dancing with Myself', the single released with his punk-pop herberts Generation X in 1980, the kind of neuron-exploding euphoric rush that had me sprinting across dance floors like a quiffed-up road runner with a firecracker stuck to its tail. I loved that song and found Billy Idol hilarious, not only an unapologetic, proper rock'n'roll star but a 2D Sex God madman, one who blasted the spirit of punk through a neon prism of pulverising, audaciously suggestive pop. He embodied a word I'd associate, throughout the decades to come, with so many of the truest Greats: *preposterous*.

Thirty-four years later . . .

Billy Idol was sitting right next to me in a restaurant alcove in the Royal Garden Hotel, Kensington when, unprompted, he rolled up his trouser leg and presented his spectacular scar. The result of his near-fatal bike crash in 1990 (he was on a two year drugs 'n' booze bender at the time), it looked like a large pink baseball wedged into his calf.

'There was a big hole where the bone exploded through,' explained Sir Billiam, nonchalantly. 'I showed Madonna when it was fresh, all purple and veiny, horrible, nasty, and she *screamed*. It was worth all the pain to make Madonna scream. Meh heh heh!'

Billy Idol, fifty-eight in 2014, had a magnificently low-slung, filthy laugh and a speaking voice almost identical to Keith Richards' (London, baritone, shredded). The sometime incorrigible crumpeteer was a different kind of hoot from the one I'd expected: less comedy buffoon (possibly insane), more mild-mannered, gentle man of mischievous bonhomie. In eyeliner and studded black T-shirt, he delicately tucked into grilled salmon and steamed veg, as befits a life-long, performance-related weight watcher. He hadn't eaten meat since he was eighteen, had been sporadically macrobiotic and like Coldplay's Chris Martin adhered to a central ethos: nobody likes a fat pop star. 'See what you make us do?' he grizzled. 'We're out there killing ourselves to look all svelte!'

Billy Idol *still* believed in the cartoon creation, inventing himself as such in Generation X in 1976, masterful doyens of dance-floor-erupting anthem-rock. Through his solo career, using the face he was born with to its full advantage via both MTV and the pop press centrefold poster, he'd become stratospherically famous, a hell-raisin', leather-assed, Disney-eyed, Elvis-lipped 'pin-up' and today, as he spoke, his upper left lip constantly curled upwards. 'It's natural, I'm not making it do it!' he insisted. His videos alone – for 'Rebel Yell', 'Flesh for Fantasy', 'White Wedding', 'Eyes Without a Face' – were testament to the extravagantly perv-kitsch, dress-up tomfoolery of the early to mid-eighties.

'My son says, "Aw Dad, I wish I'd been in my twenties when it was the eighties",' Billy reminisced that day. 'And I say, "Well, when it was going on everyone said it was crap!"'

In 1981 he was banned from (he thinks) Granada TV for performing 'Dancing with Myself' in a vampire's cape, thigh-high boots over bare legs and a stripper's leather posing pouch.

'I did the rehearsal normally, came back looking like that and it was *live*,' he chuckled. 'I can imagine the director. "Don't zoom in on his bollocks!" Good fun. Meh heh heh!'

Within three years of moving to New York in '81 he was the toast of the Washington Square drug dealers. 'If they saw me coming, they'd start calling their drugs by the name of my songs,' he chortled. '"We got that White Wedding crack, that Rebel Yell heroin, that Mony Mony marijuana ..."' Colossal fame was 'weird, claustrophobic', and by '87 he was relocating to Los Angeles where he and his inner circle practically lived inside studios, 'trapped in tiny rooms because outside the room was mayhem, I was bigger than my music really.' Naturally, he slept with legions of women, despite having a girlfriend throughout the eighties, Hot Gossip dance trouper Perri Lister (they had a son in '88 and in '89 Billy had a daughter with a different, nineteen-year-old girlfriend). Did Perri simply accept his monstrous philandering?

'She didn't really know about it,' he reasoned, unapologetically. 'Thank God there wasn't social media like there is now, it's ruined everything. Must be a pain in the arse now, all that fame and you can't be naughty! You can't even buy crack on a side street without the papers knowing. *Hopeless.*'

From '88, his life was a rock-pig playpen of booze, drugs, strippers, orgies, walking around studios naked, 'but for our biker boots and scarves', until the bike crash, followed by almost fifteen years of smack, crack and creative inertia. He came off heroin by developing a crack habit, 'but then I was stuck on cocaine for years, terrible'. He attempted rehab and lasted five days. 'Horrible, they wanted you to write essays about your addiction.' Eventually, self-discipline triumphed and today he could drink booze occasionally, 'with an evening meal, lovely', smoke 'a little pot' and stay in control. He last smoked crack in 2003.

'I had a great time but it would be so wrong for me now,' he added, mercifully. 'You wouldn't want to meet me if I'd stayed like that. People who smoke meth, coke, you're really seriously out of your mind, terrible, you lose your teeth and everything.'

Maybe vanity, in the end, saved Billy Idol from himself, a man so determined to keep his dirty-bleached spiky hairdo he had dark roots 'painted in, meh heh heh!', otherwise they'd be white. That year the punk generation, suddenly, were in the approach to sixty.

'When I was young there wasn't old rock stars,' he noted.

'Lou Reed was the oldest and he was about thirty. It was a footballer's lifespan and then playing working men's clubs up north. Or in cabaret. Terrible! So I'm just glad there's still enough people who like my music. My records do still sound quite good.'

Unfeasibly, then, the real-life Billy Idol was very far from a ruined buffoon, more a cackling kindly uncle.

'I think that's to do with coming out of the punk scene, which will keep you grounded because it was all about smashing the star system,' he concluded. 'I'm not some damaged article sitting in front of you. I'm still vibrant. I've had a great life.'

He ambled off happily, and gently, on the holey leg that made the invincible Madonna scream.

Ten years later...

June 2024. While watching the Spain v Italy Euros match on telly, Billy Idol suddenly appeared in the ad break, perched on a wrought-iron throne, flanked by a couple of large, pointy-eared spook dogs. 'I can't believe you corporate types are still at it,' he pouted. 'Just stop calling each other rock stars.' Then, he gate-crashed a meeting, hollered 'Using responsible AI doesn't make you a rock star!', before the sarky exclamation, 'Look at my data-driven insights! I'm a rock star!' He then disappeared and some alien words, to me, appeared on screen: 'Workday: Be a Finance and HR rock star.'

Workday Inc., I only then found out, is 'a cloud-based, financial management, human capital management and student information system software vendor', American of course, proponents of the Man, who've been using 'rock stars' in ads for years (Ozzy Osbourne, Joan Jett, Gwen Stefani, Blink-182 drummer Travis Barker). 'While these rock icons might not consider us to be rock stars in the traditional sense, our customers around the world are the true rock stars of business and we want to celebrate that,' bugled Workday Chief Marketing Officer Emma Chalwin of this latest advertising ruse.

I could merely laugh. In the face of that kind of corporate hokey, I hoped Billy Idol had cackled uproariously all the way to the bank. He always was, anyway, a *massive tart*.

9

I'LL SAIL THIS SHIP ALONE

1986, The Housemartins' debut album London 0 Hull 4 *makes cardigans cool forever*

Late February 1986 and I walked into an open-plan office in Carnaby Street as Staff Writer on *Smash Hits*, a profoundly unexpected, life-changing scenario which emerged from a none-more-prosaic opportunity: an ad for the job in the *Guardian* newspaper. This I applied for with a life-or-death determination born of Dundee-trapped torpor, via not so much an application letter as a paving slab-sized dossier featuring teenage work from both school magazine and *Etcetra*, all liberally sprinkled with as many *Hits*-esque jokes as I could possibly get away with. That Monday morning I was all the things you'd expect in a newly London-dwelling twenty-year-old given her actual dream job: ecstatic, terrified, naïve and bursting with chaotic energy. But by October that year, now twenty-one, I'd confidently persuaded, somehow, several of my brand-new *Smash Hits* buddies to come with me to see the Housemartins live. *In Hull.*

In '86 the Housemartins were now *my band*, one I loved

as much as I loved the Smiths, but for opposite reasons. From comically glam-free Hull, they were not only the indie underdogs but titans of acutely un-Smithsian self-deprecation, whose badges bore the slogans 'the band with nowt taken out!' (in 'homage' to an Allison's bread ad) and 'the Housemartins are quite good.' This was a band with a *Smash Hits* mentality who were simultaneously as politically righteous as the Jam, creating a genre of their own: comedy Marxist agit-pop. Jaunty musical façades belied their provocateur's inner purpose, swathing their treatise on the charity delusion ('Flag Day'), Thatcherism ('Think for a Minute'), conformity ('Sheep') and Britain's belligerently macho booze culture ('Happy Hour') in melodic, sing-along euphoria. Their searing intent was then further disguised by dishevelled cardigans, NHS spectacles and amusing ears. And in frontman Paul Heaton they had not only a born eccentric but a scandalously underrated gospel-voiced virtuoso.

That 27 October we trundled up by train, as organised by teenage Readers' Services doyen Sue 'Smiles' Miles, booked ourselves into a B&B (featuring candlewick bedspreads and doilies on bedroom dressers), before heading to Hull City Hall, piling down the front and turning limb-flailing bonkers to the be-cardiganed, gospel-tinged, protest-pop comedians who deemed themselves 'the fourth best band in Hull'. Then, we barged backstage, where the four shuffling Housemartins were 100 per cent bewildered as to why their hometown dressing room was suddenly teeming with staff members of *Smash Hits*, whose features that year more regularly starred the likes of Jon Bon Jovi, Five Star, A-ha and glam-kitsch electro-rock chancers Sigue Sigue Sputnik (whose coverline read, 'The future of rock'n'roll or a load of codswallop?'). After much awkwardness and compensatory drinking, we piled back out again, back to the candlewick bedspreads. At least, this is how I've been told it happened by Sue Miles here in the twenty-first century, because this long-mythologised trip to Hull in the autumn of '86 I have no recollection of whatsoever. None. I bet, though, it was *completely brilliant.*

Brief *Smash Hits* interviews with the band I Scottishly called 'the Hooses' ran throughout the eighties but I got to know Paul 'Heato' Heaton significantly more through his post-Housemartins troupe the Beautiful South, who were, unfeasibly, the most grog berserk band I encountered through the chaos of the Britpop era. We travelled on the road in '95, from Chicago to Seattle, an endless odyssey of boozed-up buffoonery where hotel breakfasts comprised pints of beer and large gins. As a lifestyle, it couldn't possibly last . . .

Thirteen years later . . .

Paul Heaton's northern homestead was a handsome, red-bricked semi-detached house in a serene Manchester suburb, where two low-ceilinged rooms in the windowless basement housed the Paul Heaton Collections. It was 2008 and I'd been invited into his lovely home, the UK's best-loved eccentric pop socialist having survived the bedlam of the nineties unfeasibly intact and now with his lifetime's hobby to unveil. For years, we'd known about the crisps, his Crisp Bags of the World Collection (all-time champ: Tudor's Spring Onion) but here, for the first time, he was letting public light in on his complete collection magic. And then, possibly, closing the door forever.

At forty-six this was his twenty-fifth year in 'showbiz', still dressing in northern rainwear, a trim, fit and clear-eyed running enthusiast in training for an upcoming 10k, having quit smoking and begun moderating the booze. Since the Beautiful South's continual nineties bender he'd even quit booze altogether for a five-year spell. His eyes were huge, steady, vivid blue discs and his nails even lovelier – smooth, elegant, womanly, with long, squared off white tips. 'Heaton's Got Talons,' he quipped, 'that's my show!'

Paul Heaton's Football Room would've made a ten-year-old football fanatic self-combust on contact: exquisitely presented two-tiered rails of many-coloured shirts, meticulously arranged shelving units bearing flags, trophies, badges, scarves, videos, books, programmes, annuals, wallets, patches, mugs, World Cup ash-trays, a replica World Cup, *Roy of the Rovers* comics, a tower of sticker book collections with a favourite on top, cover star George Best (1969 to 1970, price: 2'6). Next door housed the Collections Room, an eye-boggling grotto of world-wide travelling ephemera (amid vast vinyl and CD collections in alphabetical order): Do Not Disturb signs, fly swatters and shoe-horns pinched from hotel rooms hung along the walls, Polaroids from twenty-five years of photo-shoots, a large picnic hamper filled with beer mats of the world, Simpsons figurines, hooks holding bunches of Beautiful South laminated backstage passes, countless maps, postcards, coins of the world, autograph books, pristine political badges including commemorative mid-eighties Miners' Strike badges kept in a Jacob's Cream Cracker tin. Had he ever wondered, on this evidence, if there was something psychologically wrong with him?

'I think some of this is about control,' he ventured, surveying his collection kingdom, mentioning the celebrity house-guessing TV show *Through the Keyhole*. 'If I went into my house I'd say, "This person is obviously very displaced. He travels but he seems desperate, there's a map from everywhere he's been, like it's gonna be the last time he ever goes there." I am secure in meself, but I've never been secure in my job. There's a bit of, "Look what I've got", like a medal. Somebody who feels as though they're travelling in the circus but they're really only driving one of the wagons. Somebody who feels as though they're a little luckier than they should be. With a child-like want for something real. When you're displaced and not at home, you're "Who am I?" And if I grab that, I'm somebody.'

We repaired to a nearby pub, which looked like a swish hotel. In a pair of leather armchairs, a chandelier overhead, we decided to have 'a drink'.

Paul Heaton was born bonkers, in Liverpool in 1962 (his part-time electrician dad played for Birkenhead's Tranmere Rovers) with a conflicting personality: sporty and arty, earthy and dreamy, chaotic and drawn to order. The Heatons moved to Sheffield where four-year-old Paul began his marble collection, playing 'marble football' every day. 'I memorised where each marble played, and the rest of the marbles watched on the sideline in a Bournville tin.' He'd then tip the spectator marbles into the marble players at the game's conclusion, 'cos there would always be crowd trouble – and I still have all my marbles, contrary to popular belief.'

The Heatons moved to Surrey as Paul turned fourteen and any hitherto commonplace obsessive behaviour (he'd begun making lists of his favourite 'John Peel' bands and alternative versions of the Top 20 Charts) was soon eclipsed by the wilfully obscure, collecting wrappers of the Rich Tea Biscuits he'd have every day for lunch, kept inside his school desk. 'About 400 of them, everyone would lift the lid and they'd all come springing out.' Paul educated himself, was encouraged to learn at home ('I was reading William Shirer's *Rise and Fall of the Third Reich*'), became a prolific writer everywhere but in school, of short stories, sketches, lyrics, poems and amusing observations. Sent to Redhill Technical College to sit O-Levels, he met, for the first time, 'proper arty middle-class types', including Norman Cook, 'when he was Quentin', the real Christian name of the soon-to-be Housemartin and eventual Fatboy Slim.

The early eighties were as inspirational to him as they had been to me, an era of individualism and polemical art-rock brilliance. Just the era, then, for the profoundly eccentric Heato to work in a bought ledger accounts department surrounded by 'racism and ignorance'. He channelled his frustrations through his most bizarre collection yet, every hole he punched in the ledgers, 'the pieces of round paper, I kept every single one in a drawer for three years.' Mercifully, he moved to Hull in 1983 where the Housemartins formed, the band Paul saw as 'a socialist Smiths', who regularly eschewed fancy hotels for the rigours of fans' floors.

'It became absolutely ridiculous,' blinked Paul. 'We were No. 3 in the charts with "Happy Hour" and I was staying that night on the roughest estate in Dundee and they [the fans] were drinking this drink which was on fire. It was madness every night. I got the bus in the morning.'

The more successful the Housemartins became, the more collecting he did, the more gig details he wrote in his diaries and the more disorientated he became.

'I think as a protective mechanism, you put your head up your own arse,' he decided, bluntly. 'I'd come home from tour and talk to meself in front of the mirror. And say, "You are Paul. Paul. Paul. Paul." Because I'd spent eight months in the company of "Paul Heaton". The Housemartins were never any mega superband but sure enough it accelerated. They were offering helicopters. Your head's in a spin and you're thinking, "Bloody hell, I'm never gonna remember the story," there was fame, money, women, drinking, you're forgetting people's names, so I took everything off the shelves, came home and filled an empty, cold flat with junk. I became really false for two years trying to be this "ordinary lad who likes a beer",

Mr Down To Earth. I was never that. And I compromised all my eccentricities. Got rid of me long nails. I always had long nails. I was much more honest and much more eccentric in the Beautiful South.'

The Housemartins, added Paul, 'just stopped, they never really split up' (their 1988 farewell best-of album was called *Now That's What I Call Quite Good*), and from '88 to 2007 the ever-evolving Beautiful South collective were quietly colossal. These were nineteen years when the Paul Heaton worldwide ephemera collection expanded to infinity, now including his favourite collection ever, due to his profound fear of flying, the boarding card stubs from international flights. 'I just felt so proud!' Unfeasibly, he'd only flown with the Housemartins once, from London to Glasgow, after a *Top of the Pops* appearance came up on the same day as a Barrowlands show. Flight was the only option.

'So I had a bumble bee suit on, that's how I flew, with the big chest and the eyes,' chirped Paul. 'I said, look, if you get me a bumble bee suit and me brother, cos I wanted me brother with me when I died, I'll fly. And I flew.'

I reminded him of the flight we took together from Chicago to Seattle, where we drank a bottle of gin between us for 'lunch', after which I collapsed in tears over a luggage carousel in Seattle airport. The Beautiful South had been *way too tough for me.*

'I think it was … enthusiasm!' he guffawed. 'And that enthusiasm for a drink kept the band together. It was all good. We all got on so well it was just crazy. It was … Showaddywaddy with a conscience.'

We sauntered to another pub, a nearby bowling and tennis clubhouse populated by three men in their sixties. It was now 10 p.m. and Paul – who'd had one packet of discontinued KP beef flavour crisps for his lunch and no tea – was now drinking a bottle of beer with a pint of bitter as a top-up combo, 'so it's one and a half drinks.' You got the impression, if he wanted, he could still be the hardest-drinking man in showbiz. But he wasn't, not anymore.

'I still have to be careful with it,' he noted, perusing his extended pint. 'But giving up for five years gave me an insight into my drinking. I was a very, very heavy drinker, whether you call that an alcoholic or not, I don't know, but I'm able to see the warning signs now. I never went to rehab but I saw an alcohol counsellor, and he taught me that one of the reasons George Best failed was that whole AA thing of guilt and "Oh God, I've had half a lager I must now do another fifty and kill myself." If you make a mistake, don't beat yourself up about it. Things are not ideal at the moment, I'm really on it. But the big change was when I stopped smoking. That was the end of the hedonism for me.'

That year Paul was dad to two young daughters, was single again having recently split with his long-term partner (they remained on good terms) and was mid-move to a new home round the corner. He was also at the several-drinks-in stage of singing the theme tune to a Gregor Fisher sketch from *Naked Video* in a preposterous Scottish accent, 'O.H.B.C. Neeeews! The Outer Hebrides Broadcasting Company, I fucking loved that!' Approaching midnight, we went for a curry and over the poppadoms he was as politicised as ever. 'We've been living in the Golden Age of Flash!' he roared, of the hyper consumerism of the noughties. 'Nobody cares about real things anymore.' He decided today was a landmark occasion.

'I feel as though I can throw away all my collections now,' he declared. 'I feel like this has been an exorcism, I really do. New house, new band, move on.'

He was serious, considering either selling the collections for charity or giving everything away to fans. His football collection would go to Preston's National Football Museum.

'It's a bit about age and a bit about just being relaxed.'

Maybe he finally felt . . . placed?

'I do feel placed,' he smiled. 'I'm exactly comfortable with where I am. I've had the best possible career, a rapid rise and then come down really slowly. I'm glad I've shown my mementoes on my walls rather than having to say nothing happened, I feel sorry for myself and killing myself through drink or drugs or lack of recognition. And now I don't feel I need to collect anything anymore. I think the further your feet are off the ground, the more shit you grab off the trees. And now I feel put back on the ground, by life.'

Nine years later . . .

In 2017, Paul Heaton was now a married man living round the corner from his 2008 home, in a modest family house on another red-bricked, terraced street. On my arrival his front door was wide open, despite a succession of burglaries round the area that year. Nothing, then, stood between myself and the tempting swag twinkling inside his hallway, having clearly given none of it away: bunting-style football flags hanging by nails from cornices (Melbourne, AS Roma, Verviers, Sweden), a metal display cabinet featuring a model Police Box, a red London bus, football team photos, a BBC Visitor's pass, a tube of Yorkshire crisps, a Sainsbury's School Games silver medal, miniature toy monsters and several football-motived toothbrushes pinned to the cabinet front. His front window hosted a cheery spectrum of nationwide football stickers, plus 'Re-elect Jeff Smith, Labour', while a wooden woodpecker served as a chirpy doorknocker. If anything, this home was even less pop starry than his previous one, certainly the least pop starry house of a multi-million-selling pop star I'd ever seen.

'If somebody burgles my house,' pondered Paul when he finally appeared, fiddling in the kitchen with the alien concept of the kettle (he'd never drunk tea or coffee in his life), 'they'll think they've burgled the home of a successful amateur football player. I've got loads of trophies upstairs for Player of the Year, from the eighties and nineties. I've never won anything for song writing. I'm not bothered but I do get a bit envious. Everybody's got an Ivor Novello. Gary Glitter's got an Ivor Novello! But at least he's not on Spotify. You know how in football, for the kids who never win anything, they get Most Improved Player? That's the sort of thing I'd get. A special award for nobody with an award. And I'd be really happy.'

Nine years on from our previous northern rendezvous and the now fifty-five-year-old Heato remained devoted to his collections (inside info on corruption had put him off any football museum idea), no longer in designated rooms but strewn around his domestic environment with a few new additions: a map charting the destinations of his Bicycle Tours of recent years (in 2012 he'd cycled 2,500 miles from pub to pub), a cheese map of France in the diner/kitchen ('Tour de fromage'), while outside the kitchen window a fluorescent green astro-turf lawn had been newly laid in the back yard. He lived here with his two eldest daughters (he had another daughter aged six; he'd also now split from her mum) while his wife of one year, Linda (a teaching assistant) lived elsewhere in Manchester, the pair both with young families and choosing to live separately until their kids left home.

'It's romantic,' beamed Paul of this unusual domestic set-up. 'It's really nice cycling to her house and seeing her happy with her kids there and her doing the same with me.'

Soon, Linda sauntered in, a small, smiley, engagingly warm woman who immediately described herself, via her husband's time-consuming passions, 'a charts widow, a daytime TV widow and a cycling widow . . . some of us have to work for a living!'

We repaired to Paul's local pub beer garden where a merciless sun burned through his hefty black hoodie while he sipped on blackcurrant and soda, the favoured drink of three-year-olds.

'How I live is driven by trying to live modestly,' he began, a measured, cheerful man that day given to outbursts of giggling, contemplating his uniquely non-showbiz home. 'I don't like the idea of living down an enormous drive. I don't distance meself from anything. I hope people don't feel they've wasted their money buying my records just for me to spend it on that stupid astro-turf. But then you've seen me try to spend my money all on booze, d'you know what I mean?'

We talked about the Housemartins, who I'd always felt were criminally underrated. It wasn't just me: in 2016, Richard Osman, then host of TV's *Pointless* quiz and soon-to-be best-selling author, was moved to a heartfelt tweet: 'There's a fairly strong argument that the Housemartins were the greatest band of all time.'

'I thought you were gonna say "greatest band . . . *in Hull*",' chortled Heato, before deftly changing the subject to the time he was ousted from *Celebrity Pointless* with singing partner Jacqui Abbott 'in the second round'.

So . . . was Osman's tweet to be believed?

'Oh, no, no, definitely not *that*,' he cringed. 'Em. Well, it could only have happened then. People forget. My daughters will watch *Top of the Pops* from '83 and they're aghast. They say, "Did you dress like that!?" People were very flamboyant, everyone had weird keyboards, big hair and we were seen as the eccentrics with hair like this [normal], jumpers and a cardie. I think we were good for people. When we were on John Peel and not in the charts, people came up and told us stories about how we'd helped them, bedsit people and underrated people and underfed people. To some the Housemartins were just a fun band, but I still get letters from people saying we turned them onto politics.'

I posited another theory: that his voice was *unarguably* underrated. No one ever talked about Paul Heaton's stunningly emotive voice.

'Well ... thank you!' he double-cringed, before the self-deprecation returned. 'My voice isn't what it was. The high range. I'm fifty-five now! But it's ... it's the reason I do things, I suppose. Is to *sing*. When people ask me what I do, instead of "I'm a singer/songwriter," I wanna say, "I sing."'

Only Paul Heaton, then, The Singer, could create in his next band, the Beautiful South, a troupe with two lead singers other than himself (Briana Corrigan, later replaced by Jacqui Abbott, and Dave Hemingway) where he became more celebrated for his lyrics: cynical, kitchen-sink comi-tragedies on booze and barbed romance. It made him fantastically wealthy, the band travelling the world like the *Whoopee!* comic strip the Bumpkin Billionaires, giggling through champagne frenzies – 'It was like [chaotic *Emmerdale* family] The Dingles winning the lottery' – and it eventually made him borderline insane.

'No matter how stupid we were, more money seemed to be coming in,' he marvelled, savouring his toddler's drink. 'I look back on those days with a mixture of affection and dread. I hope I didn't upset too many people. But most people say we were good fun, we swept people along in a tide of ... having a laugh!'

In the end the booze caused mostly grief for himself, his habits escalating to troublesome proportions. Several wagon slips through the noughties and 2010s led to the nearest he'd come to a wilderness period, where radio ignored his solo albums. 'It was a bit depressing, that people thought I couldn't be arsed.' By 2014, the year he met Linda, he'd reconfigured his relationship with booze, now something he did only as a creative tool: on a writing trip, with Linda, to Amsterdam, he attempted writing on alcohol-free beer and 'nothing' creatively emerged. He had a drink, and the ideas immediately flowed.

'It *is* weird,' he acknowledged. 'I have to go to a deep place and alcohol helps me do that. But the good thing is, the minute I step back into that airport after the writing, that's it. I don't drink again. I can just stop. I've reprogrammed myself.'

So he went on a *drinking holiday*?

'It *is* like a drinking holiday,' he nodded. 'Linda looks after me, puts me to bed, I get the songs done, make sure I don't leave me [lyric] books anywhere and it's a very close relationship we have. And it's a relationship with her, not with drink. Controlled by both of us. We have a really good time together. The three years since has been very important in terms of change. Changing the way I am because of the ... hurt, myself and alcohol have put people through. *And* myself. To keep a steady ship. I've no intention of having a sneaky one behind my wife's back. It's a team effort.'

I'd met Paul Heaton many times by then and seen up close the conflicting variations of his shape-shifting personality. With the Housemartins (intense, cynical, volatile), with the Beautiful South (hilarious, charming, volatile), in the solo years of the noughties where he lived through relationship traumas (philosophical, analytical, volatile) and this year's Paul Heaton was by several dimensions the calmest he'd ever been. The volatility, it seemed, had disappeared. As he talked on, in fact, he was becoming less maverick by the second; not so different, in his cycling obsessions, healthy ways and belief in responsibility, as the everyday, fully mature, middle-aged man.

'It does sound remarkably immature to say you've only

reached maturity at this age, but I think I have,' he decided. 'It's weird, even getting that artificial fake fur grass, it's symbolic, spending money on meself and the house.'

The sometime irrepressible madman of the nineties was now 'very excited' to be taking driving lessons – 'I've passed me theory test as well, first time, in yor face!' – mainly so he could drive his twelve-year-old daughter to swimming training at dawn (a competitive swimmer, she swam for Manchester), his heady new ambition 'to have one of them Dad's Taxi stickers' on the back of his first car, which would be a Nissan Micra Deluxe.

'It's very maverick!' he snorted in my aghast face. 'Because what do people in my job drive? Twats' cars. Big tanks. And send their kids to private school. And that's not happening with mine.'

He saw himself as an optimist, even in these culturally chaotic times, about humanity itself.

'Incredibly optimistic about it,' he confirmed, here in the rare Mancunian sunshine. 'You can't be pessimistic, can you? If I have any input into my gravestone, I want written across it "Everywhere Was Ace". I've never been anywhere that didn't have something about it that was brilliant. It's why my football collection is geographic. And half the time it's because of the people, y'know? Half my reason for forming a band was because I wanted to go to all these places. And everywhere *was* ace.'

Backstage after a euphoric show in Warrington that night, where Heato thanked the crowd for their lifelong support 'from the bottom of my heart', possibly the most non-silly, earnest public statement he'd ever made in his life, and British pop's most optimistic oddball now sipped a non-alcoholic beer while plying everyone else with the real stuff. Was this as close as he'd ever come to actually *being a normal person?*

'You'd have to ask my wife that,' he grinned. 'She thinks I'm madder than ever! Well … *more* normal, maybe. Hmm. But then, things can be *thrown* at you, can't they?' He stopped, a mischievous smile appeared, and the deep blue discs of his striking eyes seemed momentarily full of madness once more. 'People will be reading this interview thinking, "I hope things go wrong again so he goes mad. Let's get him back on the booze!"'

As I left he wondered if I'd like some crisps 'for the journey', soon returning with a bag of Fiddler's Lancashire Crisps, with a tagline which read: 'By 'eck you'll find 'em tasty!' He sauntered off to join his beloved wife. Wherever he was going next, in life, you could be certain it would be *ace*.

In 2020 the magazine most of my Paul Heaton features had appeared in, *Q*, folded, a victim of Covid, as the music industry shut down and its advertising revenue disappeared overnight. On hearing of its demise, Paul Heaton offered a significant sum of money to its final ed, Ted Kessler, to be distributed throughout both the soon-unemployed staff and main freelance contributors. We all received £500 each. In 2021, a further unexpected windfall allowed me to refurbish my woefully broken-down kitchen and Paul's £500 was added to the kitty. Every day, therefore, his buoyant spirit sparkles in a corner of the kitchen, in the appliance I call Heato's Fridge. It was an act of then-unpublicised generosity, which would not have come from any other pop star on Earth.

Now that's what I call quite good.

Four years later …

Early summer 2024 and Paul Heaton was drinking pints of ale, really rather swiftly, in one of his local pubs in Manchester.

This was highly unexpected, as was his now regular tweeting of a specific image: a pub table-top sporting a pint of local ale and, usually, a local brand of crisp, on his travels around the country. He was drinking like a normal person once more, merely attempting to 'not drink too much', with no detectable adverse effects other than an increasingly rambunctious sense of humour. He'd simply learned to control his drinking and never drank before a show, out of 'respect' for his audience. We were mere weeks away from his Glastonbury 2024 triumph, a stunning performance applauded nationwide for the undeniable power and emotional reach of his singing pipes that day. By now he'd even won his Ivor Novello, in 2022, for Outstanding Song Collection.

'I did!' he beamed, sipping his pint. 'And I got a nice standing ovation. Very touching. And it wasn't an award just created for me being there, that's what I was most happy about, other people had won it in the past!'

We talked about a new song he'd written that year, 'National Treasure', a term he loathed.

'It's not critical enough of people like ... fookin' Judi Dench,' he snorted. 'National Treasure my arse, she's doing a money advert, in't she? What a bastard.'

The term, however, was one bestowed upon himself these days.

'Yeah, and it's absolute bollocks, that, I'd rather be a national disgrace, I'd rather be Lord Haw-Haw,' he announced, with a dastardly cackle (Lord Haw-Haw being the nickname given to the American-born, Germany-dwelling fascist William Joyce, who broadcast Nazi propaganda to the UK in an English toff's voice during the Second World War). 'Anyway [the song] starts off with a person who goes round to see someone each day, just gives them a cigarette, a hug, 50p, and those simple things can be that person's caviar. I'm really into tiny gestures, just human contact with people. I think they're worth treasuring, not some twat who's released records for forty years. I've got an award, thank you very much. I've got me Ivor fookin' Novello! I don't need national treasure now, yer bastards. Too late! *Fuck you.*'

Paul Heaton was now aged sixty-two and still putting his money where his mouth was. In 2022 he'd put £1,000 behind the bar of sixty pubs across the UK in celebration of his sixtieth birthday, and he still adhered to his £35 price-cap for concert tickets, in the era of stratospheric live show prices, alongside his donation to the unemployed *Q* personnel.

'Similar things, I just wanted to say "thanks for the support",' he explained. '*Q* supported a lot of people over the years. I've had a couple of people come up to me on photo shoots [since] saying they managed to get a little laptop or something. *You* know, from early days, it's never really felt like my money. Right from the Housemartins, to the Bumpkin Billionaires of the Beautiful South, so I've always wanted to share it a bit. I think you have to reverse-greed it. Once you start going one way and asking for higher ticket prices, you behave a little bit like *them* [the bean counters]. Coming from a punk background we were always supposed to be the opposite of them.'

He sipped some more and contemplated his worldview today, which was exactly the same as his worldview at the helm of the Socialist Smiths that 'unforgettable' night in Hull back in 1986.

'I like people on the wrong side of the tracks,' he declared. 'You hear people as they get older, "Oh I don't like people on benefits," shit like that. My thing is, "Take me taxes but don't make them fucking do anything for it." I'd rather pay people to have a good time, smoke a bit of dope, sit on their arse like I did for two years, and then they can decide what they wanna do. That's what it's about, helping other people who are less fortunate. What I've always tried to do is talk about people as though we're all part of the same community. Because *we are.*'

He finished his pint and joined his newly arrived wife, and flurry of friends, melting into the warmth of his local community pub. For the irrepressible Heato, this place, like everywhere else, was ace.

10

NOTHING COMPARES

1990, 'Nothing Compares 2 U' makes a global political figurehead of Sinéad O'Connor

'Nothing Compares 2 U' arrived as a one-off, the Prince-written song turned towering sonic obelisk through the colossally affecting vocal delivery of a tiny, damaged Irishwoman. Nineteen ninety would bring several thrilling pop moments – from Madonna's 'Vogue' to Kylie's 'Better the Devil You Know' to Snap's 'The Power' – but 'Nothing Compares 2 U' was serious pop music at its most seriously emotive.

Since '87 Sinéad O'Connor had been a beguiling presence to provincial girls like me, seeing in this elfin, beautiful, confrontational twenty-year-old a one-off warrior spirit. A fellow escapee from conventional life, she was a fully formed agitator whose voice, I'd later learn, was the sound of trauma made manifest through scorching rage. 'Mandinka', her second single, was a primal roar significantly intensified by the arresting vision it screamed from, as if beamed from a Disney storyboard: a Bambi-eyed, shaven-headed siren in hefty Doc Marten boots. Her fury was both palpable and pointed:

over the medieval Ireland she grew up in where the Church controlled women's lives financially and sexually; over her religiously warped mother who violently and sexually abused her; over the sexual abuse of children by Catholic priests, igniting her lifetime's mission to expose this scandal and the years thereafter of the Vatican's criminally shameful cover-up.

She found her alternative family in London, as so many of we circus runaways did, in musicians, Rastafarians and drag queens, singing on stage in performance artist Leigh Bowery's club Taboo, puffing on a gasper, can of lager dangling in hand. It was almost by accident when, in 1990, she became the most famous pop star on Earth via 'Nothing Compares 2 U', its searing interpretation of loss made all the more personally powerful by the sudden loss in my own young life of both my brother Ronnie (from a pulmonary embolism in '87) and dad (from bowel cancer, in '89). The central scene in the song's indelible video – a single teardrop trickling down that stunning, alabaster face, at the memory of the terrorising mother she'd newly lost – connected to millions worldwide: No. 1 in fifteen countries, it was crowned Billboard's World Single of the Year and handed Sinéad O'Connor, the formidably fearless activist, a globe-sized megaphone of incendiary indignation.

Nineteen years later . . .

The Library Room of the five-star Dylan Hotel in Dublin was an elegant drawing room starring a grand, white, 'John Lennon' piano, several stately grey bookcases featuring theological, velvet-bound tomes and a golden-curtained sitting area gracefully bedecked in a three-piece, white leather suite. Into this sumptuous opulence shambled Sinéad O'Connor as if she'd just returned from several years living in an upturned wheelbarrow in Glastonbury's Babylon Uprising tent. It was 2009 and her no-longer-shaven head was crowned with a dark brown, unwashed, grown-out shoulder-length bob, wearing a pink knitted hooded jumper, shapeless jeans and an oversized brown hooded parka. She couldn't have looked less '2009' if she was a creel basket weaver in Donegal in 1909. Then again, Sinéad O'Connor was all *about* not fitting in.

That year she was defined, still, by the *Saturday Night Live* incident of 1992 where she ended her performance of Bob Marley's 'War' by ripping up a photo of Pope John Paul II and declaring, vehemently, 'fight the *real enemy*', causing the *New York Daily News* to print the headline 'HOLY TERROR'.

'It didn't hurt my career, as such,' she pondered of the Incident, now seated on the white leather sofa. 'Because here I am. Other people had desires for my career, the label, the publicist, so my career was downgraded, but that's where I wanted it to be cos I couldn't fit into that "pop star" mould. To me, success is I actually still pay my bills, and I have some self-esteem, and I know who I am. I'm not a project for other people to make a living out of, y'know?'

She had zero regrets.

'I don't regret anything profoundly but my one regret about the "controversial" things I said and did is that I gave too much of a *shoite* what everybody else thought,' she announced, in her profoundly Irish way. 'At that age you haven't a strong sense of identity anyway and when you get famous your sense of identity is impossible to find cos suddenly you become this thing in other people's eyes. Everyone's relating to this projection. That can make you feel quite lonesome.'

Back in '91, she'd been nominated for four Grammys and boycotted the show. There wasn't an artist alive in 2009, or any year since, who would've done the same.

'I saw myself as someone who artistically represented child

abuse survivors because that's where I had come from,' she explained. 'And places like the Grammy Awards were all about record sales. So I said, "shove the Grammys". So much of the music business is about materialism and vanity, it's all a big wank, and nobody was saying jack shit about jack shit.' By then Sinéad had four children, aged two to twenty-two, and talked especially affectionately about her second youngest, Shane, then aged five.

'He's an angel but he's terrible and because he's so cute he gets a-fucking-way with murder,' she beamed. 'He has a storybook face, seven sets of dimples, this cute smile and these big blue eyes that just look up at you. He's very intelligent but he won't do a *thing* he's asked to do, which I don't mind but his bloody teachers do. Do I think he might have a rebel streak? He bloody *does*, yes.'

Two years later . . .

Throughout 2011, Sinéad O'Connor had been carousing through one of the most outré personal episodes of her already uniquely edgy life, something she'd publicly documented, with a merry enthusiasm, on social media. We were back in Dublin, squeezed together in a cupboard-sized meeting room in the Radisson Hotel where she was theorising over the purpose of the proper pop star. 'We do your madness for you. Otherwise, you would all end up in the nut house.' She was surely only doing her job, then, when she wed her fourth husband in Las Vegas on 8 December 2011 (her forty-fifth birthday), thirty-eight-year-old Irishman Barry Herridge, only to end the marriage sixteen days later, citing 'intense pressure' from Herridge's family and 'a wild ride I took us on looking for weed on me wedding night (which led to a crack dealer) and my husband was very badly affected'. As he might be, being a drugs counsellor for disaffected teenagers. Nine days later, on 4 January 2012 (twenty-three days after we met in the Radisson cupboard), she tweeted their reconciliation via a series of exuberant bugles:

'Yay!!! we decided to be boyfriend and girlfriend again . . .'

'An be sickenly happy an go counsellin an move in like yr regular people'

'Yay!!! Me husband is a big hairy cave man an came to claim me with his club :)'

'Yay!! We both go panto!'

'YAAAAAAAAAAAAAYYYYYYYY!!!!!'

'Tee-hee.'

If it had all been an extravagant publicity prank (as some would inevitably judge) it didn't seem so on 20 December 2011, the day of our rendezvous, when Sinéad was just twelve days married, before any of this subsequent madness. She was encouragingly cheerful, wearing a style-free moss-green hoodie and stubbing endless snouts into a rapidly-filling glass tumbler. Two years on from our opulent drawing room summit and she was transformed: shaven-headed once more, two stone lighter and considerably jollier (and speedier), the result of coming off medication for bipolarity in summer 2011 after eight years' misdiagnosis. That August, following the end of her third, eight-month marriage, she'd advertised for a new boyfriend in her Irish newspaper column 'to cheer myself up'. This involved the kind of bawdy tomfoolery hitherto unassociated with the sometime stern-faced Pope-bothering militant. She bluntly wrote she was 'desperate for sex', contemplating fruit 'n' veg coitus ('yams are looking like the winners'), while on Twitter pronounced herself 'a suicidal Tourette's ridden fat ugly lunatic with a big fat flappy fanny', now specifically seeking anal sex or, as she dubbed it, 'the difficult brown'. Mercy!

She remained *profoundly* Irish, cursing like a salty seadog, officially declaring there was nothing neurologically wrong with her: 'No.' Her misdiagnosis had come about through circumstance: the father of her then newborn baby wanted nothing to do with the child and a distressed Sinéad turned to a GP.

'And because I'm me, I'm made out to be mental, y'know?' she pointed out. 'The doctor rings the local nut house, me in the office, says, "I've got Sinéad O'Connor here, she says she's suicidal, what'll I do?" And your man goes, "Well, from what I read about her I'd say she's bipolar, so give her the bipolar drugs."' She laughed ruefully. 'It did the trick, but it began to have the opposite effect. It's such a relief, it was a long time to be on heavy fucking drugs.'

In her most important life's work she'd now also been vindicated: in 2010 Pope Benedict XVI had finally apologised to Ireland for the Catholic Church's cover-up of decades of sexual abuse of minors by priests (as proven in the 2009 Murphy Report). 'Mad' Sinéad O'Connor had known the truth all along and Facebook petitions had called ever since for the Vatican to 'apologise to Sinéad O'Connor'.

'They should apologise to the Holy Spirit,' she responded, puffing on her cigarette. 'It's not me there was harm done to. But yeah, it's been fan-fucking-tastic.'

We talked about a very different lifetime highlight: the time Frank Sinatra threatened to 'kick her ass' for refusing to have 'The Star-Spangled Banner' played before her New Jersey concert in 1990.

'How cool is that!?' she cackled. 'And he was staying in the same hotel as me. I was imagining this scenario where I was gonna get in the lift and was gonna have to kick the shit out of Frank Sinatra. Cos if he lifts his foot to me, I'm gonna have to brain him, obviously. That'd be a right head-fuck, wouldn't it, if you found yourself panned in the face by Frank Sinatra in the lift at the Waldorf Astoria.'

By 2011, the concept of the controversial pop star had receded even further into history, leaving Sinéad in a minority of one. Did she have any theories as to why?

'It's just all become about being famous and materially successful and being thought of *well*,' she decided. 'Nobody particularly wants to be challenged or beaten up or treated like a fucking lunatic for twelve years either. It's tough if you're gonna stick your head above the parapet, unfortunately. But that's what music used to be for. To me, the job of the artist is to vocalise on behalf of people. Hip-hop went from a powerful controversial voice to MC Hammer and *Cribs* on MTV. The Gallagher brothers had tea with Tony Blair. You set foot in Downing Street, you're fucked as an artist. You can't become part of the shit-stem.'

But then Noel – and it was just Noel – always said he did that a) for a laugh, amused he could attend in the first place possibly on cocaine, and b) to make his mum proud, because his family were always Labour.

'I think it's just vanity,' she countered. 'We artists are very vain. We want to feel real fucking important and be like John Lennon. So, we think if the Queen or Tony Blair invites us round, we're powerful and important musicians and of course we're not. Tony Blair just wants to shut you up.'

We addressed her scandalising of Ireland by making public pleas for sex. Why did she do that?

'Mischief,' she twinkled. 'It was amusing, because we're still a very repressed country about sexuality. It was hilarious, reactions and reactions, six weeks of complete fucking mayhem which was just the best six weeks I've ever had in me life. My favourite headline was "Sinead Admits Sex With Popular Fruit". What was lovely was, I was on the radio and there were phone-ins, and these lovely old men rang in, in their eighties, saying this was the best thing they'd ever fucking heard. They'd had wives and never once did a woman ever suggest they actually *wanted* sex. They'd fucking love a woman to be running around with her arse in the air.'

It's fairly extreme, mind you, to see in a tweet from a permanently famous person: 'If you're not interested in the difficult brown, don't apply.'

'Oh, if you're gonna advertise, tell the universe exactly what you want!' she guffawed, her shoulders shaking with mirth, miming writing out her sex list. 'It's funny too because I'd always been this very serious person, probably the last person anyone would expect to suddenly do all this stupid, crazy, childish, adolescent shit. There were five hundred replies, all manner of psycho and sweetheart. My favourite chat-up line was this American guy [Californian accent], "Hi I'm John, I'm a great ass rammer!" Yeeeeeah! But the only one I went to meet was my husband. We wrote to each other for six, seven weeks beforehand. He's a very unusual character. We call him Wednesday, out of *The Addams Family*, because he has this mad thing where he's convinced he's gonna die in three years. I keep laughing, doing this [she crossed her arms over her chest, bending backwards, as if lying in a coffin]. He asked me to marry him on the first date. He said, "Because I'll need you to do this, that, with my ashes." We're working out the funeral every day. He's completely and utterly nuts in a very safe way. I'm having a great time. It's grand!'

After three previously failed marriages, she evidently remained a romantic.

'I guess,' she supposed. 'I had an enormous aversion to marrying again but he changed my mind. I dunno, ask Rod Stewart. No one seems to mind when it's fellas. It's like the four kids with four different men thing. Fuck off. Men can have babies whenever the fuck they like and nobody says a word. I get a lot of "I pity your children" emails. I don't give a shit. I love my little unconventional twenty-first-century family.'

Were women in their mid-forties, as she'd stated, really in their sexual prime?

'Definitely,' she confirmed. 'There's so much I would've liked to do when I was younger, and I was too fucking miserable *and* Irish. A *Playboy* shoot is on my Bucket List. I like the idea of doing some interview in weird sex gear, talking about something really serious. The economy! You can talk about serious issues while you're bollock naked. On all fours in your dog collar.'

What did her fifteen-year-old daughter, Roisin, make of all this filth!?

'I don't say it in front of her!' she cringed. 'She's worse than me anyway. She is determined to marry the singer from Muse, despite his being married to Kate Hudson. She has Muse carved into the side of her head.'

She had a furnished shed at her home where she'd encourage her older kids to have their parties. Was this the passive control thing of the rock'n'roll parent?

'Oh, I'm not letting them do anything out there they shouldn't be doing!' she assured. 'There's no drink or drugs or shagging, no, Christ, their parents would kill me! But yeah, it's so I can keep a bloody eye on them.'

So, she's in the house smoking dope and her children aren't allowed to?

'Oh, the kids don't know I smoke dope!' she spluttered. 'I just sneak down the garden. But kids now, they're very anti-drink and drugs and cigarettes. Roisin is sixteen in March, and I have an agreement that the first few times she drinks, she'll do it at home. So she knows whether she's the type who's gonna have her knickers round her fucking ankles after a bottle of vodka walking down the high street. With the older one and his mates, yeah, they were smoking dope, but they were eighteen, nineteen. But now I wouldn't allow it. Best to not encourage them. With teenagers you can lose them *like that*, down a tunnel.'

Did she think she might have finally found happiness in her so-called troubled soul?

'Well, I always liked the idea that you listened to my records like reading the diaries of someone recovering from some very severe fucking abuse,' she responded, in her blisteringly candid way. 'A journey documented musically and the whole point of the journey is to get fucking happy. There's no point taking the journey if, at the end of it, you're gonna be fucking miserable. But it's all down to the cock, obviously. As it always is.'

Two years later . . .

Sinéad O'Connor was once more seated inside a foyer, this time in a posh South Kensington hotel in London. Her beguiling face now bore the red-ink outlines of the tattooed letters 'B' and 'Q' on either cheek, still clearly visible since their removal earlier that year. Originally a cautionary, dramatic reminder to herself of romantic betrayal by a man called Brendon Quinlan, she'd since decided they were 'stupid shit on my face'. She was now sporting a tapestry of new-ish tattoos, the famed Jesus on her breastplate just visible above a shapeless, Jesus-motived grey sweatshirt, now accompanied by back-of-hand tattoos, one reading 'the lion of Judah shall break every chain' (a line from scriptures, lyrically adopted by Bob Marley). We all understand tattoos, I began, but . . . on her *face?* 'Musicians have the freedom to do what they like, we work for ourselves!' she snorted, merrily. We then contemplated another new-ish, arresting tattoo, on the other kind of cheeks from a very different kind of pop star, Cheryl (then) Cole.

'I think if you have a rose garden on your arse, it's a message for the fellas,' surmised Sinéad, before a vivid contemplation of what that, in her mind, surely implied. She was leading us back then, within minutes, to the *difficult brown*. She was, I told her, surely the *definition* of the word maverick.

'The word equals lone wolf and I think of myself as a lone wolf,' she nodded. 'Sometimes my kids ask me, "Are you famous?" and I say, "I'm infamous." I prefer infamous.'

By 2014 Sinéad O'Connor had been a lone wolf for almost thirty years, the firebrand radical who'd materialised in the midst of the PWL-dominated, eighties Kylie 'n' Jason era, and become ever since, if anything, even *more* radical, and even more continually 'crazied'.

'If a woman isn't propping up the system, she's a dangerous creature,' observed Sinéad that day. 'If you can't tempt her into behaving herself, you have to "crazy" her. They need to disempower you that way. Musicians are very dangerous people, because we're the heroes of the young.'

Since we last met there'd been a reconciliation with Barry Herridge before they'd split up again in mid-January 2012, for good, culminating in a series of alarming tweets from a suicidal Sinéad – 'I'm in serious danger,' she wrote – stabilised by medication for emotional distress and blaming the 'evil' tabloids for destroying her marriage. 'I will never again associate myself romantically with anyone,' she insisted, even if she remained amused by the furore over her desperately-seeking-sex ads.

'The more scandalised people were, the funnier I thought it was,' she confided, looking back. 'What people don't understand is musicians are filthy, crude people. We like toilet humour, we're disgusting. He [she motioned to her nearby manager] told me a great joke yesterday. What's the difference between Joan Collins and a Kit-Kat? You only get four fingers in a Kit-Kat. See, I was cryin' laughin' and a regular person would find that too fucking much. We're very limited where we can be brought to dinner. The more formal a situation the more degenerate we are. It's a mild Tourette's. We are *all* degenerates!'

Talking to Sinéad through the years was an education in several ways, not least in the aggressively repressive nature of the Irish constitution which decreed, until fairly recently, that when a woman married, she must give up work.

'Men had the entire say in fucking everything,' she cursed in Kensington, now sipping a café latte. 'It was only in the early eighties that women got to go to work. Ireland has remained fifty years behind everywhere else, at all times.'

When she became a truant and habitual shoplifter at fifteen (encouraged by her family), she was sent to a corrective school, the infamous Magdalene asylum run by nuns, where a sympathetic volunteer encouraged her musical gifts, leading to her record deal with Ensign. 'I was seventeen, eighteen so I was financially independent from men straight away, which in Ireland was staggering.' Sinéad was nineteen when her mother was killed in a car crash, after which she turned ever more intensely to music.

'Growing up, music was all about rebellion,' she reminded me. 'That's what was attractive about it to me, a safe place to say stuff that couldn't be said anywhere else. Songs like "Idiot Wind" by Bob Dylan. [Widely acknowledged as both a self-lacerating break-up song and a searing study of fame.] Myself, Kurt Cobain and Roseanne Barr were the first people talking about child abuse without being in shadow. It was a difficult thing to be, a hot potato, and you got a kicking for being it. I was aware of actions having consequences, the main one being isolation. There's a price to pay for everything, y'know? Somebody wrote at the time, "there's nothing so dangerous as an artist who has no sense of self-preservation."'

After the 'great' Sinéad O'Connor witch-burning campaign of the early nineties (even fellow Pope-botherer Madonna mocked her), she 'retired' in '94, pulling a premature ripcord on a still stratospheric career. She was 'crazied' for that, too.

'If you walk away from fame, fortune and material shit, tell it to go fuck itself, reject the very stuff everyone wants, you're holding up to everybody else a mirror,' she coolly stated. 'Without even meaning to, you're telling them they're full of shit. People aren't gonna like that.'

For twenty minutes she plunged us into political darkness, alleging an establishment cover-up of a 'Westminster paedophile ring', which she'd forensically researched 'off stage', before further allegations of global child trafficking, with anecdotally detailed evidence which she insisted were no conspiracy theories, 'which I don't buy into, I like fact.' On my return to London Sinéad then emailed, called and sent me corroborating links, hoping I could somehow help her exposé. Back in Kensington, I had the Fear. Why wouldn't she be right? She was right about the Vatican.

'I didn't used to believe in Satan and now I fucking do,' she proclaimed. 'The nearest thing there is to God is a child. None of us have any power over this but I do believe there is nothing hidden that will not be revealed. It rains and the Earth spills out its secrets. It's a horrific world. But if you think about it too much you're fucked.'

We were very far away, now, from jokes about Joan Collins. As we finished up that day I wondered if the forty-eight-year-old Sinéad O'Connor, eighteen months shy of her fiftieth birthday, could possibly be in danger of becoming an elder rock'n'roll stateswoman?

'I don't think so!' she hooted, comically appalled. 'I think I'm still perceived, and happily so, as a loose cannon. Loose cannons don't make stateswoman category. I like to be the pirate queen.'

Eight years later . . .

When news arrived in 2022 of the suicide of Sinéad's son Shane, then seventeen years old, I was distraught, as we all were. Her public response was devastating, saying this of the child she'd told me was both an angel and a rebel: 'You will always be my light. We will always be together. No boundary can separate us.'

On 17 July 2023 she made public more sorrowful words on Twitter. 'Been living as undead night creature since,' she wrote. 'He was the love of my life, the lamp of my soul. We were one soul in two halves. He was the only person who ever loved me unconditionally. I am lost in the bardo without him.'

On 26 July, having posted just days before an unfeasibly upbeat video looking ahead to a new start in London, Sinéad O'Connor went to sleep and did not wake up again, aged just fifty-six. She died, the coroner confirmed in January 2024, of 'natural causes', details emerging later that year citing degenerative lung disease COPD. A smoking-related disease, it was compounded, surely, by a broken heart. Or, maybe there's only so much struggle you can take, so much energy you have for the fight. Maybe, after everything, her energy simply *ran out*. But her lone wolf legacy lives on, in today's increasingly progressive Ireland, and beyond. In 2022, in Kathryn Ferguson's *Nothing Compares* documentary, the final words from Sinéad would prove a fitting epitaph for the deathless spirit of Ireland's peerless pirate queen.

'They tried to bury me,' she said. 'They didn't realise I was a seed.'

11

THEIR LAW

1991, 'Charly' introduces planet pop to The Prodigy via a cartoon cat

When the Prodigy's 'Charly' single arrived in clubland in 1991 it made an instant connection with seventies-raised kids like me. From '73 onwards a series of government-produced Public Information ads beamed from the telly featuring an animated ginger cat called Charly warning said kids about everyday perils, from creepy strangers to ominous ponds to flaming matches. Voiced by the late, brilliant, subversive Kenny Everett, whose absurdly anarchic TV shows I'd loved as a kid, 'Charly' would prove the perfect breakout foil for the brilliant, subversive Prodigy, a dastardly mewl from a cartoon cat at the centre of this bonkers, techno-rock din. I found the track hilarious, even if the techno purists were sceptical, the cover of then-influential *Mixmag* asking on a '92 cover, 'Did Charly kill rave?' (featuring founder member Liam Howlett enraged on the cover with a pistol pressed to his temple, an image which would possibly imprison any editor today).

By '91 I was a freelancer, having left a now-struggling *Smash*

Hits in the era of 'faceless dance music', with mainstream pop now dubiously dominated by Chesney Hawkes' 'The One and Only', Jason Donovan's 'Any Dream Will Do', Right Said Fred's 'I'm Too Sexy' and Bryan Adams' 'Everything I Do (I Do It for You') at No. 1 for approximately 398 weeks. That year I was immersed, instead, in the Past, newly obsessed with the Small Faces, Scott Walker and Gordon Lightfoot's 'If You Could Read My Mind', one of the greatest blubsome ballads ever written. In thrilling contrast to all this, then, the Prodigy's 'Charly' came to me as a rare blast of contemporary fright-pop energy while knowing nothing about the mysterious dudes who made it, dudes so righteous they vowed never to appear, as the Clash before them never did, on *Top of the Pops*. I'd always assumed, therefore, they were glum-faced doyens of the pop resistance, never up for the comedy caper . . .

Four years later . . .

Late December 1995 and it was minus 20 outdoors in icebound Livingston, Scotland. Inside the Forum venue, however, the Prodigy were not so much warming the cockles as blowtorching them off the broiling crowd with their deafening breakbeat-hip-hop thrash, a pulverising musical anomaly as perky Britpop revelled on. By then, they'd sold almost one million copies of their second album, *Music for the Jilted Generation* (1994), propelling them, unstoppably, towards People's Heroes status. One sweat-drenched young fellow next to me, T-shirt off and roped around his waist, announced that this was the kind of experience, 'that makes you think, "right, I'm gettin' the fuck out of this shithole."' The Prodigy, evidently, were the kind of band that changed lives.

Up on stage, through a kaleidoscope of lasers, searchlights and a gigantic hamster wheel, their techno-tune wizard, Liam

Howlett, grinned behind his bank of glittering decks wearing the actual shirt off my back (which he'd bargained for back in the dressing room), rapper MC Maxim stalked the stage with his neon-blue'n'yellow Devil's Cat contact lenses ablaze, while the towering spectre of Leeroy Thornhill, 6' 6", and the purple'n'green-haired Keith Flint both shrieked alternate yelps of 'hey!', 'yaargh!' and 'Oh my Gaaaad!' through the blistering blast of 'Poison'. Keith was clearly the star, adorned that night in a shredded, silver-and-black skirt and matching jacket two-piece, twirling and leering like some speed-fried drag queen straight off the limo from Saturn. He was having his first go at 'singing' the ferocious pound of new song 'Firestarter', beginning its pop-art bullseye all the way to No. 1 in the March of '96. They looked like the scariest men on Earth. By now, though, both life and the inner workings of the rock'n'roll circus had led me to a theory, which survives to this day: that the least threatening people you ever meet in life are the ones who look most frightening, because their madness is all on the outside, not the inside where the danger lies.

Several hours earlier, the staff in the foyer of the Hilton hotel, nonetheless, were shifting nervously as the 'scary' men tumbled into reception like Bash Street Kids on day one of the school holidays, where they noisily loitered before the Livingston show that night. Rapper Maxim, the sometime reggae-toaster, was a believer in ghosts, had seen 'loads' and began absentmindedly whistling into a novelty, miked-up pint glass causing a relentless feedback rumpus. Leeroy, the tallest man in 'pop', both dancer and qualified electrician, was declaring how much he hated Christmas: 'Cos you have to change your life for it, don't you? Just cos some geezer in a red suit comes along. "I don't care who you are, you fat bastard, get your reindeer off me roof!"'

Keith, fast becoming A Legend, was the ex-traveller,

snowboarder and parachuting enthusiast whose nose and tongue-bolted, purple'n'green-haired likeness was now immortalised on the bodies of Prodigy fans. Once, he stage-dived right out of his trousers, boxers included, then surfed on the heads of punters who repeatedly tried, he cringed, to 'grab my lunch'. He talked like Jools Holland and looked like Vivian off *The Young Ones* back in 1984. He took a fancy to my fluffy white fake-fur jacket piled on a chair, pounced on it, impersonated a Rottweiler, and wrestled the innocent garment to the floor. And here was Liam, the sometime teenage musical 'prodigy' (hence the name), player of piano since age six, lover of hip-hop at fourteen, who met Keith while DJing at a beach party in the golden summer of 1990, and collector of fancy sports cars.

All of these men would prove, then, *permanently* up for the comedy caper, possessed of wide-open, huge-grinned charm. Equally unexpectedly, they were all exceptionally good-looking, despite their devil's-eyeing, Day-Glo hair-dying, scary bolt-piercing attempts to make you believe otherwise. All four, however, were hopeless at explaining their own phenomenal success, attempts at self-analysis culminating in the chewy chestnuts of ancient rock'n'roll cliché. To 'wit': 'The press just build you up to tear you down.' 'I don't write for anybody else except myself.' 'We'd love to be able to go and see ourselves.' 'You'll never ever be able to manufacture what we've got.' 'We're not into categorisation; it's just Prodigy music.' In other words, they were punk rock to the bone. They were also profoundly uncompromising, earnest Essex Boys in their mid-twenties, still inhabitants of Braintree where they set out in '91 to 'rock the crowd'. Their deepest horror was being perceived as a Pop Sensation, even if *Music for the Jilted Generation* had been No. 1, featured nine hit singles, including two top five. All this despite never going on *Top of the Pops*. And they still never would.

'Everyone that goes on there,' snorted Liam, 'is trying to get their little angle across, wearing Oasis T-shirts when they're in Blur, it's all bollocks and I'm not playing the game. Fuck it.'

They must've known, though, they had twelve-year-old fans who loved them for their great big catchy pop numbers, scary or otherwise?

'That's true,' nodded Liam, 'but I don't see how they can possibly understand what we're about. Keith doesn't want young kids going, "Oh, Keith! Waah, I touched him!" and trying to rip his clothes off.'

Well, tough bananas cos it's looming any second.

'Well, you can't diss every twelve to fourteen-year-old to be honest . . .' conceded Keith, putting a word in for the pop kids, 'cos you get into older brothers' music. I was into the Jam at that age and that was cool. But it's about whether you take the piss or not.'

As a freelancer that year I was still friends with my *Smash Hits* buddies on staff and knew, therefore, that the Hits had lobbied for a Prodigy front cover around eighteen months previously.

Maxim (astonished): 'Really? Not having that, man. Really?'

Liam (horrified): 'Well, you'd get a picture of my nuts on the front cover.'

Soon, the Prodigy were preparing to 'rock the crowd'. In a modest backstage dressing room, strewn with beer 'n' crisps, Liam took such a shine to my untastefully garish fluorescent orange shirt he asked to 'borrow' it for the show. I obliged, whipping it off behind a Christmas tree in exchange for a purple-piped white T-shirt (which ran after one wash).

It was the start of a year of planetary touring and Keith, for one, could not wait.

'It's ideal for me,' he chirped. 'Cos I love being surrounded by people and I'm always in a pickle anyway. If I'm in the hotel I'm in a mess, if I'm at home I'm in a mess, I'm a muddle and this is the muddle I'm in at the moment and I'll be muddled on me way out and muddled when I wake up again and that's just me. I like being lost an' that. Y'know? I tell you what, can I be frank with you for a second?'

Here, he bellowed an impressive impersonation of Frank Butcher off *EastEnders*, who'd newly returned to the show: 'Jan-eeeen-ah! Rick-ai-eee-ah!' I told them Liam Gallagher had recently said the Prodigy's music 'does me head in cos it's too hard'.

'At least he's honest!' responded Liam, delighted.

Did they understand why Oasis allowed themselves to be Pop Stars?

The Prodigy in unison: 'Money. Yeah!'

Leeroy: 'Why else would they approve a 12-pound calendar in Our Price?'

So, there isn't a 1996 Prodigy topless calendar extravaganza winging into the shops as we speak?

Keith: 'Well, actually I've done a hose edition where I do fireman poses in a very tight leather G-string holding the hose in various interesting positions ...'

Leeroy: 'And there's me in the Lycra spiderman suit ...'

Maxim: 'And the cowboy suit ...'

Keith: 'With the hole in the buttocks ...'

Liam: 'And the long jump towards the camera naked ...'

Five years later...

After an unexpectedly long hiatus the Prodigy were back on tour, on a bus, hurtling through the German countryside away from their headline show at the huge Bizarre Festival (Germany's Reading Festival). The show, in the middle of a field in August 2001, had been riotous, at midnight, in an ex-military airbase, where a permanently moshing 60,000 people had bawled in unison, ' …fuck 'em all … an' their laaaw!' The boys were *spectacularly* refreshed, several crates of Moët & Chandon sliding around the tour-bus lounge area floor, skunkweed spliffs perfuming the air, Keith's eyeliner melting down his face, his barnet a striking black and white skunk do. 'I'm very …' he persevered with the word, 'DRUNK.'

It was 2 a.m. somewhere on an autobahn on rock's lost highway and the three core Prodigy members were in a state of post-performance euphoria (limb-quaking dance doyen Leeroy had now left, though they remained good mates). Visually, they remained arresting, all silver bike-chain wrist accoutrements and all-over 'menacing' tattoos. Keith's on-stage biker jacket had the number 17969 stencilled on the front, his date of birth. 'How d'you know that?!' he wanted to know, glacial blue eyes a-twinkle. 'A guess? Fackin' 'ell!' Liam was still grinning, a fin-haired twenty-nine-year-old with a silver tooth on one side, gold on the other, all deeply pervlicious sex eyes, wearing a denim jacket and huge, blue, kickboxer trews motived with red stars. 2001 was their tenth anniversary: from the hard-core, rave-sampling, Essex electro-ghouls of '91 to the composite, global rock'n'roll entity which had now sold almost fourteen million albums. They hadn't played Britain for three years, had played nowhere in the world for two and released no new records for four. What could they possibly have been up to?

'I feel like I've just come off stage from the last gig,' blinked Liam, 'and just gone on to a new gig. I don't even know what I've done for two years. I'm serious!'

Keith then delivered the speech of a seventeen-year-old skateboarding stoner.

'I tell you what,' he trilled, 'this is very kind of spiritual …but it's just reality! It's boys from the street and that's the thing.

No, serious! Being from the street is not just about how much graffiti you've done, it's about your state of mind and what you're about and the gang that you're in. Cos ... that's it! And that's why it works!'

Twenty minutes later he was unconscious, legs hoisted up the wall, fluorescent orange trainers dangling a foot from the ceiling with imaginary Tweetie-Pies, surely, twirling around his head.

One thing Liam had done, famously, was become engaged to Natalie Appleton, now former All Saint and Celebrity Pop Tart forever cavorting in showbiz beanerie the Met Bar. Perhaps it wasn't so surprising: back in '97, Liam had made it known, 'We like All Saints. We *really* like All Saints. Especially the one with the lips.' This was highly intriguing pop gossip, given the Prodigy remained the most anti-pop, anti-celebrity rock'n'roll group on Earth. In 2001, they'd *still* never played *Top of the Pops*, still refused to be 'fake' or 'compromise' their punk rock spirit. Sometime in the middle of 2000, then, Liam met Natalie Appleton (not, in actual fact, 'the one with the lips', who was Melanie Blatt, but the one Julie Burchill once deemed 'the most beautiful woman in the world'). So, I naturally wanted to know, how was the lovely Natalie?

Liam: 'Well, I don't talk about my private life ...'

I know you don't ...

Liam: 'But it's great! She's the best and that's that.'

Weird, eh? You lot 'rubbing up' against pop celebrity ...

Liam: 'To be honest, I don't really wanna talk about it, cos that ain't gonna go nowhere. I'm as surprised as you are. You can't fuck with love, at the end of the day. D'youknowhatImean? That's real.'

Natalie's sister Nicole was, in 2001, 'stepping out' with Liam Gallagher and so, one day, Liam Howlett could become Liam Gallagher's brother-in-law ...

Liam: 'Shit ... yeah. But you can't fuck with love! And he's a good lad!'

Then there was rumour of a dalliance between Leeroy and DJ Sara Cox. (The pair were, in fact, engaged in the late nineties and split up in 2000.)

Liam: 'Well, you can't fuck with love!'

With Liam and Natalie there would, I carried on, probably be many 'New Posh 'n' Becks' jokes – but I doubted Liam would care.

Liam: 'No, but the thing is she don't give a shit either. She don't want that shit, she's dragged into it. She's just like me. That's why I get on with her, been with her a year now and ... that's ... y'know ... I love her.'

Sometime in the previous year, Liam had 'nearly burnt down' Nicole Appleton's house, twice, on a visit: first time via a fag left burning on a flammable surface in the bathroom, the second via some bread in a plastic bag on top of her switched-on cooker ring. Reaction of his future sister-in-law: 'She thought it was fuckin' hilarious!'

Three years of cultural disappearance equated, on planet pop, to an epoch. The Prodigy knew nothing about the Strokes or the White Stripes, Liam had gone off hip-hop – 'R&B's more hip-hop than hip-hop, that's where the real streetness is' – and they collectively 'hated' dance music.

'I can say,' yodelled Liam, 'I've sat, for the last two years, and thought every single piece of music that's come out is a piece of shit. I haven't doubted what we do once. Nothing is taking our place, d'youknowhatImean?'

That week, So Solid Crew were No. 1 in the UK.

Keith: '*Who*'s at Number One? Who's that?!'

What you lot do, really, is scary pop.

Liam: 'Accidentally. Accidental scary pop!'

Maxim, appalled: 'What is scary pop, though!?'

Bloody . . . scary pop! Like you. And the Aphex Twin! Sort of . . .

Maxim: 'I don't see it as scary pop. That's a category you just made up!'

I know!

Liam: 'Eminem? Scary pop?'

Absolutely. Some of the best pop in the world is scary pop!

Liam: 'Well you could put us in that category, but it's all accidental. Our whole career's accidental!'

'Firestarter' is one of the best scary-pop records ever made!

Liam: 'Well it's just people are scared of the word pop, I personally am not, but I'm not interested in the charts or any shit like that, I'm just interested in playing live. Hurgh! It's like Kurt Cobain, he made pop records, but it was real shit, real punk rock, so I don't think pop's wrong, I think it's a by-product of what you do. Good records are transformed to pop by the public.'

Here, he grabbed my tape recorder and bawled into the microphone with his evidently definitive statement.

'Good records are transformed to pop by the public! So, it's their own fault, OK? Bye!'

The assembled, by now, were crumbling. Like a multiple, cross-table MC battle, Keith was still reinventing 'reality!' while Liam, a spend-up enthusiast who once said, 'money does strange things to other people's heads, I just fucking spend it,' revealed a brand new purchase obsession, beyond the sports cars and technotronic gadgetry.

'I tried to buy Emu,' he beamed, of the infamous life-size puppet once affixed to the arm of comedian Rod Hull. 'Emu's quality, and his son owns it and he wouldn't sell. Tried to buy Zippy as well the other day [the zip-mouthed puppet from seventies/eighties kids' TV caper *Rainbow*], on the internet, on sale at Sotheby's for ten grand. I bailed out at five grand . . . But

I've got the [Duchess] Sarah Ferguson Spitting Image puppet! Cheap, two grand! The original, it's got loads of jewellery and a shell-suit, you should've seen Nat's face, she'd never seen it before. I've got Jesse Jackson's head as well! Went for Arnie [Schwarzenegger] but it was fucking twelve grand or something. There comes a point where you think, "How much do I want this shit, d'youknowhatImean?"'

From here, he veered off on an unfathomable tangent, with Maxim joining in.

'Y'know that one out of Atomic Kitten with the fucking cheeks? She really fucking annoys me ...'

Maxim: 'I don't hate anybody, man, but that guy out of Steps, H ...'

Liam: 'Nah, the one with the dark hair's worse! H is the red coat, the Butlins guy ...'

Keith: ' ....'

By now, Keith was so appalled by the pop talk he stood up, wobbled, and bolted down the front of the bus.

Liam: 'We started to talk about Steps and Keith's gone ...'

Ten minutes later ...

Liam: 'Since I met Nat, right, d'you know what I watch? *Family Fortunes*. On Play TV. Les Dennis is the biggest twat on TV. But no one else could do that show! We sit there, right, and we fucking watch the day-time episode and the night-time episode and we laugh our fucking heads off! [Here, he was momentarily distracted.] What day is it today? I'm thirty on Tuesday! What's it all about, being thirty?!'

Soon, it was 5 a.m. in Keith's room in the Radisson Hotel, Dusseldorf. As dawn approached on another no doubt eventful day in his real-life rock'n'roll dream, Liam Howlett was no longer a bona fide 'prodigy', he'd turned into a bona fide grown-up. Sort of. Despite his puppet-purchasing efforts.

'When you get older,' he contemplated, sliding half way

down the back of Keith's sofa, while Keith had finally collapsed in the nearby bed, 'you realise the shit that matters. And it's the simple things. Like love and family, d'youknowhatImean? Happiness is a precious time. Cos it's rare. For me, it's rare to be happy. So you've gotta hold onto your happiness. Even though it's something we don't understand.'

*

Tragically and shockingly, the adorable Keith Flint took his own life in March 2019. He was forty-nine years old. On the fourth anniversary of his death, in March 2023, Liam posted what had now become his annual tribute:

'Four years gone. We miss you so much brother. Yes, in body you ain't with us but in spirit, through our music and what me and Maxim represent on stage, you are and always will be fully fucking there. Massive. Your spirit living, breathing and snarling deep within the beats, bass and heart of the band, unfadable and undeniable. You live forever Flinty.'

12

MY DRUG BUDDY

1992, The Lemonheads' fifth album, It's a Shame About Ray, *makes an international poster boy of Evan Dando overnight*

In the year the KLF threw a dead sheep on stage at the Brit Awards, when Whitney Houston was No. 1 in the UK for ten weeks with the yodelsome 'I Will Always Love You' and the post-Thatcher Conservatives *still* won the election with John Major (*Sun* newspaper headline: 'IT'S THE SUN WOT WON IT'), the most dominant musical force on Earth was glum-faced US grunge. I'd no truck with the non-glam, fame-shy, anti-pop phenomenon, a 'movement' fuelled by smack, Prozac and an existential crisis should your single scrape the hem of the 'sell-out' top 100. Then, overnight, *salvation*. I knew nothing of a band called the Lemonheads until their fifth album *It's a Shame About Ray*, immediately beguiled by its sun-stroked, country-folk alt-pop allure, melodic adventures in drug buddy hilarity and shaggy dog narrative charm. Only *then* did I see him: frontman Evan Dando, all plunging dirty blond tresses, expansive, guileless blue eyes and a smile, as he'd come to describe it himself, 'like a dolphin'.

He could've been designed by a cackling AI algorithm, cynically conjured to entrance and ensnare the kind of girly-sap romantic who loved a bumbling, freewheelin', guitar-strumming sensitive poet – i.e. a girly-sap romantic like me. Instead, Evan Dando did this all by himself. Best of all, like no one else from the grim grunge era, he was *funny*: in '92 they released a thrash-punk version of 'Mrs Robinson', its B-side, 'Being Around' a beautifully crafted, poetic comic ode. By December '92 they were on *Top of the Pops* with 'Mrs Robinson', the nation now transfixed by the incandescently good-looking twenty-five-year-old Bostonite, who embellished the song with a yodelling impersonation of Morrissey, for a laugh. Overnight, myself and every other glitter-eyed dreamer on planet pop would see in the Disney-faced Dando what he would soon say about himself: 'a jolly child of the universe'. After six years in the US alt-rock cul-de-sac, the Lemonheads were finally properly famous. Or, at least, Evan Dando was.

And so, The Madness began.

Two months later . . .

Early '93 and by now I'd built up a highly romanticised perception of this enchanting, smiling hobo-dude, who loved Gram Parsons and lived beyond the material plane, a flower child too pure for the grizzly grunge world bestrewn with junkies, neurotics and harrowing songs about rape, suicide and Hell. He was the dreamer's dreamer, the stoner's drifter, known to wear T-shirts bearing the words 'Be A Friend'. The New Dylan had come among us – the one off *The Magic Roundabout.* He'd initially joined a band, he told me on the phone from Australia, so he could return to being a kid, when he went 'surfing every summer', a man-child who lived by the loose-grooved mantra, 'no doubt the universe is unfolding as it should be.' A gentle soul, he identified with women more than men.

'I would hope to be more like a woman than a man actually,' he nodded, winningly. 'Right now, women should be listened to more, because men have proved that they can't really be cool.'

What he'd learned from women, he meandered, was 'how to put my hair up in a towel after a shower – that, and patience', while he was convinced fame could never destroy him, as it had done (I ventured, flirtatiously) Valentino.

'Wow, it could kill me, too, we'll see what happens,' he pondered. 'But every day I remember that I'm doing this because I love to play guitar and sing. I haven't changed at all. And I'm not gonna. I'm a jolly child of the universe. *I am.*'

One month later ...

In a tiny central London hotel room I finally met Evan Dando in real life, for twenty minutes, just one of a succession of speed-questioning, junketing journos there to observe this curious new American rock star, as if an exotic chimp sent around the world for viewing in a gilded cage. Tall and sturdily built, he had the wound-up demeanour of a man enduring cabin fever, slightly manic, though enthusiastic enough, all wafting hair, signature smile and tales of lost shoes. The worldwide media had now officially dubbed him Dippy Dando, the Bubble-Grunge Slacker 'Alternahunk', who made the girlies wibble and their boyfriends sick, not least when he appeared naked on the cover of prestigious *Interview* magazine in a bathtub with three hundred lemons.

Peculiar eccentricities were now emerging. He was hysterically giggly, definitely stoned – laughing with a hillbilly gurgle 'hurgh! hurgh!' – his favourite words being 'wow!', 'cool!' and, occasionally, 'dodecahedron'. Away from the unfolding universe of his rootless hippie dimension, we now knew he was an elite-schooled Bostonite of 'groover' parents, mum a sometime model, dad a wealthy property attorney, both pot-smoking, roller-skating surfers. He'd been a child model himself aged six in a Jello TV commercial. He quoted William Blake when musing on his lack of need for a watch: 'Who needs time when you've got angels in the trees?' He loved the telephone: 'Cos when it rings, like, man, that's the unknown!' He had five 'tenets of life' by which he lived and could say in German, which he did, and then translated: 'The cat has green eyes', 'Where is the playground?', 'Life is beautiful', 'The sun is shining in a cloudless sky' and the definitely unexpected, 'Is your father a chemist?'

I'd studied German at school for two years, loathed it (mostly because I loathed the po-faced, authoritarian teacher, Miss Paton) and learned more German in twenty minutes from a wasted American stoner who probably didn't know what country he was in than I ever did from Ver System, man.

A further two months later...

Evan Dando had, already, alarmingly unravelled. He was now everywhere, both his image and his physical self, placed on an ever-speedier promo conveyor belt more befitting the likes of Take That. He was seated in a London hotel bathroom, on the toilet seat, *with his shirt off*, having his plunging, newly darkened hair trimmed before his latest *Top of the Pops* appearance. The dolphin smile had swum away, now wearing a permanent glower, his voice incoherent and aggressive. 'Electricity,' he blurted out, 'comes from other planets.' (A line from the Velvet Underground's 'Temptation Inside Your

Heart'.) 'Lou told me. You can hear it too, for cripe's sake! Cripes. Crepes! Graci! Stouski!' He bellowed a dramatically fake laugh: 'Hurghurghurgh!' Drugs were surely involved.

He insisted we do the interview in this tiny bathroom, where the only perching place for me was *inside* the bath. His now beleaguered PR, the normally invincibly optimistic Tony Linkin, not only an agreeable rock'n'roll stalwart but a seasoned chaos-absorber, told me Evan was having an acutely sensitive day. Evan then confirmed he was upset, because of 'war and violence, everything's messed up'. That morning he'd taken $350 from his wallet, cut the notes into tiny pieces with scissors, then cut up his wallet and his driver's licence. During rehearsals earlier for *Top of the Pops* he'd stolen the 'Phil Collins' dressing-room sign and shredded that, too. His emotions were chaotic, pinballing in twenty minutes between hilarity, boredom, paranoia, enthusiasm, aggression, giggliness, rudeness, anger and deep sarcasm. He couldn't hear me properly. 'I can't understand what you're saying, if you're gonna move your mouth make it happen for me cos all I can say is "what?"' he sniffed, as my tenderly nurtured Rock Star Fantasy Crush dissolved into vaporised atoms. 'Hurgh, hurgh!' he now gurgled, manically. 'OK. Um. Well, honesty's the best policy. Like, um, coo, whoops, like, um, wow man, like, cool, stupid, whoops, darn it. And that's my answer.'

He'd never, he alleged, even in his Jello ad model phase, thought about being a good-looking person. 'But I learned that I could be packaged.'

His only high school qualification was that he could 'laugh, without smiling', which he demonstrated, setting his face to stone, with starey eyes, in huge chest-heaving convulsions. 'Huh. Huh. Huuuhuh. Uhuh,' he heaved, now thumping his knees. 'Huhuhuh! Huhuhuuhuh! This is a strange, horrible thing that I do sometimes to amuse my friends.

It makes me laugh, anyway, like ... [louder] uuuhuhuh. Huhuhuhuuhuuuhuh!! HUUUHUHUHURGHUH!!' It was the most disturbingly bonkers thing I'd ever seen a rock star do.

The hotel phone rang, he cursed into the receiver and hung up. It rang again. 'Don't answer that! Just turn it off! Or go away!' I asked him if he was OK. 'No. I'm sad. I'm sad about my *haircut*.'

He asked to have his photo taken on the bed, but wouldn't sit still, splayed out on the bed, then bounced off and spread-eagled himself on the carpet.

'It's ... hard to be in a band!' he roared, facedown.

He picked up his guitar and began strumming a Dinosaur Jr song as we headed for the door. 'I'm sorry,' he said into the strings of his guitar, 'I'm not a bad person.'

Within hours, during his eventual, croaky-voiced *Top of the Pops* performance of the hitherto bewitching 'Into Your Arms', Evan took the shredded $350 from a plastic bag at his feet and showered the contents like confetti over the cheering, swooning crowd. Within weeks, he was conducting interviews mute, detailing his LA-cultivated crack and smack addictions in public, which had wrecked his voice. Instructed by his doctor to stop smoking, drinking, drugging, singing and talking, he was now writing 'permanent damage' on sheets of paper for the still-incoming procession of international journalists.

The following year, 1994, he began hanging around with Oasis, becoming a kind of unofficial roadie, which was, of course, exactly what a disintegrating psyche bedevilled by fame and narcotics would need to relocate his sanity. By the end of '94, the once jolly child of the universe was a stumbling, pitiable drug-bum, forever gate-crashing festivals in search of someone else's action, usually the newly starburst Oasis boys, forever lurching around their stage wafting a tambourine like some unpaid slacker Bez, wearing a ripped and stained overcoat once belonging, apparently, to his recently deceased friend,

Kurt Cobain. He carried his acoustic guitar everywhere like a minstrel, playing impromptu camp-fire sing-a-longs for some still devoted fans (usually girls). The music media howled its derision. Evan Dando was not only, by now, the interloper Buffoon of Britpop but subject of a new US fanzine named, mercilessly, *Die Evan Dando, Die*, which loathed, among much else, his famously girly pronouncements. Its creator Jeff Fox justified himself thus: 'We're not saying he just bashes men to try to get women to sleep with him, but let's face it, he probably does.'

Far more questionable pronouncements were now legion: Evan blamed his many-hours lateness for TV shows on taking Mandrax 'too soon' before a flight, described a heroin session 'with two lesbians', explained how he'd been kicked off a flight for taking Polaroids of the air stewardesses while enquiring after their mothers' maiden names, and instructed the world in print on how to smoke Mexican tar heroin off tinfoil, which can lead to Alzheimer's disease and/or kill you. 'I've always done dumb things on purpose,' he said at the time. Furthermore, he witheringly stated, 'I wasn't too concerned about dying, but I could really have fucked up my career.'

By Glastonbury '95 he was the chaos figurehead in a cultural year *built* on chaos, who missed his main stage slot, was then squeezed on before triphop alchemists Portishead, whose fans bottled him off, spending the rest of the evening drinking with the assembled peak-nineties revellers – Oasis, Pulp, Robbie Williams, Elastica – before a two-man campfire Kumbaya with Noely G.

And finally, he disappeared.

One year later . . .

September 1996, and the Staggeringly Swift Downfall of Evan Dando had become the cautionary rock'n'roll fable of the era – and there had been *many* downfalls of the era. But that autumn, the US alt-rock jungle-drums decreed the erstwhile Dippy Dando had been off all hard drugs for a full six months (via family intervention and rehab), recovered enough to write an album, the acutely confessional *Car Button Cloth*, documenting drugs, hospital and madness. He was giving interviews again so myself, esteemed photographer Kevin Westenberg and Evan's still-beleaguered but ever-optimistic PR Tony Linkin flew to his current hometown, Martha's Vineyard, the holiday island off Boston where *Jaws* was filmed, then favoured by President Clinton and Princess Diana. There he had a family beach house, in Gay Head, where he'd spent summers with his dad from age eleven, the year his parents divorced.

Landing in Boston, news arrived from his US publicist: Evan couldn't be photographed, he'd had an allergic reaction, his face was 'all swollen up'. Arriving at his beach house anyway – a light, wooden, one-bedroom bungalow with a surfboard propped against the back-door porch – we were confronted not with a throbbing pumpkin head, but a swollen top lip.

'It's all puffed up, I'm sorry,' drawled the languid, unshaven, barefooted Evan, rising slowly from a huge, dirty-white sofa, wearing a faded, rust corduroy shirt held together by a safety pin. His jeans, up close, you could actually *smell* (mould). 'I'd rather not do the story than look weird.' The sometime most celebrated hair in stoner rock history no longer plunged like waterfalls, now a dark brown home-hacked bob. Always tall and never skinny, he was heavier than before, slower, his demeanour as glum as any of his ghoulish grunge brethren. 'It was a reaction to this,' Evan told us, wiggling a gnarly old hash pipe, 'there's some bad old resin lodged up in there . . .'

Sly Stone and Curtis Mayfield slunk from the nearby sound system in a living area littered with tapes, CDs, drinking glasses and scrolls of paper, the plain walls hosting a few spidery written scrawls, the largest wondering, 'Can a phone call change your life?' The kitchen was strewn with empty 1.75-litre bottles of Jack Daniel's and on the dining room table sat a naked blade. A few friends wandered in and out, girls in bikinis, boys with flyaway hair. This was evidently a party house, currently missing its host. We decided we'd do the interview anyway, pass some time until a newly prescribed anti-swelling drug kicked in. Evan settled on his sofa; I perched on a matching dirty white armchair.

On his own, his friends and PR gone, he was twice as morose as before, no serenade here to his unfeasible comeback, his voice monotone, his facial expression limp, the sometime smiling dolphin now Droopy, the very sad dog. Almost comatose on the sofa, he moved only to light endless Camels or steadily puff on powerful grass from a makeshift Coke can bong, his sentences stretched to breaking by enormous pauses, thinner and thinner, like broken, over-rolled dough.

'I guess,' he finally managed, 'I got a little lost there for a while. However skewed my wiring was when I went into this whole pop star fiasco, it got a lot worse during and after.'

We talked about his adventures with Oasis, about how, in '94, post-Lemonheads tour, he simply 'jumped in the van with those guys and lugged gear cos I didn't want to stop'. Was he aware of being perceived as the unwanted Bez who wasn't on the payroll?

'Yeah yeah yeah,' he nodded, finally finding his voice, a newly reflective one, burnished with self-awareness. 'In the back of my mind, I knew that all this stuff doesn't come without a cost.

I wanted to live out the rock'n'roll myth, just once, to the hilt. And it's much more fun to be famous if you're high on drugs. I tried to say the most obtuse, flaky stuff because I thought hiding the real me was the best idea, so I played the idiot. And I don't regret it cos it was very funny. One tabloid said I had a Mustang and I lived in tents in people's gardens, and I was gonna buy the actual original site of Woodstock. Very funny. I was just ... "Thank God I'm not me".'

He thought *Die Evan Dando, Die* was 'hilarious'. '"Evan Dando's head and a pointed wooden stick – any ideas?" *Hurgh*. I was going to thank them on the record.'

He felt much of the scorn towards him was born of envy.

'I think I was a little too lucky for people to swallow,' he reflected. 'I came from an upper middle-class background, was exposed to things like Kafka's *Diaries* when I was in tenth grade, people knew I had myself a real interesting life. And I have a very expensive imagination. I didn't care other than I didn't want to make it impossible for me to continue making music. So, I'm excited that I can. And now I'll do what's required. I am a professional.'

Here, he coughed. And so I laughed. He didn't laugh back.

One year earlier in 1995 and professionalism was the last thing on Evan Dando's mind. He had in fact lost his mind, in Sydney, Australia, trying to fly home to New York. He'd been up for three days on a concoction of drugs and on the third day took acid, just as the withdrawal symptoms from heroin kicked in. He knew it was dumb, he just, you know, forgot he was withdrawing, and the third day is when the terrors really start to come. He was looking at the back of a dollar bill, where it says, 'In God We Trust', thinking, 'What does that have to do with money?' He started thinking about credit cards and how it doesn't say, 'In God We Trust' on those. He looked at his airline ticket and it said, 'Not for use in magnetic strip reader' so now he was thinking, 'They're not gonna let me back because credit cards are God. Because they don't have the information needed!'

He went to the airport anyway with his ticket and passport, but he'd left his luggage back at his friend's house. So, he hailed a taxi and just, you know, forgot to pay the driver and the next thing he's in this police car back at the airport, handcuffed, and his wrists are bleeding all over the handcuffs, so the policemen put rubber gloves on his hands and made him drink water. He saw they were worried and thought, 'That's a very heroic thing to be, a good cop.' His outbound flight had been booked from New York to London to Sydney, his flight back home to New York via LA and he cancelled it, insisted on it, he had to fully retrace his steps, find whatever it was he'd lost because he knew: something had gone horribly wrong.

'I lost my marbles down there in Australia,' confirmed Evan back in his Vineyard beach house. 'I was going off on this private conspiracy theory, learning weird handshakes and feeding coins into grates thinking I was gonna "pooooof!" back home. I lost it so hard. And looking back, I'm glad I lost my mind completely, once. As long as you get it back it's a wild experience, I highly suggest [sic] it. And my friend Mandy [Mandrax] came with me, the whole way, just to bring Evan home, so God bless her, she saved my life. Pretty much. Shwoooooo . . .'

He let out an almighty sigh, reached over and switched the tape recorder off. 'Let's take a little break there . . .' And he left the room.

Evan Dando didn't use drugs in a Liam Gallagher 'top fookin' buzz, man' kind of a way, to let the good things out, it was more to stop the bad things getting in.

'Why I take drugs ...' he ruminated, now back on his grubby sofa. 'You see people around you that have some sort of membrane that doesn't let the real world in, that keeps them content. It's like an ozone. And there's a big hole in my soul membrane. My ozone layer. I let too much in and it's overwhelming. And to create a false forcefield, a false sense of well-adjustedness, there's nothing better than smack. So, there's ways to cope and for me it's singing and playing and listening to music and reading books.'

He'd had a sleeping disorder since age seven after 'a little bit of a car accident'. He woke up in a trance state every couple of months, had terrible nightmares with his eyes open. Child psychologists suggested drug therapy, 'long-term, like Prozac', but he'd rather accept the problem as 'part of me'. At school he was known as Mr Popularity. 'They were being ironic. I was the loner on the swings.' He thought the condition was funny sometimes, 'when I wake up and I'm running down the street in my underpants'. Things hadn't improved and he now suffered an additional, sporadic syndrome, where 'for two weeks I leave my body, I just disappear, then I come back all of a sudden, it's a chemical thing.' In the last year, he sighed, 'crazy amounts of my friends have committed suicide'. One of them did the very thing Evan once contemplated himself, driving up to the Blue Mountains in Australia and jumping off a cliff. The supposed suicide of another had led to a murder inquiry. On the very day we talked he'd heard another friend died of cancer. 'It's all turning into a Jim Carroll song before my eyes.' You couldn't really blame him for not dancing atop his surfboard with a pawpaw on his head.

'I get freaked out when sad things happen,' he added, melting back into the sofa, 'because I love life so much. So now that I know what it feels like to think, "I could've done that" [suicide], I don't wanna pin that on people, I could never do that. I have too many great friends and my family. I'm not staying alive particularly for myself, but I am for other people.'

He was still single.

'Mainly it's random victims these days,' he said, ruefully. 'I hope that I'm alert enough to recognise true love when ... if I ever happen to run into it. C'mon, let me show you my drum kit ...'

We wandered down to his basement where, for several minutes, he expertly pounded on a beautiful, original, sixties retro drum kit. Afterwards, he changed from his stinky jeans into a striking pair of orange and fawn tweed sixties-era trousers, deciding his lip, at last, was fit for public perusal. He drove us around Martha's Vineyard in his battered old jeep littered with rubbish: bottles, cans, papers, packets, food cartons, clothing, broken forks, tapes labelled 'Wig Out At Dando's'. In the front passenger seat the litter was piled knee-high, and the dashboard ashtray could've been a work of art: hundreds of cigarette butts in a majestic multi-pronged stalagmite.

We found some kids' swings and Evan wandered off alone, swinging to and fro, bare feet scuffing the sand, still the loner on the swings after all these years. He spotted a carefree youngster on a bike and said, 'I used to be one of those.'

Back at the house, with the press ordeal over and the dope wearing off, he perked up no end. A girl called Maya had dropped by and left him a huge leaf as a gift, which he placed, delighted, on his head. He put a fluorescent pink fluffy lobster on top of that, grinned, started playing his guitar and talked about a new lyric idea, about 'God's own jelly-bean jar'. He played Marvin Gaye's *What's Going On?* album and poured us a glass of red wine with the toast, 'drinking gay wine in Gay Head to Marvin Gaye.' He wandered onto his porch and looked out to where the sea met the sky, where everything had 'gone purple' (it really had) and contemplated whether the road of excess really does lead to the palace of wisdom.

'Yeah,' he finally decided, sliding down onto the floor of his porch, 'I would say I'm a little wiser. And a little less intelligent. I've learned a bunch of tricks to keep things . . . barely OK.'

It sounded like his expectations were pretty low.

'*Hurghurgh* [a trace of the dolphin smile]. The really good times are never planned, and the really bad times are never planned, so the stuff you plan you better plan to, at best, be OK.'

Did he remember those tenets of life he used to live by, the ones he could say in German?

'Oh yeah. Yeah yeah yeah. *Wo ist der Spielplatz? Die Katze hat grüne augen. Lieben ist schön. Die Sonne sheint aus einem wolkenlosen Himmel. Ist dein Vater ein Apotheker?* Where is the playground? The cat has green eyes. Life is beautiful. The sun is shining in a cloudless sky. Is your father a chemist? I've no new ones.'

And was life still beautiful?

'Of course it's beautiful. It hasn't really been much better than this ever, for me. Well. Except maybe when I was five.'

Twenty-three years later . . .

The Holiday Inn, Camden, North London is quite some distance, both geographically and spiritually, from the millionaire's paradise island of Martha's Vineyard, Massachusetts. It was early 2019, weeks before Evan Dando turned fifty-two, and he was seated by his hotel room window, acoustic guitar on his lap. He had aged since those Vineyard days by approximately one hundred years.

'What about Pete Shelley dying? He was *the best* . . .' was the first thing he exclaimed, still digesting the recent death of Buzzcocks' frontman, as I sat down on an adjacent seat.

He struck a chord – struuuuuum! – and struck several others, trying to find the right key, as the unmistakable chord sequence to Buzzcocks' 'I Don't Mind' came strumming from his fingers. He then sang, in deep-throated, wistful tones, the famed opening lyrics: 'Reality's a dream ...'

I was glad he was alive, and still musical, and could still speak, even if he resembled that day, much more than any average middle-aged rock star, a busking itinerant beach bum who possibly lived in an upturned canoe. Despite the guitar in his lap, I could clearly see a large, oblong hole in the crotch of his turquoise corduroys. 'Oh shit,' he exclaimed, when I mentioned it, 'I forgot ... I wear underwear though!' Those once-silky, blond, plummeting curtains were now congealed, light brown slats, he had one foot bare, one wearing a black sock, his bed strewn with a scattered jumble of clothes. His teeth were tobacco stained, his intonation often unclear, his once cartoon-beautiful face now lined and weathered as he absentmindedly strummed and burst into occasional song.

There was no sign that day, though, of the heroin/crack-addicted loose cannon he'd sporadically been these last two decades, often hostile to media intruders. He'd developed a rum reputation as a difficult man, a no-show interviewee and when he did show up was often irascibly rude, once inspiring the headline 'The Cuntoid is a Lemminghead!' He was erratic, certainly, but he was on time, in buoyant spirits, prone to his hyuck-hyuck comedy gurgle and tangents of ill-advised honesty.

The still freewheelin' Evan Dando, a man more likely to sabotage commercial success than chase it, barely acknowledged the Lemonheads' new covers album – 'there's a new album, which is handy' was the sum of his self-promotion – and was keen to show me his paintings instead, scrolling through his smartphone.

'They're crap but fun, I give 'em away,' he enthused. 'This one's kinda cool.'

He proffered his phone, showing a bold abstract of plants in a large brushstroke. 'Oh, this is good!' he then announced, presenting a black background glistening with a milky-white wash, perhaps a galactic constellation.

'Like a galaxy, right? It's coke, see! It's a photo, so you can pretend, it's a placebo, beautiful . . .'

This, then, was Dippy Dando in his fifties, still obsessed with music and drugs, if decades away from the kind of global fame that had crocked him. His now lengthy life story was yet more compelling evidence not only of what extreme fame can do, but what drugs, success, money, women and adulation can do to a human being with an ill-equipped, sensitive psyche. During those 'alternahunk' years, he'd been one of *People* magazine's '50 Most Beautiful People in the World', while teenage bible *Sassy* magazine swoonfully anointed him 'His Beautiful Blond Sadness'.

'The looks thing was not good,' surmised Evan by the window, with no trace of either self-pity or regret. '*Reluctant babe magnet.* The music was what it was all about so I thought, if I can hide behind this bimbo thing maybe it's . . . subterfuge.'

As he'd intimated back in '96, he'd wilfully created a beauty-blurring, chaotic façade via drug-fuelled hedonism.

'I definitely embraced that,' he acknowledged. 'Because it's a ridiculous thing, to be a . . . pop star. And I'm . . . *really real.* I have a perverse streak, but I've always been true to my idea of freedom.'

Evan Dando was never daft, a well-educated, privileged kid whose prestigious Commonwealth High School in Boston was where his first punk band rehearsed, in a room hung with original masterpieces by Rembrandt, Pissarro and Picasso. He was, he reminded me, 'a loner, always the sad kid', who still had the sleeping disorder. Just two years ago, sleepwalking back home in Martha's Vineyard, he smashed an arm through a window. He pulled up his pink, seventies-retro shirtsleeve to trace around several deep scars: 'Luckily Gibby from the Butthole Surfers was there and drove me to hospital, cos it was really bad.' He'd been literary forever, loved the beat poets and narcotic extremists, obsessed with Dylan Thomas, Kafka, Coleridge, Burroughs.

'Everyone I loved went the way of excess,' he pointed out. 'So, I was always gonna take drugs. Since I was ten years old that was pretty much my MO. My parents got divorced. I was in pain, I guess. I didn't see my dad for a year. I learned to comfort myself by playing music. I definitely choose chaos. Or it chooses me.'

He still looked back fondly on the Oasis years, loved the piss-take banter of the Mancunian wags, 'and I learned how to make a chip butty.'

He addressed his infamous Glastonbury moments. 'Just looking for excitement,' he now decided. 'That was my only rule in life, since I was little. My song was "You can't catch me, I'm the gingerbread man". I thought I was bulletproof. And found out I wasn't.'

Astoundingly, he remembered meticulous details about our meeting twenty-three years previously.

'I had my bass player Farley's grandmother's pants on,' he recalled, something I didn't know at the time, of his winningly sixties trousers. 'We drank red wine. That was a fun house. Ended up Keith Mooning it that summer. Like, broke the whole house. Stupid. We started drinking vodka pretending it was water. Ended up having to spend a hundred grand [to fix it up]. My poor stepmother came in, there was blood all over and cocaine and mushrooms and pot and glass everywhere.'

I recited to him his own eloquent reasoning behind his drug use, about the hole in his ozone layer: 'I let too much in and it's overwhelming. And to create a false force-field, a false sense of well-adjustedness, there's nothing better than smack.'

'I'm pretty smart, actually!' he responded, delighted. 'Well, I don't wanna do that anymore. I can't. It's too much hassle on tour. I was on it, like, a month ago. But I've been OK for a month. I'll always have struggles with it. But I always wanna stop and I always *do* stop. I'm lucky that way. Because it's ... Satanic. But I didn't get a bad drug problem till I was in my thirties. And it isolates you.'

In '97, the year he turned thirty, after seven Lemonheads albums, Evan's output of original music dropped away like an anvil off a cliff-face, though he'd regularly toured. He'd written new songs, too, for the next original Lemonheads album, thirteen years after the last, some with his vocalist/Hammond-playing girlfriend Marciana Jones. (The pair had a side-project in 2016, The Sandwich Police, with guitarist Willy Mason, both then musicians in the Lemonheads.)

'But she's not touring,' he lamented. 'She's not ... in reality enough to tour. My muse, my girlfriend and I, we kinda broke up. Together a coupla years. It's really sad, my hope for the future was making music with her. She's one of my best friends' wife. Willy Mason's wife.'

This was startling news to me, now fully understanding their side-project's curious name.

'They're married still,' he added. 'We did the Fleetwood Mac thing, y'know? Willy was fine, it was all good. I moved in with them a coupla years ago. It was interesting. Well, it's kinda like the seventies on the Vineyard ...'

By 2019 we were deep into cancel culture and #metoo, its lens newly trained on Americana folk-poet Ryan Adams over allegations surrounding sex-related abuse-of-power with young girls and women. (Allegations denied by Adams, who tweeted: 'I would never have inappropriate interactions with someone I thought was underage. Period.') Back in 2012, he'd collaborated with Evan on an eventually aborted album.

'Oh, it sucks,' said Evan, of the allegations. 'Ryan was always a megalomaniac. But d'you know what? It doesn't matter to me *at all* what a human being does with their lives, outside their art. I *refuse* to do this modern thing. Where would we be with Roald Dahl? He was a fucking Nazi. And will always be one of my favourite writers. I don't give a fuck. We can't know what they're really like. Who cares? A lot of the best artists have been criminals and fucking reprobates of all kinds. And people fucking *like* that they're a little bit . . . evil.'

I wondered if Evan ever worried about a #metoo-ing himself: back in the nineties girls were forming queues the length of the equator.

'Nope, no I don't,' he replied. 'Because I would never fucking do anything to someone. That they didn't want to happen.'

Was he more likely to be fending off the attention?

'That's the thing,' he nodded. 'During the whole sex symbol shit, I was celibate for eight months. It turned me off. I was into it for a little while, "Oh, this is fun," and then it was "This isn't fun *at all*." This isn't intimacy, this isn't warmth, this isn't comfort. Who knows, I could've gotten in trouble if I'd continued being like a rock pig or whatever, y'know? But people make too much of this man/woman thing. I think the less separation between the sexes the better. I like the androgynous thing.'

In 2019 he was now 'a country person', living in the Vineyard doing what he hoped to do for the rest of his leisurely life: fishing, painting, hanging out with friends, smoking pot, trying to stay off heroin, playing his guitar by the lapping shoreline, possibly in a hammock. Had he squandered his talent?

'Bullshit!' he cackled, happily. 'I made the *most* of it. I'm not very talented. I may have *some* talent. But you also have to be lucky. My friends call me lucky. I went fishing once near Papua New Guinea, caught a thousand-pound black marlin in an hour. Guys were "In five years you don't see a fish half that size!" I got a hole in one in golf once. I don't play golf! I have good … intuition.'

He didn't feel damaged by the extreme life he'd chosen – 'I'd be a lot more damaged if I'd worked as a coffee barista,' he assured – intending to stay freewheelin' forever, living only for personal and creative freedom.

'That's what it's all about,' he smiled. 'Doing what you love makes you healthy, I don't have any grey hair, look, I'm fifty-one!'

Financially, he'd lived on investments made in the nineties, 'and I go on tour if I need money.' His parents, still alive that year, had always supported his musical dreams but refused to bankroll his lifestyle.

'My pop lived by that, he's smart,' noted Evan. 'If he had, I wouldn't even have wanted to do it.'

Twenty-three years on could he still remember the five tenets of life he used to say in German?

'Oh yes,' he said, reciting them all once more. '*Wo ist der Spielplatz?* Where is the playground …' but missed out, this time, which I pointed out, 'the sun is shining in a cloudless sky.'

'That wasn't me,' he swore (it *was*) and now stared upwards through the window, his next declaration sounding like a perfect impersonation of Liam Gallagher.

'The soon's joost up there … the soon's joost oop thur!'

Back in the nineties, he and Liam Gallagher had looked uncannily similar, facially. Did he notice?

'We used to trip out about that!' exclaimed Evan, adding they had a family name in common, Griffiths, and were convinced they might be related. 'We'd do coke in the bathroom and look in the mirror. Liam would go "your nose [he mimed Liam fondling his nose], it's like mine man!" Liam's so funny. It's a good thing those guys aren't getting #metoo'd. But they're gentlemen, they had a female tour manager, that says a lot.'

He saw me out with a song, seventies folk-poet Richard Thompson's 'Dimming of the Day', a melodic, mournful lament. I left him blanketed in the comfort of music, still in some ways the sad kid, in others the jolly child of the universe, with the hole in his trousers and the permanent hole in the ozone membrane of his soul.

It had been good to see him again. Good to know he was where he wanted to be, and what he needed to be: free. Whatever the cost.

13

VIOLENTLY HAPPY

1993, Björk's Debut album turns her into Iceland's first (and only) pop superstar

Two enormous hit singles defined the mainstream in the pop-curious year of 1993: Meat Loaf's blaringly bombastic 'I'd Do Anything For Love (But I Won't Do That)' and Mr Blobby's 'Mr Blobby', the inevitable result of Noel Edmond's *Noel's House Party*, featuring the hideous Blobby gonk at core, becoming the BBC's most irksome Saturday night TV 'sensation' possibly of all time. Elsewhere in pop, Take That were No. 1 as usual (this time with 'Babe'), electronic dance music was bouncing onto dance floors via 2 Unlimited's 'No Limit' and Ace of Base's 'All That She Wants', while crude tomfoolery erupted throughout school playgrounds courtesy of TV's Beavis and Butthead. Into this dubious cultural quagmire beamed Björk, as if from outer space, both as spook-pop antidote and as significant a lone female figure as Kate Bush had been a generation before her.

It wasn't just me who spent hours on dance floors wafting imaginary diaphanous sleeves to the spectral tinkles of 'Venus as a Boy' from her *Debut* album, just as I had in 1978 to the epic, soaring soprano of Kate Bush's debut single 'Wuthering Heights'. Still working as a freelancer out-in-the-field, I knew she'd been inching towards us since '86, fronting experimental punk-pop combo the Sugarcubes until '92, after which, in '93, she became that rarest of phenomena – a profoundly experimental art-pop outsider who couldn't help but create, and consistently so, irresistible, unique hit singles. Much like Kate Bush. Planet Pop had never known an Icelandic pop star before, soon dubbed by the tabloids 'Bjonkers!', a perception I'd soon have the opportunity to investigate for myself...

Two years later...

Nineteen ninety-five and Björk was showing me around her lovely home, a nosy person's pleasure you would never be afforded by the famously reclusive Kate Bush. She was hovering by an artwork and ... What did you just say, Björk?

'As you can see, it looks like a disco cunt,' announced the Icelandic sorceress fully named Björk Guðmundsdóttir, addressing an oval-shaped sculpture shelved on a wall, made from outer concrete and inner flecks of blue glass. 'It's modelled on a shell,' she explained. 'My friend in Iceland makes them.'

Her beautiful, strange, West London home was an open-plan, three-story house which looked like the inside of a ship. Everything here screamed 'traveller'. Upstairs was the airy, floorboarded living-room with a mile-high, white beam-held triangular-shaped ceiling, a room featuring a collection of hand-crafted sailing ships, a sea chest crusted all over in shells and a white triangular slatted chair which looked like a yacht. Her TV was a projector screen, the kind you found on planes in the olden days, the projector hanging from the ceiling like a side-on traffic light, beaming images onto the wall-mounted screen: 'It costs the same as a normal TV. Wicked!'

On her answerphone a message blinked from Jarvis Cocker, who'd newly returned from holiday in Iceland; Björk, who barely knew him, had bumped into him at *Top of the Pops* and given him the keys to her Icelandic home to spare him a vibeless hotel. Videos, CDs and tapes were shelf-stacked in abundance while one wall was dominated by a huge, glass-fronted map of the Earth which illuminated wherever the sun was currently shining. It was a unique domestic setting which made a nonsense of the old Stone Roses adage: 'It's not where you're from, it's where you're at.' Björk couldn't come from anywhere *but* Iceland, the island which invented the first-ever democracy in history through sheer bloody-minded Viking self-preservation, romanticism and passion for life.

'There was this survey done around the world,' mused Björk, now munching on a hunk of cheese, 'where people were asked one hundred standard questions and one of them was "What do you believe in?" The people of Iceland stood out because they all said "Myself". That's very deep in our character, in history we were the biggest rebels on the planet. It's always said that the reason we don't have an army is because it would be impossible for everyone to walk in rhythm, everyone would have to walk differently.'

She was also, unlike the British, very keen on talking about sex. To rid herself of sexual frustration she practised karate, swam and masturbated every day. Sexually, she called herself 'outrageously greedy'. She threw herself into love, as you could hear on her latest single 'It's Oh So Quiet', a cover of the 1951 big band number by Betty Hutton.

'People think my version is over the top, but hers makes mine the ambient version! I guess the song describes pretty well what being in love feels like because it's in and out, innit?'

Certainly is, mate.

'Wahahah!'

So, what about right now, was it in, or was it out?

'Nah!' spluttered Björk, who was famously reticent about romantic entanglements. 'That's a secret! It's delicate. I could come out with a bag of lies and tell you I sleep with three transvestites every night. But I'm not going to lie. Everything's ... OK.'

One year later ...

Björk was 'plastered'. It was 1996 and on a rare day off from her punishing touring schedule she was letting loose on the dance floor of a mobbed Norwegian discotheque. Mid-freak-out she was approached by a posse of lairy lads, who danced in front of her, taunting her about being 'famous ... we know who you are'. She ignored them. It didn't work. Annoyed, she told them, 'It's my night off, OK?' That didn't work either, the loudest now frothing, 'I should ask you for your autograph, shouldn't I?' She'd had enough, told him to 'Fuck off!' It worked. He apologised, said he'd always liked her music, and would she do him an autograph, no hard feelings? Of course she would. He proffered a piece of paper, she took it, smiled angelically, crunched it up in one hand and threw it into her mouth. Munch! Munch! Munch! Gulp! Leering into his face, eyeball to eyeball, she then snatched his pen and bit the top off. Crunch! And the rest of it. Crunch! Crunch! Crunch! Gulp! Then, she swiped the pint from his hand – Glug! Glug! Glug! Down in one! – smacked her lips, handed him back the empty glass, turned around and marched straight back onto the dance floor. To coin her own most favoured phrase that year: one-nil.

'It was a pen like that,' chortled the tangerine-haired Björk, now thirty, nodding to a standard Bic lying on a café pavement round the corner from the strange and beautiful home I'd visited the previous year.

'But to wash it down with his own pint, that really got to him,' she cackled. 'You should have seen him, this big guy, he just crumpled down to nothing. Heheheh! Of course, the next day [she clutched her stomach] I was in total pain, but it was worth it. Even just to see my friends on the floor laughing their heads off. I was on the phone to Goldie [then her new-ish boyfriend] telling him and he was going, "Go on! That's my girl!" I was going, "But sometimes it's so hard to be hard!"'

But she made it look so easy. A few months on from the pen-munching incident, Björk appeared across the planet's news channels pulling a journalist by her hair across the floor of Bangkok airport. The tabloids were thrilled, now anointing her 'Bjonkers!', the woman already eulogised by *Spitting Image* as the hysterically squalling maniac who sang to fax machines. To Björk it had simply been maternal instinct: the journo was harassing her ten-year-old son.

'It's probably the third time in my whole life I lost my temper,' she pondered that summer in her curious Icelandic/cockney accent. 'Last time it was protecting my brother. I'm not proud but I would do the same thing today. The best thing about it is the woman was offered a commercial for a hairspray thing in Asia. It was going to be, "I get battered by pop stars all the time but I use this hairspray, and it keeps my hair in place!" And she said *no*. I was gonna call her and say, "Do it!" I thought that was very funny.'

We were seated on the café's outdoor patio, Björk enthusiastically ploughing through fresh fruit salad and Greek yoghurt. You couldn't miss her, as ever, in fluorescent orange jumper and white shiny trews, reflecting on a bout, last night, of restless body syndrome. To wear herself out, she ran round and round her garden wondering what was wrong with her until she saw the full moon overhead. 'Aha,' she thought, 'so that's it.'

That summer she was headlining the Phoenix Festival, enlisting the help of a fireworks expert called Kristoff, a 'French pyromaniac fucking terrorist', who previously created displays for the Olympics and was organising a round-the-world, time difference-considered, year 2000 extravaganza.

'He's brilliant,' marvelled Björk. 'All fireworks I've ever seen so far are like a punk song, it's all, "Let's buy loads and PSHOOOO! Just put them all in the air NOW!" But this guy, he's modern, he does patterns, it's not [here, she sang like, er, fireworks], "Peu peu peu pee pchkschckkcpsh!" His is all kind of [she waved her hands around] patterns and it might not do anything for a few songs and then suddenly just ... *shimmer*. He's all scars and scruffy hair and lives in a barn with another barn full of powders ... he's a scientist! Outrageous!'

It was, she felt, an 'accident' she'd now become a phenomenon.

'I never thought I'd be playing so big places,' she blinked. 'I've always looked at my music as kind of for headphones, really, introvert music so the fact I'm headlining festivals is just hysterical.'

Björk didn't see herself as a futurist. Like Goldie, the Prodigy, Underworld and so many doyens of nineties dance, she was creating the 'sound of the world today'. She believed her music was 'taking reality and making it into magic'.

'Which is the bravest thing in the world to say,' she added, rubbing her hands all over her face, minuscule fingers poking randomly up her nose. '"Oh, me with my most gorgeous tits riding a white horse on Saturn", it's very easy to make that into magic. But making fucking *this* [here, she belted her saucer, which wobbled up and down] and *that* [she pointed to a bus roaring by], these noises that most people find ugly, into something pretty is just, I'm sorry, fucking heroic. It's ... one-nil. Against boredom. One-nil against death. One-nil for love. People say techno music is cold. Fuck 'em. Crap! You're blocking out half of your life, being a coward.'

Perhaps inevitably, the old-school guitar boys of Britpop she'd no time for. Especially Oasis.

'Britpop,' she felt, 'for me is middle-of-the-road. Stagnation and normality. If we were talking food, it'd be something very boring I don't really like, like bread. Potatoes. No taste, but it fills you up. Then some of the good things you get with so-called dance music is … cherries! And tequilas! The extremes. Chocolate mousse with nine thousand billion fucking calories and a bloody steak with it. That's what I like in food, very spicy, fucking Indian madras. Don't give me toast and cornflakes and potato salad and a roast dinner and greasy pub foods.'

Funny that: this was all very British 'cuisine'.

'Yeah!' she guffawed, 'and everybody hates British food. And that's what Britpop is to me, boring and bland and egg and chips and beer. I don't understand beer, it's like drinking wood, it doesn't get you anywhere. I'd rather skip it altogether or do a fucking bottle of Cognac and go the whole way.'

I contemplated her orange jumper. She was always wearing orange; in colour psychology orange is the colour of healing. What did that say about her?

'Well, obviously I'm very *ill*.'

Until three years previously, Björk had lived with 'no money'. Life was 'two jobs, working-class, single mother, hardcore'. Moving to London, followed by the supernova success of *Debut*, changed her life. She'd been in bands from childhood, supplementing her ethos of 'no compromise, brave music, taking risks' with work in antique shops, fish factories and a stint as an accomplished, er, thief.

'I once nicked a swimming pool,' she confessed, breezily. 'It was from a supermarket, an inflatable one, cos we needed a bath, we didn't have one where we were renting. And I nicked a disco ball! In Reykjavik. A massive one, off the ceiling and got it out the club, got away with it! I used to do that sometimes when I was bored. Obviously hysterically drunk.'

Goldie had already told me that year that he and Björk's relationship had been 'fated', their coming together 'a big set-up by some fucker'. What did Björk think? For the first time there came a dramatic pause. (She remained notoriously private, being a secretive double Scorpio, astrology fans.)

'Um,' she quavered. 'I'm pretty anti-fate cos I want to know that you've got options. But it is very tempting to think it is. It feels like it anyway. Which is something I wouldn't admit to . . . a lot of things.'

Their similarities were bordering on the 'Bjönkers!': they were both thirty, both parents, both spook-pop pioneers, both spiritually obsessed, both spoke in complex metaphors, both were 'misunderstood', both possessed of one name in fame.

'I've tried to explain it to myself,' she agreed. 'But when you try to explain those really important things in life, it's just not logic, is it? It's just the force of nature. We're talking waterfalls and volcanoes, y'know?'

They'd known each other by sight and reputation for years, met across clubland but it was the Björk/Goldie tour of '95 when they finally felt *the vibe*.

'It was quite good, the way we fell in love,' she unexpectedly blabbed. 'We'd been touring together for a few months, which is quite intimate.'

Goldie was the touring rookie, Björk the almost-veteran who, by the end, was 'crashing physically, he saw me doing shows at forty degrees fever, crying my eyes out, finished, and I saw him at the beginning, we ended up supporting each other.' By the tour's end love had bloomed. 'We realised we'd built something up that we couldn't live without. It's good because . . .' Suddenly, a fulsome grin. 'It's uphill from here, innit? Aw, now I've gone shy. I'm cautious about it. It's *important*.'

What did being in real deal love do to her head?

'Nine thousand pros and cons,' she decided, unhelpfully. 'It's instinct, the primal needs one has. Your body creates all these things and if you don't put them somewhere you go mad. In my case, I have to sing. Some people have to tell stories. And one of the things you wake up with every morning in your lap is very romantic love, innit? So, it's about finding a channel for it. And when you find someone, I guess you've found someone to fax to. To phone to. People who aren't very happy are maybe running around with ninety-seven Safeway bags full of love and they just don't know where to put it. And I guess when you find the right person, you've got somewhere to put it.'

Was the right person the person with enough room for your ninety-seven bags then? Or was it that the bags fit that person because they're the right shape? Or something? Otherwise, you could just give the bags to anyone, and we know that doesn't work . . .

'Yeah, that's the riddle innit!? And it ain't solved yet. It's like going to a restaurant and wondering if they'll have what you want on the menu. "Well, today I feel like three bungee jumps and having a very intimate talk with somebody I've known for eleven years."'

And all they've got left is a broken catapult and the nutter at the 29 bus stop?

'It's the same thing with the Safeway bags. It's like best friends. Why do you have best friends that you've had for ten years? I dunno. Free for all. Free jazz! Improvise!'

Goldie, I told her, was a birrova Sexy Beast, wasn't he?

'Coo-*or*!' slavered Björk and then rolled around her seat in mirthful silence. There was nothing more to be said, then, except *lucky bastards*.

*

Björk was, and doubtless remains today, as unique an individual as her ancestral Icelandic DNA dictates. She wrote her first song aged four: 'Little songs, things like, "Pete likes raisins too much, I think he should actually kiss Shirley today" and then the chorus would go, "If Pete and Shirley would kiss, I would giggle. Giggle, giggle, giggle till I die".' She was a mathematical boffin at school and a student of musical theory 'forever'. She was as versed in the orchestral classics as the back catalogue of Jimi Hendrix, who her parents played every day. 'So by age seven I was "enough is enough", the classic rebel.' She married aged twenty 'because my boyfriend needed contact lenses': the Icelandic government operated a young person's pension scheme where high interest savings could be claimed back when you either reached twenty-five or married. When they married, he got his contact lenses, they divorced and were still friends. That same year she performed on Icelandic TV as a bare-stomached, seven-months-pregnant punk provocateur with no eyebrows, and caused a seventy-nine-year-old woman to have a heart attack in front of the TV.

'She didn't die!' roared Björk. 'But I was nearly sued.'

She'd been making 'my own music' for twenty years already and only realised last year, as she exclaimed, 'My God, I'm actually a fucking professional' and 'obsessed with truth and integrity.' On tour, to get over the lack of sex, she drank 'twenty-seven tequilas for that physical kick', swam for two hours every day – 'not paddling, fucking swimming!' – to rid herself of 'the madness of boredom and sitting around and doing nothing'.

In 1996 she was a global superstar who dominated the airwaves, dined with Michael Stipe and Madonna and … Christ on a bike!

No it wasn't, it was Robbie Williams wobbling past us on

his bicycle, looking distinctly dishevelled and '1996' in his crumpled blue tracksuit, hair on end.

'Hiya!' hollered the people's pop hero.

'Did you go to Heaven last night?' wondered Björk, surveying the human carnage.

'No, but I feel like it,' quipped the man who'd behaved, that year, like the sixth member of Oasis. 'I've been in Italy, fookin' mad! I've got to go to bed, I've got to sleep . . .'

He wobbled off into the horizon. I'd heard a story about Björk and Robbie: that she once drank him under the table to the extent he needed a Vitamin B jab in the morning to wake him from the dead.

'Yeah, heheheh!' she confirmed. 'It was the Berlin MTV awards about two years ago. I think we drank each other into oblivion, actually. It wasn't just us two, there were a few of us, but I got the blame from the managers. That was one of my favourite nights actually, all the clubs were going on and it was just terrible, so pretentious and rock'n'roll and gross, so I found some German jungle kids and them and Naomi Campbell and Take That and some of my friends went back to the Holiday Inn disco. Naomi flirted with the DJ and got him out of the DJ booth, got the jungle kids in and got Take That on the dance floor. Top night out! One-nil!'

There were some things Björk couldn't deal with: her phenomenon, her money and hysterical adoration by fans. 'If I think about it,' she shuddered, 'I have to call the ambulance because I am insane.' Her money went 'back into the music where it belongs' and her greatest achievement was living 'with no compromise: I'd rather be in the bravest band in Iceland that no one knows about and do two jobs than make music to pay the rent. I won't use music as a whore.' She did much 'spring cleaning' and it was nothing to do with Marigold gloves.

'I try to be as much in the here and now as possible,' she

explained. 'I think it's cowardice to live in the past, or the future, so I try to be brave and spring clean and take with me only what matters. I try to make sure that in a year's time I'll be just as lost as I am now.'

She saw the immediate future of music as 'chamber music mentality, spiritual and free, my new thing', wrote her own string arrangements on a laptop and eulogised over its 'revolutionary relevance' and historical re-emergence at the beginning and end of each century.

'It will be the opposite of your old rock'n'roll tune,' she levitated, 'which is traditional and conservative, God and the Devil, like the Bible, the oldest story ever told. Now, if you want to go into aliens and somewhere you've never been before you end up with some kind of chamber music atmosphere, not earthbound. We don't want any of that earthbound now, do we? We wanna get lost! We wanna get fucked! Lost and fucked!'

As might a gentleman who now approached her.

'I'm sorry to bother you . . .'

This, then, was the universal opening gambit of your standard autograph hunter. A gangly city gent in a suit, his tie askew in the balm of this summer's afternoon, he was holding a Filofax page aloft.

'I know that you must get people coming up and asking you all the time, but I really am a big fan and . . .'

Björk reached into her bag, swiftly located a pair of nail scissors, snipped off his tie and *ate it!*

Except, sadly, she didn't. She smiled angelically once again, became eerily quiet, wrote her autograph in the tiniest swirl dead in the centre of the page and handed it back, lips tight shut. He left, embarrassed by the silence, which was its purpose in the first place. He would never know how lucky he was.

'One day,' grinned Björk, springing back into life, mouthing behind her hand while striding into the café to pay for our luncheon herself, 'I might just eat someone's camera . . .'

14

SHIZZLE MY NIZZLE

1993, Snoop Dogg's 'Who Am I (What's My Name?)' brings West Coast stoner-rap to the mainstream

In 1993 the first green shoots of the incoming Britpop phenomenon became visible in the otherwise barren cultural landscape (Björk aside): the release of Blur's *Modern Life Is Rubbish*, Suede on the cover of *Select* magazine in front of a photoshopped Union flag with the words 'Yanks go home!', Oasis signing to Creation records after a tiny gig in Glasgow was accidentally attended by Creation boss Alan McGee. *Smash Hits* had now tragically lost its way, its cover stars (beyond Take That) a procession of US TV/movie star 'hunks', from Keanu Reeves, Christian Slater and *Baywatch* surfer dude David Charvet clutching a rose for a Valentine's Special issue, to the UK's non-hunks Chris Evans, Toby Anstis and Andi Peters in a 'kidnap' plot by the Channel 4 Zig and Zag gonks. Still occasionally freelancing for ver *Hits*, I was sent on a cover story assignment to Paris with 'Joey' from US teen-sap sitcom *Blossom*, a trip I remember nothing about except blubbing in a cab at the architectural splendour of a curving Parisian street.

Into the void, mercifully, came a benchmark wave of American hip-hop, now edging towards the mainstream via the incoming impact of the Wu-Tang Clan, De La Soul and A Tribe Called Quest. Most visible of them all, though, was Snoop Dogg, who you couldn't miss in '93 and not only because he was approximately nine feet tall: possessed of a cartoon pretty face and neatest braided hair, he was a gangsta-rap gamechanger who singlehandedly realigned the very sound of hip-hop with his deviously mewling, effortlessly languid style. No wonder adolescents globally were sashaying through playgrounds blaring the comedy chorus to his breakthrough single 'Who Am I (What's My Name?)': 'Da-da-da-da-dah ... Daaaawg!' (from his debut album *Doggystyle*). All this, too, in the year he was arrested and charged with a gangland murder, before his acquittal in '96.

To me he was a comically shady hip-hop caricature with an intriguingly charismatic presence. Nonetheless, I've no recollection of an interview we endured around '95 other than the mockery of his surrounding crew: listening in, a coterie of his chums found my Caledonian whinny worthy of relentless impersonation. To them, as I could clearly hear, I sounded like Groundskeeper Willie off *The Simpsons* ...

Sixteen years later...

By 2011 hip-hop was global youth culture's dominant sound and Snoop had been a superstar for years, much loved in Britain – one reason he held his World Press Conference that May in London. He'd also finally had his British visa reinstated in 2010, details of which had never been made public, after his visa was revoked in 2007 for a catalogue of misdemeanours. His venue of choice was West End stripper joint Platinum Lace and I was one of a press pack numbering around forty, mostly stubbly men in beards with man bags, several paparazzi and one hyperventilating fan, possibly Italian, frothing 'Snoop Dogg, he is coming!' Another, from Rock Feedback TV, wondered on camera if Snoop would receive 'a warm welcome, after being banned from Britain in 2007 for smashing up an airport!'

This wasn't strictly true. There had been several altercations that year: fights outside BA's First Class lounge with police officers injured; arrests in America for possession of a collapsible baton, marijuana and a handgun; arrests in Sweden for possession of drugs; his previous US criminal records involving drugs and handguns resulting in a revoked visa and ban from the UK Home Office 'for life'.

The man christened Calvin Broadus was, as he once described himself, 'a businessman first and foremost'. Seller of forty million albums worldwide, he was now worth a reported £60 million, his near-twenty years in the rap game augmented by a clothing line, video games, porn DVDs, a *Pimp Juice* drink, a range of pet accessories, commercials for both Adidas and Pepsi Max and a movie career. The sometime teenage McDonald's worker was now both a self-mythologising, cartoon gangsta-rap superhero who called himself 'Snooperman', who pretty much invented the comedy hip-hop suffix 'izzle', and a married family man with three kids (two sons, one daughter, then aged sixteen, thirteen and eleven). He was involved in his Snoop Youth Football Team and David Beckham had personally taught his sons to play. 'If you taste success,' he once said, 'make sure it's from a tall glass.'

Down in the basement of the moodily red-lit stripper club lounge, a white leather upholstered golden throne sat empty on a stage alongside a roof-high silvery pole, atop which twirled a foxy lady, upside down, in a Platinum Lace all-in-one bodysuit. As she slid around the pole, tracks boomed from Snoop's latest album *Doggumentary*, featuring the irresistibizzle song titles 'I Don't Need No Bitch', 'My Fuccn House' and 'Gangbang Rookie'. Irksome press restrictions were announced: questions today, informed a tense PR from the stage, would be 'all about the music, nothing about being banned [from Britain].' She said this more in hope than expectation, seeing as the press horde included the *Sun*, the *News of the World* and *Sky News*. A plume of greenest herbal smoke then snaked, Bisto-style, into the basement, announcing his imminent arrival.

At 4.30 p.m. precisely, the fragrant Snoop Dogg loped through a side door, moving like mercury towards his throne in a fluorescent sky-blue Adidas tracksuit, wearing black-out mirrored shades and silvery silken scarf, draped in *twelve* foxy ladies. Introduced by a jolly, Fearne Cotton-style compere, he seemed considerably relaxed.

'Thank you very much,' twinkled Snoop, now turning to his departing glamorous assistants. 'Ladies? Thank you for doing what you do. And thank y'all for having me out here, especially the people who fought to get me back into the UK.'

He held aloft a Union Jack mug, practically a *demand* for the unspeakable question, and quipped in faux-cockney, 'Fancy some tea?'

Rock Feedback TV reporter: 'The UK seems special to you. Why?'

Snoop: 'When I was a young rapper, the UK showed me so much love and respect ...' he began, eulogising over his British fans for at least three dreary minutes. 'It feels good to be home!'

Jolly Compere: 'That's what I like to hear!'

SBTV: 'This is your eleventh studio album, how do you stay relevant?' (snip!)

This would never do. Fifteen minutes creaked by in a

cliché-led informational void, concerning album collaborations and 'vocal inspirations.' This was *Snoop Doggy Dogg*. We wanted blunts, bitches, 'shizzle my nizzle' and sticking it to The Man in the Home Office. Come on, tabloids, I inwardly beseeched, do your job!

B2 magazine, Norway: 'Do you think you could have created anything without smoking?'

Snoop: 'I created three babies without smoking. Heheh!'

BBC News: 'How much has the music industry changed since *Doggystyle* and how's it changed the way you make records?'

Snoop: 'The music industry since *Doggystyle* has become more commercialised and more open to rappers and hip-hop. When I first came, hip-hop was the bad boy of music, the scapegoats. Now, hip-hop is a part of everything, sports, TV, entertainment, if you have hip-hop on your thing, it's gonna sell.'

Here, a lively query arrived from *Time Out* on whether young rappers today should be reacting against 'forty-year-old rappers rapping about Gucci', to which a smiling Snoop replied, 'for those who have something negative to say about hip-hop, suck a fat baby's dick.'

This was more like it! Inspired, I ventured a query.

Me: 'You're perceived as something of a cartoon character these days. Liam Gallagher once said: "I don't mind being a cartoon. As long as it's a good one." D'you feel the same?'

Here, Snoop sat back on his throne, evidently pleased.

'I am a cartoon character, baby,' he told me, promisingly. 'Lemme break this shit down for you. There was a cartoon created by Charles Schultz called *Charlie Brown*, right? There was a little white dog, Snoopy, but what Charlie didn't know was that Snoopy had a black brother, named Snoop Dogg. But he couldn't bring him home because the white family didn't really like black folks back then. So, he kicked me out, I went to the hood, he gave me a few dollars and my little white brother Snoopy told me, "You have a cartoon mind and you will succeed." And I have succeeded.'

Here, because we were getting along fairly well and the *Sun* had evidently gone soft in the head, I risked the forbidden question.

'Do you know exactly why your ban from Britain was lifted? What were the details?'

Jolly Compere, appalled: 'Actually, we've only got time for one . . .'

Here, Snoop shouted something indecipherable featuring the word 'gangsta!' so I blurted out, for a laugh, 'Who let the Dogg in?!'

Our breezy discourse was then crushed by Jolly Compere's insistence on a final question 'about the album!' Snoop then revealed his latest entrepreneurial ambition, 'a chain of supermarkets called Snoopermarkets', rose from his gilded throne and padded away, blowing a theatrical kiss goodbye.

Swizzle!

Two years later . . .

Snoop Dogg had undergone a dramatic transformation. The sometime renegade ghetto kid from Long Beach, LA, the former teenage crack-dealing felon turned self-styled D.O. Double G, was now A Massive Hippie. Or, at least, a reggae artist, announcing in early 2012 his reggae album, *Reincarnated*, written and recorded in Jamaica on a month-long pilgrimage to explore Rastafari culture, promote reggae music and become 'a better man' devoted to 'peace and love'.

Central to the project was his flourishing friendship with Bunny Wailer, last remaining member of Bob Marley and the

Wailers, who recorded vocals for *Reincarnated* and renamed his newly beloved Rasta brother Lion (magnificently pronounced by Wailer as 'Lie-yon'). But by January 2013, the peace and love had gone up in mintiest smoke: Bunny Wailer, in an interview, denounced Snoop Lion's 'outright fraudulent use of Rastafari Community's personalities and symbolism' while the Rastafari Millennium Council, a sort of Reggae Police Bureau which Wailer headed, released a statement saying, 'Smoking weed and loving Bob Marley is not what defines the Rastafari indigenous culture!' It claimed to have sent Snoop Lion a seven-page list of demands seeking fulfilment of both 'financial' and 'moral' commitments, threatening a lawsuit should he continue to call himself Lion. This, then, was the murky backdrop to our 2013 summit in his hometown of Los Angeles. The tension would surely be palpable ...

Snoop Lion floated towards me as if on a magic carpet of marijuana fumes, singing his head off, 'a song from my new reggae album, yes baby!' Around his neck sparkled a black crystal pendant in the shape of a Lion's head wearing a jaunty crown, no outward trouble detectable in his newfound Rasta paradise. We were in the Blues BBQ bistro on LA's Santa Monica Boulevard, in a curtained-off back room featuring a Henry VIII-style wooden banquet table where Snoop Lion sat under a large taxidermied cow's head. A feast lay before him – ribs, burger, fries, shrimp – all of which he ignored as we addressed what Quentin Tarantino might have 'dubbed' The Bunny Wailer Situation.

'I have nothing but love and respect for Bunny Wailer,' he assured me evenly, twenty minutes into a conversation where he'd stared directly into the middle distance, avoiding any eye contact whatsoever. 'I match negativity with love. So, there is no drama.'

Why would Bunny Wailer suddenly see the Snoop Lion project as 'fraudulent'?

'I can't explain that. The last I seen and heard from him was in Jamaica and we was all love and it was beautiful.'

He finally met my gaze and his liquid almond eyes looked genuinely forlorn.

'I don't believe what people write until I hear what the person say,' he coolly continued. 'Someone could be trumping this shit up. A sabotage. Writing this for him, out of spite, or their own anger and jealousy.'

Did he ever receive a seven-page letter of stipulations?

'No,' he frowned, his calm demeanour evaporating. 'No. No. *No-no-no-no*, I don't have no *stipulations*. First of all, I'm from East Side, Long Beach. *Period*. I don't answer to *no* man. *Period*. The spirit called me to Jamaica so no *man* can throw a stick. Everything that I've done was out of love and I'm gonna continue to do it out of love. For example, we created the Mind Gardens programme, you need to be asking me about *that*.'

Snoop always knew there'd be cynicism over his comically extreme volte-face – 'I knew the job was dangerous when I took it' – attempting to stem accusations of one-way reggae-robbery (today we'd call it cultural appropriation) through his non-profit Mind Gardens project, building community gardens so impoverished families could access (and sell as produce) fresh fruit and vegetables. 'As opposed to just take the music and run away and make money,' he noted, pointedly. Was he convinced those words *weren't* from Bunny Wailer?

'It *couldn't* have been him!' came his howl of dismay. 'Our relationship was *genuine*. I don't know how to fake. I'm one hundred per cent.'

Maybe he should contact the man himself?

(Heavily frowning) '*Why?* It should be *the other way around.*

Listen listen listen listen *listen*. Why should I reach out when I'm the one being attacked? He should reach out to clear his name. If he doesn't reach out, he must be saying this shit. Because if someone said, "Snoop Dogg is saying this about you," Snoop Dogg's gonna get on the phone and say, "Hey homie, I didn't say that shit" and then I'm gonna tell the media, "Fuck y'all, y'all lying, I didn't say that shit." If I *did* say it, I *meant* it, so *fuck* you. But if I didn't, I would reach out.'

He sat up, rolled his shoulder blades as if kneading out gnarly knots of tension. By now I was yearning for the good old days of 'shizzle my nizzle' and comedy gangsta-pimp capers . . .

Calvin Cordozar Broadus Jr was now forty-one years old, and I had a theory as to why the Dogg had become the Lion: at forty, Westernised humans tended to ask the what's-it-all-about-man Big Picture questions. I'd watched a succession of veteran performers, after youthful years of extreme success, fame and money, routinely turn to 'spirituality', seek more meaningful things (usually a family), declare 'all you need is love' and urgently wish to 'give back'.

'Well, when you reach the pinnacle,' agreed Snoop, 'you finally wake up, put aside childish ways and want to do something positive. You can affect people. You have kids and you understand what life is about.'

I reminded him of his cartoony self back in 2011 in London, all blunts, strippers and 'Gangbang Rookie'.

'I was having fun with that persona that people loved,' he now decided. 'Wearing my uniform one more time before I become somebody new.'

This might also have been rap's first celebrity mid-life crisis, in reverse.

'Yeah, at forty most men decide to live wild and crazy

because they've been so conservative all along,' he smiled. 'Me, I've been living wild and crazy my whole life!'

He was also, perhaps, consumed with regret, needing to right the wrongs of old.

'I have no regrets,' he countered, before thinking again, contemplating the day in '93 he witnessed a gang-related fatal shooting and was held on a murder charge. 'The only regret I have is that I was a part of a day where someone lost their life. I wish that man could still be alive, and I wouldn't have that on my life.'

Around 2003 the already vastly famous, successful and wealthy rap icon Snoop Dogg decided to give himself what we'd call a side-hustle today: he became a professional pimp. I wondered if this, too, was something he might regret; it had never made sense to me.

'It didn't make sense because you didn't understand where I came from,' he instructed. 'Where I come from the people that we looked up to were the pimps. The people who were the ghetto superstars. Who had all the money. All the cars.'

But he was already that himself, though.

'Yeah, but that still doesn't tickle your fancy as far as your infatuation with who you want to be. If you listen to my rapping, from the beginning, there was always a pimp inside of that rap. And I finally became what I wanted to be as a kid. And once I was able to live it, full-fledged, year in, year out, day to day, I began to understand that it wasn't for me. It was a man living out a child fantasy.'

Those must've been very weird years for his wife.

'Her father was the biggest pimp in Long Beach, *ever*!' he scoffed, incredulously. 'Cecile "Doc" Pimpin' Ass Fuller. I grew up wanting to be like her father. Her father had a blue Rolls Royce with a cherry curtain and the steering wheel was on the other side. This was in the eighties, when a motherfucker didn't even know what a Rolls Royce *was*. He'd ride through Long Beach in a Rolls Royce with major money and had his own nightclub and bitches and he was *the one*. So, my wife understands the dynamics. She never loved it, she always hated it, but she loved *me*. And supported me. If you marry someone you love 'em for good or worse, thick and thin, till death do us part.'

Back in 2011 Snoop lost a lifelong close friend, Nate Dogg, who died suddenly from stroke complications. Perhaps this shock had given him the most profound life-changing epiphany of them all.

'That's just how life works,' responded Snoop, matter-of-factly. 'I never thought I'd bury *him*. My close friend. You think you're friends to the end, somebody who you started off dreaming with and you see both of your dreams come true. Me 'n' Nate stayed a block away from each other. It just hurts. And money can't fix it.'

In 2013 Snoop remained fantastically wealthy, his fortune accumulated not only through his forty million album sales but starring roles in fourteen TV shows, fifteen films and endorsement deals with Adidas, AOL, Chrysler, Pepsi Max, *FIFA 13* and Wonderful Pistachios (Get Crackin'). Now he was a 'Rasta' – a central tenet being the rejection of 'Babylonian' materialism – shouldn't he be giving all his money away?

'If I give it all away, I give it to my people!' he balked. 'Make sure others are happy when I'm gone. That was the whole purpose of me getting it. It's never been me-me-me; it's about us-us-us. I'm not one hundred per cent Rastafarian. Doesn't matter. I'm learning.'

So he definitely wasn't giving it all away?

'No! It's been through my God-given talent!'

How about 'peace and love' for all mankind? Was that plausible given our barbaric history for the last ten thousand years?

'But we have evolved!' came his enthusiastic response, before a fulsome speech on 'the peaceful people' now living in 'Berlin, Iraq, Palestine, Israel, Saudi Arabia, it's about touching one person, changing a mentality' (from today's perspective, a horrifically depressing reply). He cited his own example.

'Imagine all the times I made records about killin' a motherfucker, fuckin' somebody up, slappin' a bitch, takin' somebody's money, being negative and everybody buying into it, "Yeah, we like this, more, more!" Now, when I say peace and love? They'll say, "More more more!"'

He ruminated on kids today compared to kids like him, born in 1971.

'I grew up where white people was over there, Mexican people was with us, Asian motherfuckers is over there,' he pointed out. 'Now, the kids, their friends are white, Asian, black, Hispanic. My kids' friends? It's like the United Nations!'

In the sixties, he added, he and I would be forced to walk on opposite sides of the street.

'I could be killed, looking at a white woman,' he reminded me. 'Now? You could be *my* woman. We could have kids together! Guess what? You can even be gay now! Gay-bashing? My kids don't even know what that shit *means*. We're doing *awesome*.'

He had just turned into a big hippie, hadn't he?

'My oldest son is a hippie!' he yelped. 'The Spanky Danky hippie era. [Corde Calvin Broadus, then eighteen, recorded under the name Spanky Danky.] He's got it tattooed on his chest: HIPPIE ERA. He likes hippie shit! Janis Joplin, all that.'

Did he just get bored of the Snoop Dogg persona?

'Not bored,' he decided, as our chipper new hippie friend suddenly morphed into someone else, again, namechecking basketball player Michael Jordan's catastrophic foray into baseball, acknowledged as one of sporting history's greatest blunders.

'It's like Michael Jordan,' he announced, merrily. 'He won three basketball championships and decided to take a year off to play baseball cos he loved it. He struck out, terrible, and people were "Mike, you gotta put that 23 [jersey] back on!" And he put that motherfucking number 23 back on and won three more championships in a row. So, to me? I'm at that stage where I won so many championships in rap that I wanna see if I can win a championship in reggae. And if it don't work out, I could always go grab my jersey, put it back on, go back to the rap world. And dominate. Again!'

And it wouldn't, I wondered, bewildered, be a different, more 'evolved' version of rap?

'Not really. Because people love me for being me.'

Whoever that was.

Perhaps fittingly for a supposed hippie, Snoop Lion now wanted to show me his favourite weed store, the Alternative Herbal Health Services, West Hollywood's longest-serving legal weed clinic for medical marijuana, established in 2003. Here, he sold his own brand paraphernalia and was greeted like a homecoming hero. A trinkety emporium, this was olden days Glastonbury epitomised: pink paper love hearts dangled from the ceiling, counters displayed cannabis lollies, Rice Krispy Treats, pipes, grinders, *Clear Eyes* eye drops while glass-fronted cabinets twinkled with enticing pre-packs called 'Diesel Skunk', 'Sweet Pussy' and 'Charlie Sheen', with an ATM machine parked against the wall. The proprietor, Dr Dina, was here, Snoop's friend and business associate for twenty years.

'Come on back to our office, fellas,' instructed Snoop,

directing myself, photographer and assistant through a door disguised as a brick wall into the Growing Room where rows of three-feet-tall cannabis plants bloomed under low-hanging lights. Among friends, he was now the playful buffoon, puffing a ready rolled blunt, peering into a plant wearing special-vision shades: 'You can see *everything* on this fucking bud … crystals!' Our photographer's assistant, a regular weed smoker, speed-puffed on Snoop's blunt to blow smoke-effects across his face and soon boggled out loud, eyes like Jupiter's moons, 'I am … *so* … *stoned*. Totally hallucinating.' Dina revealed their latest entrepreneurial venture, the Snoop Lion Weed Growing Box: a metal box the size and shape of a chest freezer, emblazoned with Snoop Lion motifs in red, gold and green, which housed lights and an automated watering mechanism. 'We want six different design options of the Snoop Lion series,' Dina told him. 'We wanna sell a lotta boxes.'

'This,' marvelled Snoop, who was still, evidently, a businessman first and foremost, 'is the sick …'

Jamaica is a beautiful country, with a smiley people specialising in bliss, where a local once told me, on enquiring the time of day, 'There is *no time* in Jamaaaaiiiiica.' It's also a developing world economy prone to corruption where the locals are known to go along with the whims of outsiders if they're willing to pick up the tab. On my return to the UK, news arrived that Bunny Wailer was releasing two albums imminently, appearing on Jamaica's Irie FM to both promote his music and clarify his Snoop position (no original statement denial forthcoming). A significantly less robust criticism, he observed 'Snoop is a Dogg first,' affirmed he was 'not really satisfied' that Snoop had 'emphasised from being a Dogg to a Lion' and merely wished 'that he does things that are Lion-like.'

Back at the LA weed store, a young member of staff had somehow failed to recognise any version of Snoop as he initially approached the counter. 'Do you smoke?' she wondered. An incredulous second passed. 'I'm Snoop Dogg!' he roared, with a gallery-pleasing, flamboyantly showbiz cackle.

The Lion had left the building.

15

ROCK'N'ROLL STAR

1994, Oasis release 'Supersonic' and redefine not only the 90s but rock 'n' roll, Manchester and the long-forgotten skill of a well-flung V-sign

We all romanticise our heroes. I certainly romanticised Liam Gallagher, from the moment I first saw him, or heard him, on *The Chart Show* in April 1994, in the actual hour I learned of the suicide of Kurt Cobain whose bullet took the grim grunge era with it. 'Supersonic' was the scorching song, Liam's strikingly beautiful head stock still, framed by a cartoon mod-u-like haircut, unblinking deep blue eyes telling you absolutely nothing through tinted, circular glasses. Such beauty can be enough on its own, but it was the delivery that did it: the attitude, the insolence, the not giving a fuckness which ignited in me a full-on projection of Liam Gallagher as a fantastical, insubordinate outlaw.

This was the year the outsiders took over, the now burgeoning Britpop era dominated by a kaleidoscopic spectrum of oddballs barging in from the margins and redefining what a No. 1 pop star could be. Even as Wet Wet Wet remained No. 1 for *fifteen weeks* with the indestructible 'Love Is All Around', the weirdos were winning, the years '94 and '95 bringing era-defining albums, often No. 1, not only from Oasis, Pulp and Blur but the Prodigy, Massive Attack, Elastica, Supergrass, the Charlatans, Portishead, Leftfield, Black Grape and the Chemical Brothers. In a DIY era characterised by limitless ambition, fearless audacity and live-forever hedonism no wonder Noel Gallagher once said, about the very purpose of Oasis, 'It's a celebration of the euphoria of life.' Liam, naturally, had his own take: 'Oasis is all about freedom.' I loved Oasis interviews so much I'd take the day off to read them in the pub. They were mostly dual affairs featuring the Gallaghers doling out decimating appraisals of both each other and the prevailing culture, Liam 'n' Noel the spiralling double helix at the centre of the funniest rock'n'roll concept caper I'd ever known.

I'd joined the *NME* freelance ranks in June '94, which sounds like dropping onto a pin-point cultural bullseye of rock'n'roll insanity. From here on in, any newbie journo would've imagined, it would be on-ver-road with the Gallaghers in a supernova of chop, bubbly 'n' amusing punch-ups, several lost months with Alex out of Blur on the absinthe in the Groucho Club and endless japes with Jarvis careering round Britain in his canary-yellow Hillman Imp. In truth, my *NME* Britpop years, '94 to '97, were mostly spent carousing with the hobos of everyone who *wasn't* Oasis, Blur or Pulp, i.e. the marauding hordes of exuberant opportunists who convened around Camden Town. While the *NME* boys were gathering those epoch-defining quotes from the Gallaghers, I'd be down the boozer with the likes of Northern Uproar, 3 Colours Red and Menswear. It was Oasis, though, the ultimate Dreamers Band, a band who wrote music not for men, but for romantics, who became *my* band.

Twelve years later . . .

September 2007, 10 a.m., and Liam Gallagher bowled into his management office like a sunbeam blazing through a crack in the doorway, a fizzing kinetic forcefield dancing straight towards me, all four limbs at a jaunty angle. Wearing a knee-length black leather coat buttoned all the way up to the neck, his newly famed, black leather man bag was slung across his body. Clean shaven with tanned, flawless skin, no shades obscured the steady discs of those enormous deep blue eyes, while his hair simply astonished: a shaggy, brown, sun-kissed mane, heading towards his shoulders. His hair, I told him, was bananas.

'What d'yer mean?' he wanted to know. 'It's gonna go longer! I'm going for the full-on Lennon, man. Madferrit. Well, it's your last chance innit, before you know it, you'll be fookin' bald.'

By 2007, I'd interviewed Liam twice before, with Noel, both early noughties encounters dominated by the garrulous older brother, Liam as amused as I was at Noel's then-hilarious addresses-to-the-nation on the disintegration of popular culture. In 2001 no shrift was given to Coldplay's Chris Martin, whose security detail, he imagined, included 'Afghan poodles', while in 2002, in Aberdeen, Noel was particularly appalled by now omnipresent Celebrity Culture, noting the recent confessions of Geri Halliwell who'd gone on a bulimia-related frenzied search for chocolate cake, 'raking through George Michael's fookin' bins'. Liam, sitting back listening, chortled throughout this tirade while tucking into a bag of smuggled in chips 'n' curry sauce in the swanky foyer of our tartan-tweedy hotel. Generously, he proffered the bag: 'Want one?'

There had been zero chance in those circumstances of any insights into the soul of the nation's most infamous frontman, anointed even then as the last of the truly great rock'n'roll stars. In 2007, though, came an opportunity to attempt to get to know him, even slightly, a then-rare solo interview while Noel was otherwise engaged, awaiting the imminent birth of his second child. Who was this man I'd elevated into the People's Hero, and how did he get here?

It was now thirteen years since 'Supersonic' had announced him as the most searing, primal vocalist of his generation, and since then we'd witnessed many Liams: the impudent cryptic surrealist of '95 who threatened to play 'golf off George Harrison's head'; the belligerent human cyclone of '96 who addressed a narcotic-questioning policeman with, 'What's it got to do with you, cuntybollocks?'; the sober penitent family man of '99, devoted to his son Lennon (from his marriage to now ex-wife Patsy Kensit); the peer-deflating swaggering Superstar of 2005 who deemed Coldplay's Chris Martin 'a plant pot'. Over 90 minutes that day, on his own, Liam would prove himself an 'up' sort of person who was also, simultaneously, acutely media-wary: as you would be if you'd been caricatured for years through the pulsing prism of our hysterical tabloid press as a perma-cursing madman, a *Wacky Races* character barrelling along in a dust cloud, two V-signs cocked to the sky.

We were now seated side by side on a spongy blue sofa in a side office and at no point did his coat come off, or his bag, which remained slung across his body like an instinctive, psychological shield. Slowly, his initial reticence melted away, easing into a multi-dimensional personality: blunt, unapologetic, philosophical, comically sweet and future-facing ('me memory's fookin' shockin''). He was almost thirty-five, had been out in the woods jogging that morning at 6.30 a.m. and had thus far smoked one cigarette. 'All that feeling shit's over,' he declared, after two decades of booze and narcotic bedlam. 'I'd rather go for a walk with me kid, y'knowhatImean? It's top, man. I wanna live forever, me.'

Back in the early eighties, as Thatcher, unemployment, New Romantics and jangling indie pop ruled, the young Liam Gallagher had no interest in music, believing music fanatics, including Noel, were 'weird bastards'. He had vague notions about becoming a footballer but if not, 'a butcher, maybe, and just sink into normal life.' Like Morrissey and Marr, his parents were Irish immigrants into post-war Manchester: dad, Tommy, a builder, and mum, Peggy, variously a cleaner, dinner lady and McVitie's factory worker who plucked misshapen Penguins and Jaffa Cakes off the production line. Tommy, always openly recalled by the brothers as a violent alcoholic, who sporadically beat Peggy, Noel and oldest brother Paul (Noel took the worst of it), while Liam, the youngest by five years, remained untouched – only because a beating might have killed him. Peggy eventually left Tommy 'with nothing but a mattress'. Liam left school at fifteen without taking a single exam – 'I just swerved school, didn't like the hours' – then worked, briefly, in a garden centre until he was asked to clean out a Portakabin toilet – 'I just said, "Fuck you" and fucked off' – and signed on the dole instead.

'I weren't a dark kid, I was out all the time 'til ten playing football,' he noted, his teenage dole years spent in the park with mates, drinking, smoking, 'sitting on the bowling green, top.' He shared a spartan room with Noel, two single beds, a stereo, no fresh wallpaper on peeling walls, where the brothers made their individual marks: football posters for Liam, bands for Noel, while both scribbled the sacred words 'Man City'. Noel was the melancholy brother, sitting up all night with his acoustic guitar, writing songs from age sixteen.

'You could tell he was a bit different,' reflected Liam.

'I thought he was pretty clever actually. I admired both my brothers. I suppose they did look after me, but it was me mam that looked after us all really.'

He contemplated the violence at home.

'It was mainly him [Noel] and Paul, he'd be giving it the pair of 'em,' he confirmed, of his dad's assaults. 'And I'd get off with it really. *Course* it was scary, man. Well, that's why I'm the way I am, aren't I? Even to this day. That's where my anger is and that's what makes me fucking *attack* that mic, y'knowhatImean? Cos it's just all boiled up. I'm glad it's not ever been … resolved, in a way. I wouldn't change a fucking thing. Me mam was great, but it was *shit* at home and I needed to get in … not a gang, but a group of summat.'

The Stone Roses saved him. 'They took me away from it, I thought "there's a place there, that I can go and be part of".' Liam joined his mates' band, Rain, suggested the Oasis name change, asked Noel if he fancied joining, which he did, with the stipulation that he wrote the tunes, 'and that was cool with me, cos we didn't have any tunes!' Those immortal songs which became Oasis' multi-platinum-selling debut *Definitely Maybe*, those world class songs about dreams, yearning and escape, about friendship, hedonism and hope, sung by Liam with such resonating reach, he had no idea the meaning of. 'Didn't fucking care. They just sounded good!' Perhaps even more astonishingly, he now 'hated' his voice on the early songs, 'I sound like fucking Tweetie Bird.' After my yelping protests, he reconsidered.

'Alright, besides a couple of tunes!' he conceded. '"Slide Away", that's a fucking tune, that's a vocal. "Supersonic", that's alright. "Live Forever", some of the high bits I just think [head in hands], "Fuck that". "Whatever", I despise that. It's shite. I was young. I was nineteen, twenty.'

Liam was always a good-looking boy. At twenty-one he was

a good-looking rock'n'roll star and a household name with a No. 1 debut album. I wondered what the impact had been on his life, of being a very beautiful young man?

'Being what,' he retorted, mortified. *'Beautiful?* What d'yer mean, the impact? I never looked at meself as beautiful. No!'

He never thought, 'I'm a bit good-looking, me'?

'Depends who you're stood next to, innit? *Nah.* I was totally into *the look.* Of being in a band! Was fucking *obsessed* with hair, man, and always have been. I don't look at myself as being beautiful. I think of meself as [bawling] fucking God-like!'

But you were so very pretty.

'Was I?'

Yes.

Here, he picked at flecks which did not exist on his immaculate leather coat.

'Well. Them's the fucking breaks, innit?'

Oasis were enormous almost immediately, which Liam easily absorbed.

'Everything just felt right,' he nodded. 'A lot of bands now, Arctic Monkeys, some of 'em feel uncomfortable [with fame] and I think "Where's your head at, man?" Just *en-fucking-joy it.* It was deserved and I fucking loved it. It was the place for me to be. On a stage with loads of people going nuts. And even though it was all mad and it was one thing after a-fucking-nother, you're young and that's what it's meant to be like. You want to be getting into ... trouble. Don't fucking grow up *now,* grow up later, if you're gonna grow up at all.'

It was never even slightly scary, that level of sudden attention?

'No, I loved it, man. *I fucking loved it.* Meeting people, having a few quid, seeing the world. And I think you were able to tell I fucking loved it.'

Simultaneously, the Liam 'n' Noel soap opera was now as big

a story as the music. Did he know, looking back, what fuelled the constant fighting?

'But it just would be between brothers,' he insisted. 'Everyone fights anyway, not even brothers, Pete Doherty and Carl, Mick Jagger and Keith, if you're in that thing all the time. I was certainly never worried about it. [Lengthy pause.] I've never really thought about anything! *Really*. Just get up and do it. Just fucking *be*, man.'

Before meeting Liam that day I'd reread the transcript of the famed 'Wibbling Rivalry' interview of '94, the classic Gallagher Brothers verbal brawl, much of it centred on the band being booted off a ferry in Holland for fighting with Chelsea football fans (other than Noel, who was asleep), resulting in arrests, a deportation and a cancelled gig in Amsterdam. Liam thought this was really funny and Noel was appalled. Noel thought Liam was a 'headcase'. Liam thought Noel was 'born to be a priest'.

'Yeah! How old was his head? Fifty!?'

I put it to him that he wanted his brother to be his playpal, whereas Noel wanted to work, maybe because time for him (at twenty-seven), was running out. Is that what it was all about?

'Totally! I don't regret it. Didn't do us any harm, did it?'

From the mid-nineties onwards, Oasis became the nation's favourite rock'n'roll cartoon caper, a travelling circus of incalculable chaos which Liam described as 'the best soap on TV – I don't mind being a cartoon, as long as it's a good one.' Before inventing Oasis, Liam's lifetime's work had comprised those three weeks in the garden centre; from age twenty-one he'd been living in a rock star's bubble. His attitude to reality ever since, I ventured, was one of *'see yer later'*.

'Reality, man, fuck that!' he hooted. 'I remember doing the first Maine Road gig [of two Manchester City stadium shows in 1996]. I was still living at me mam's that day, first gig, come back home, sitting on me bed. That same bed. "Fucking hell, man, just played that gig, insane." The next day, I moved in with Patsy [Kensit]. Moved out of me mam's house into a fucking million-pound house in St John's Wood. *That* was good. I haven't been back since. Why would you go back *there*, man? *Fuck that.*'

His marriage to Patsy Kensit was no stabilising influence: that year there was a road rage incident, he was banned from Cathay Pacific airlines for life (an argument over a scone) and headbutted a fan in Australia. Cocaine was surely involved.

'Probably,' he shrugged. 'Maybe I weren't ready to get married. But I got a kid out of it [Lennon, born in 1999] so that'll do me. But it wasn't like I'd just gone out and headbutted people, started with some Cathay Pacific person. I don't class myself as a cunt, I class myself as an alright geezer. Who, if people wanna fuck with me, I'm gonna fuck with them back. I've only ever stood up for meself. And there's no way I'm ever gonna change that because if that gets taken away from me, there's no point being me is there? But I think I've grown up a little bit. I like who I am.'

By 2007, Oasis' best years were clearly behind them. What would Liam do if Oasis split up?

'I'd go in-fookin'-sane wouldn't I? Cos it's your life. I'm dreading the day. Just concentrate on one year at a time. One day at a time.'

In late 2006 Liam bought a new house in Henley-on-Thames, South Oxfordshire, where George Harrison lived for decades and where toffs in rowing boats have convened every year for the Henley Regatta since 1939. His life there was serene-ish and domestic – 'I just hang out with me missus [Nicole Appleton, former All Saint] and the kids.' He went to the pub occasionally, visited Nicole's sister Natalie Appleton and her husband Liam Howlett from the Prodigy – 'he's a geezer, man, we go to theirs, make a mess and get off' – but barely saw Noel and his partner Sara MacDonald. ('We're not the fucking Monkees.') His house had recently been renovated into Beatles-themed splendour.

'I've got a Beatles Bar,' confirmed Liam, proudly. 'It's black holes all over the ceiling and a submarine flying through it. I'm getting a collage of John Lennon with a guitar, my favourite picture, on the living room wall. I've got Beatles pictures, and I can afford frames these days. The bar is just Beatles everywhere, it's got that [pulls imaginary pint] and optics. Bar stools. Jukebox. Beatles, Stones, Pistols, all the classics, new music doesn't inspire me at all. Booze everywhere. It's fucking top. Our kid [Noel] was like that, "Are you not over that Scouse cunt yet?" No!'

Why did Liam love John Lennon so much?

'Because I know he's just like me – a shit-kicker from Liverpool, human.'

A typical morning round Liam's Henley Beatles house consisted of a cup of tea, *The Jeremy Kyle Show* ('he's a geezer'), followed by *Loose Women* ('the Loose Women are havin' it, man'). The house wasn't a party house in the way Noel's Supernova Heights was back in the revelling nineties. 'No chance. No famous people. Just mates.' When they moved in, they had a New Year's party with bouncy castles, which Liam and Nicole had a go on, 'And Nic broke her ankle didn't she, the fucking lunatic,' the woman he called 'me best mate, she's not got a bad bone in her, man.'

She once said Liam had a heart of gold as well.

'So I have. I just keep it hidden.'

Their son, Gene, was now a six-year-old with long, golden hair, which Liam tended to everyday. 'I'm like that [he mimed brushing Gene's hair over and over again], he's like, "Don't!" and I'm "The comb is your *friend*."'

Was Liam the kind of wayward soul who'd always needed responsibility?

'I suppose. Listen, I was always gonna go a bit nuts. But I don't think I was that fucking bad, actually. I ain't got no drug habit. I'm not an alcoholic.'

Despite everything, he'd never pressed all that hard on the self-destruct button. He wasn't exactly Shane MacGowan, was he?

'No disrespect to him, man, but I'd be on the piss if I was that ugly.' (Enormous bellow of laughter.)

What stopped him going down that road?

'Me mam. Gotta be, innit? I ring my mam every fucking day, man. Cos she's on her own. So as long as she knows I haven't changed, that's all that matters to me, couldn't give a fuck what anybody else thinks. People are "he's this, he's that", I don't give a fuck mate, whatever sells your papers, but as long as she knows she can still relate to me, that'll do me. She's "What you up to?" "Fuck all, wanna speak to the kids? How's Aunty Anne?" Shooting the breeze, man, checking in with that life, y'knowhatImean?'

It was different days, I noted, from turning up on Peggy's doorstep with an arm and a leg in a cast, an air-rifle down his back and cricket bat injuries all over his body, the result of the infamous Rockfield Studios Liam/Noel bust-up of '95 during the recording of *What's the Story (Morning Glory)?* in Wales. Here, Liam impersonated the profoundly Irish Peggy, aghast, as she opened the front door: 'What kind of fockin' record are yer *makin'* up dair!?'

Before he left that day he showed me the contents of his man bag.

'Bills!' he blared, holding envelopes aloft. 'Fucking TV licence! I've got to give it to one of the girls in there [management office], it's the final reminder . . .'

Or there'd be no more *Jeremy Kyle*.

'And no more fookin' SpongeBob.'

One week later...

In a North London pub at 3 p.m. Liam was drinking a large glass of rosé wine, followed by three more in rapid succession. 'I still drink,' he noted, 'just not every day.' Around his neck a black scarf was tied together with a large, flat-surfaced silver ring (Nicole's) bearing the words 'GIVE LOVE'. 'Oh, I'm not shy to give love, man,' he grinned. Today's Liam, just-add-booze, was exactly the same as last week's Liam, only increasingly louder and considerably bawdier. Suddenly, he fell silent.

'The fucking boys are playing,' he signalled, as Blur's 'Parklife' clattered out of the jukebox. 'Let's have a minute's silence here, man. I met him the other day, Phil Daniels [guest vocalist on 'Parklife']. I was running, he was running, coming towards me in the middle of the woods and he went [arms straight out to the side, roaring] "Alright geezer!" Jimmy in *Quadrophenia*, my hero. I don't mind Blur, I'm over it. It was a laugh, man, that's what you do when you're young. When I see Damon Albarn, I buzz off him. If I was still caught up in it now, I would be a right wanker.'

I wondered what he'd looked like on crystal meth, Oasis' drug of choice on the first calamitous American tour of '94, culminating in Liam pranging his tambourine off a wasted Noel's head and a band-threatening temporary split. Liam demonstrated by dropping to the floor and clamping his entire jaw around the edge of the wooden table.

'Not into that no more!' he hollered. 'Mushrooms were the best, when we were fifteen, sixteen. I had my best nights when I weren't in a band. On the dole. No one was looking at me for a fucking start. A normal bod just bouncing around. Half my mates doing normal jobs, they were rock stars in their own right. They knew how to have a good time. They've just got shit voices. Haven't we all?' (Uproarious cackling ensued.)

Noel once said Liam was a glass half-empty person and he was glass half-full. To me, Liam had as big a positive spirit as Noel had.

'Is that what's he's been saying then? That he's the positive guy? That's bollocks for a start. You wanna fucking try 'n' work with the cunt! Basically, he's the band bully. Fucking is, man! Believe you me, I'm the most positive person in the fucking world. He says these things as a form of jealousy. He wishes he was me! As much as I wish I was him. So he is exactly fucking wrong. You ask anyone around us! I'm always up, man.'

Where did that attitude come from?

'From being the Enlightened One. It's fucking true!'

Is it true that Liam growing his hair long really annoyed Noel?

[Huge grin] 'Who told you that? Cos he asked me mam. He said, "How fucking long's he growing it?" Is that *true*, that? [Delighted.] If *that's* the case I'm growing it down *there*, man! [Indicated the floor.] I'm gonna have to have pageboys, it'll take me about an hour to get on stage! [He leapt out of his seat to demonstrate a pageboy carrying hair like a bridal train.] "Fuckin' in the Bushes" is on. "You'll have to play that again, only half his head's on stage!"'

He cackled some more and pondered his contribution to the sum of human happiness.

'Oh, I have *thoroughly* enjoyed myself!' he blared. 'And I think the Oasis lot did too. Everyone got something out of it. I think this world's a better place for having me in it.'

Two years later, in August 2009, Oasis split up.

*

Sixteen months later...

December 2010, and it was now almost four years since Liam Gallagher told me he'd 'go in-fookin'-sane' should Oasis split up. He'd surely underestimated himself, if not the forces of the universe itself. He was now in a new band, Beady Eye, with three former Oasis members, bassist turned guitarist Andy Bell, guitarist Gem Archer and drummer Chris Sharrock. In a photo studio in London the full band spent several high-octane minutes addressing the run-up to the Oasis implosion and its crescendo, the tabloid-anointed 'Wonderbrawl' at the Rock en Seine Festival in Paris in August 2009, where guitars were smashed and plums were pelted at walls. Keen to get this over with, Liam rapidly summarised the events.

'We got there, went backstage, me and him [Noel] had an argument about some fookin' stupid little twat and that was it,' he raced on. 'He smashed my guitar that was bought as a present by my lovely wife and it was signed by my kid. Gene and Nic. But regardless of that, I thought, "Fuck it. He's been a tit for the last fookin' six months on this tour." Blowing hot and cold. So I thought "Fuck this shit, you're getting one of your guitars." He got off and that was it.'

His last words to Noel, he added, were, 'You go and fookin' stand behind your big security guard,' while Andy Bell interjected, 'The bottom line is, Noel just wasn't into being in this rock'n'roll band anymore, but we *are*.'

I'd long held a theory: that Liam, throughout his life, might have been suppressed, or at least felt suppressed, by his domineering brother Noel.

'Fuck that,' was Liam's immediate response. 'Oasis were one of the free-est bands ever. Best years of my fookin' life, man. It wasn't like [comedy German accent] Oz-Vitch [Auschwitz], d'youknowhatImean?! There is a bit more freedom now because anything that goes out [creatively] all of us have OK'd it, whereas Noel would before. And it's all immense. And that ain't bravado. It's fookin' . . . it's El Dorado. [A fulsome cackle ensued.] Listen, me and our kid didn't hang out, it wasn't like we were best buddies and then summat happened. We'd be like that if we worked in a butcher's together. He left the band, that's it.'

His eye alighted on a large glass of red wine now perched in front of me. Mischief had come among us. 'I dare you to neck that glass of wine in one,' he taunted. 'It's Christmas, innit? Coom on!' I caved in and agreed, only if they'd do likewise with newly arrived bottles of Corona. Exactly nine, silent seconds of five-way down-in-ones later, the universe exploded. Heading towards the nearby toilet, I walked straight into a glass wall, which Liam found hilarious, before I accidently stood on his exquisite, own-brand Pretty Green moccasins, 'Me fookin' suede-ies, I'm calling the cops!' Minutes later we were all bowling around an upstairs bar, Liam now drinking shots of 'Petroleum' tequila. He was looking forward, already, to turning forty in September 2012: 'I've got more enthusiasm than a twenty-year-old. The twenty-year-olds are all potheads sat on their arses all day playing *Space Invaders*.' He then affixed a hearty slap to my backside. He had very powerful hands. 'It's called passion,' he grinned and administered the same to Chris, 'none of that sexist bollocks.' Close-up, his skin was incandescently flawless.

'Nah, I've got bad skin, man,' he glimmered. 'I've got psoriasis all over my fookin' body. I have, man. Everywhere, except for me face. And every now and again on me head. I'll tell you a story, right. One time at Glastonbury I looked like I had dandruff. Everyone's backstage and this geezer comes up to me off his tits going, "I ain't seen Oasis for fookin' years, fookin' great" and he goes to his mate, "Look, Steve, he's even got cocaine in his hair!" And he pulls a bit of shit out of me hair and he's going [mimed geezer snorting flakes of Liam Gallagher's psoriasis straight up both nostrils]. On my fookin' life it's true!'

This story he thought so good he told it thrice, to Chris and then Andy, by which time the tale had expanded, 'and he's [finger on teeth] rubbing it in his gums!' It was the kind of rock'n'roll comedian moment we'd more usually witness in crowd-pleasing raconteur Noel Gallagher. After an hour of ribald tomfoolery and boisterous bear hugs, Liam left first around 4 p.m. with a chandelier-shattering 'Merry Christmas!'

What would be happening, I asked Gem, if Noel was still here?

'Well, nobody's assuming the Noel role of, "You shouldn't be drinking tonight",' observed Gem, 'so Liam would probably be here 'til midnight, just to prove a fucking point.'

I asked him if he agreed with my theory that Noel, perhaps even subconsciously, had suppressed Liam. 'Course he has,' he firmly replied. 'Not all his life. But look, in some ways, the best thing has been suppressing him. Because Liam could *really* have fucked his own life up. D'youknowhatImean?'

It seemed to me that Liam had always wanted to be the Entertainer and was only capable of being so – of really being *himself* – when Noel wasn't around.

'You're right,' nodded Gem.

'Hence,' added Chris that winningly chaotic afternoon, 'Liam's always in a good mood.' He smiled, expansively. 'Liam's like having Elvis walking around.'

Beady Eye was a short-lived endeavour. Liam's resurrection as a solo artist then arrived in 2017, after three wilderness years which saw him, it certainly seemed, finally go *in-fookin'-sane*. He split with Nicole, confessed to a 'love child' with a US journalist and publicly apologised for 'hurting a lot of people'. He remains engaged to PA/PR Debbie Gwyther, Noel is divorced from Sara and in August 2024 the brothers announced the Oasis Live '25 reunion tour to explosive global excitement, shows which were then defined by the most staggering level of multi-generational joy in rock'n'roll comeback history. Before then, only Liam had become a singular force on Twitter/X and only Liam had been enormous enough on his own to play Knebworth, twice, in 2022, to 170,000 people, shows which were, naturally, 'biblical'.

Today, Oasis are more famous and adored than they've possibly ever been and I know all I need to know about who Liam Gallagher is, and how he got here. I don't romanticise him anymore, nor see him as any kind of fantasy. A second-generation Irish immigrant, born into violence and chaos, with zero education and little hope, who forged his own spectacular life through passion, determination, talent, unapologetic belligerence and irrepressible personality. A geezer. A shit-kicker from Manchester. Human.

A working-class hero is something to be.

16

INNER MEET ME

1998, The Beta Band release the critically adored 'Three EPs' and, soon enough, go completely mad

By 1998 the Britpop fire had turned to smouldering embers. With three No. 1 singles, the Spice Girls were the biggest band in Britain, as the late nineties musical swing-o-meter deviated dramatically away from guitar bands towards the shiny shenanigans of pop. When the Spices weren't No. 1 Cher was, with the fabulous 'Believe' (for seven weeks), while irksome Irish pop manager Louis Walsh had created a mimsy-pop colossus in Boyzone during the years Robbie Williams, post-Take That, was the biggest solo star in Britain.

Over in the US, Britney Spears' 'Baby One More Time' and *NSYNC's 'I Want You Back' began the global teen-pop takeover while Madonna's mighty *Ray of Light* album proved the international comeback thriller of the year.

Into this predominantly glam-pop atmosphere shuffled ramshackle four-piece the Beta Band, from east coast Scotland, whose first three EPs were released together in September '98 as *The Three EPs*. To me they felt miraculous, a peerless art-pop troupe conjuring an Alice in Wonderland rabbit out of the moth-eaten Britpop hat, an indefinable distillation of dub-folk-hip-hop-psychedelic-jingle-dance-electro-acoustic-cosmic rock'n'roll (predating the genre-fluid, multi-hyphenates of today by over two decades). Their grooved-out possibilities were endless, featuring duck whistles, pots and pans, toy horns, a ship's bell, a steel drum, a shoebox and anything else bashable (including, possibly, themselves). They dressed up in karate suits, or as African kings, made films for live shows featuring the band being abducted by giant parrots, or inexplicable footage of a bloke in a sleeping bag on a hill. On stage, clutching their curious instruments, they stood amid swathes of foliage, palm trees and rubber plants like the David Attenborough In-House Band. Still working for the *NME* that year, I loved them immediately, a beacon of true pop subversion among the ruling pop class of the time, and if the day ever came when they'd 'grace' the paper's cover I knew I'd hustle for the job with a journalistic mission: to make them significantly more famous than they currently were – i.e. not at all.

One year later...

In 1999 the Beta Band had finally made their debut album proper, *The Beta Band*, a bendy-mirrored spook-palace of sprawly instrumental wig-outs, tragic-comic lyrical brilliance, homestead rap, parping hilarity and melancholic, dream-pop splendour. It did, however, sound like it was recorded at the bottom of the sea. Nonetheless, the *NME* were granting them a cover story and sent me on assignment, the ruling class now shinier than ever, the year tots' and teen-pop fully took over via Steps, S Club 7, Britney Spears, Christine Aguilera, B*Witched, 5ive and Louis Walsh's even drippier Boyzone clones Westlife. Nineteen ninety-nine would be the year the now chart-throttling Brian from Westlife told me, as I blubbed into my tape recorder, how 'sad' I seemed, that 'everything's turned from rock to pop – we'll write you a rock song, that'll make yer sad alroight!'

My mission to regain some art-pop ground began in an incongruous setting – a posho lunch in the sky-high brasserie of London's OXO Tower. Here, the four members of the Beta Band were seated amid the clouds and the kind of business-lunching clientele who wielded golden Amex credit cards, all the swifter to pay for their ostrich steaklets in coriander and sesame seed brine (£17.50 – a non-snip worth £38.01 today). Swathed in their practical camping-wear 'chic', the skew-haired Scottish quartet stuck out from the braying toffs like itinerant, penniless buskers and for this ditch-dweller's aesthetic alone, aside from their beguiling grooved-up psychedelia, they were more heroic to me than ever. Disastrously, however, like the Stone Roses in '89, they famously could not speak, bearing a collective and impenetrable dance DJ's horror of self-analytical speech. Nothing, however, prepared me for the stony-faced, comprehensive silence of singer, guitarist and percussionist Steve Mason (wearing a cagoul and sensitive fringe). Eventually, he delivered his opening pronouncement on the culmination thus far of his artistic life, debut album *The Beta Band*.

Steve (into his pint, in the world's most underwater mumble): 'I think it's fucking awful.'

He actually hated it?

'It's definitely the worst record we've ever made and it's probably one of the worst records that'll come out this year.'

So, where had it all gone wrong in his ears?

'Picked the wrong guy to help us produce it. We've ended up with what sounds, to me, like ten demos. Recorded by a guy who's obsessed with the Beach Boys and sixties production styles. Which is totally irrelevant, in this day and age.'

But but but, I spluttered, this shouldn't have been allowed to happen! Because the Beta Band are special!

'I don't think that's true. We're not doing anything that hasn't been done before. We're not making any kind of new sound. [Sharp intake of breath from rest of the band.] All we've got is some slightly different arrangements. What is it that's so interesting about it?'

It is, I insisted, brim-full of imagination and soul and gorgeousness! The percussion isn't done anywhere else, particularly, for a start!

'Not done particularly well, either.'

Ten minutes ensued of unresolved discourse between Steve, drums/percussion vibesman Robin, bass player Richard and DJ/keyboard player John over who was to 'blame'.

Did Steve really think the Beta Band were not special?

'Yeah. There'll be another band along for you all to get excited about in about six months' time. The pinnacle of achievement for this month is . . . dress up as wacky next-door neighbours and hit pots and pans and have strange production styles and next month it'll be riding round on a bike with bananas tied to your feet.'

The Beta Band, then, were the first band in history the British music press had built up only to knock *themselves* down, out, unconscious and set fire to their own life-support machine. At no other point in history had the phrase 'we're the best band in the world' seemed so appealing. In that Friday-evening drinkerie, expensively suited executives were now guffawing so loudly we reconvened to a nearby park, only to be constantly disturbed by stone-pelting children and footballs whizzing past our heads.

'Chaos,' sighed John, a-seat on the grass. 'It always has been.'

'We've been put to sea,' described Richard, 'in a very

hastily constructed ship with all the rivets missing and we're constantly bailing water out the bottom just to keep the thing going and chucking money over the side and wondering why we've got nothing. And we've used up all the bread. Nothing to eat!'

Twenty minutes later I learned a supposedly forthcoming Beta Band 'new era' visuals concept would involve less pastoral man-in-a-sleeping-bag footage, more 'industrial, urban, gritty realism'. And 'violent sexual transport'.

No more abducting parrots, then?

Steve: 'Fuck the parrots.'

Richard: 'We'd just like to say the fucking funny days of the Beta Band are over. Anyone fucks with us now ... they might as well step to the Wu-Tang Clan before they step to us. We're gonna start bustin' heads pretty fucking soon. We're like the kid who got beaten up in school and went and had loads of kung fu lessons and then thought "fuck it" and bought a huge gun instead and came back and shot everyone. Not that I'm suggesting anyone should shoot anyone at schools anywhere in the world.'

Steve: 'That's gonna be the big word thing [pull-out quote], that. *Oh no.*'

It was now time, I ventured, for the Beta Band to tell the public exactly what it was they were trying to say as a band because no one had a clue.

The Beta Band, in unison: 'We're not trying to say anything!'

Steve: 'I am. No drugs! I'm the band ... spokesmouth.'

John: 'I need the toilet. I need to go home!'

Richard: 'Can we go home now?'

John: 'Please!?'

The Beta Band now sprang, as one, up from the grass and barrelled back towards the public house toilet.

Sprinting after them, I insisted this was ridiculous, that

there must be something they were trying to tell us, because that's what was fabulous about music?

Richard: 'No it's not! The great thing about music is hearing it!'

But there was all the other stuff, I hollered. Stuff to believe in, who someone is, what they say, what they stand for, the mindset you align yourself with and it makes your world a better place!

Richard (appalled): 'Well that's wrong! *It's wrong it's wrong it's wrong.* You're basing your hopes on something else that doesn't exist! Rather than believing in yourself!'

Steve: 'Believe in someone else.'

Believe in someone else!? And that's the Beta Band's last word on the Beta Band!?

Steve: 'Yes!'

Pthrhthrt!

Sixteen years later . . .

'Believe in someone else!'

Steve Mason's stubbly face was creased in cackling laughter. It was late December 2015, eleven years since the Beta Band split up in 2004, £1.2m in debt to EMI. We were seated at the tiny dining table of his rented, red-bricked terraced house in coastal Hove, by Brighton. 'I was talking about that interview last night,' he smiled, hand-rolling a Golden Virginia, now a forty-two-year-old man of engaging self-assurance. 'It's probably the single greatest example of a self-destructive musician, the *dictionary definition*,' he chortled. 'Cover story: "Don't buy our album, it's rubbish!" I was *insane . . .*'

By then Steve Mason had been a musical renegade for over two decades, whose pioneering Beta Band had been, as he defined them that day, 'punk rock anti-heroes who didn't want to be famous; I wanted to be part of an amazing art *happening*.' After the Beta Band imploded, he released music as King Biscuit Time and Black Affair, had released albums under his own name since 2010 and in 2016 was releasing his third, *Meet the Humans*, his most epic, affecting and joyously euphoric since the Beta Band's mythologised *Three E.P.s*. Maybe this year – at last! – he would fully emerge from the cul-de-sac of obscurity. Lyrically, he was yearning, breaking through 'the darkness', his music the definition of melancholy beauty.

'That's what I do,' nodded this robustly reconstructed version of Steve Mason, sipping a strong tea. 'Every album I put out, and this sounds ridiculous, I *expect* it to change the world. And it doesn't happen. And it breaks your heart every time.'

Eighteen months previously, Steve had changed his own world, moving to Hove because he didn't feel insane anymore. Since 2002 he'd lived in rural Scotland 'in isolation', first in a coastal village, then seven years of his thirties entirely alone in a cottage in the woods, sporadically making music while resetting his aggressively destructive mind, a successful ten-year process culminating in 'reintroducing myself to society' (hence the new album title). The high-ceilinged, rectangular living room we were sitting in was a makeshift studio housing old Beta Band instruments (he'd no money for anything new), a single man's room spartanly sprinkled with books (Plato's *Republic*), CDs (Link Wray), DVDs (*The Jean-Luc Godard Collection Volume 1*), vinyl albums (compilations from seventies-to-nineties African liberation station Radio Freedom) and one pork pie hat, the sort 'Heisenberg' wore in *Breaking Bad*. Brighton he'd chosen both for its creative energies and already resident friends, including Primal Scream's Martin Duffy, 'truly, a genius' (who we tragically lost to an accidental fall in his Brighton home in late 2022, aged fifty-five). He sipped more of his tea, a strident, intense, dramatically honest character.

'It's still a novelty,' he noted, of his newly populated life. 'I can walk to the pub, the record shop. There's women in this town I can meet! It's not just me and the turnips and the sheep.'

Growing up, Steve had been 'a kid like any other, a bit dark but I laughed a lot'. He'd been a drummer in bands from age thirteen and became a car mechanic by trade. At nineteen, his parents split up, overnight: his mum walked into his bedroom, out of the blue, and told him of his dad's affair. The emotional shock triggered clinical depression, which deepened into 'manic depression and agoraphobia', then worsened by an increasing impulse for hallucinogenic drugs. He denounced his father 'forever', endured violent manic outbursts, smashed up instruments and possessions, started boozed-up fights in pubs and battled increasingly acute suicidal thoughts. His nadir arrived in 2006, a 'monumental breakdown', which included jumping in a river, drunk, before finding sustained professional help in a three-way recovery approach: anti-depressants, therapy and six-hour sessions of deep self-analysis through conscious hypnotherapy. 'It's fucking exhausting,' he admitted, of the gruelling hypnotherapy. 'Battling against yourself, it's far harder than batting against anything else, *far* harder.' Once, in an anger relapse, he booted over the bin outside his woodland cottage, 'and a deer popped its head up, rabbits went flying off, but at least I wasn't smashing up my own possessions anymore.'

I wondered what he did every night all on his own?

'You masturbate. Heheheh!'

His life in the woods, on heavy medication, had meant permanent 'lethargy': up at 11 a.m., breakfast, 'have a few fags', internet, 'a few more fags', TV, film, dinner, fall asleep, wake up, 'work on music till 4 a.m., but what I was really doing was sorting my head out.' He was now 'completely reconciled' with his dad. 'You realise your parents are just people, they make mistakes, fall in and out of love, crash cars and fart, just like everyone else.' He felt, he added, 'genuinely happy, for the first time, I'm old and I love it.' Then came a pause. 'I'd still like success though!'

Three years previously he'd come off the anti-depressants completely, 'like that [he snapped his fingers] which is very dangerous, it often leads to suicide.' Instead, he was in psychological, musical and perhaps even romantic renaissance.

'I want an actual proper relationship now,' he chuckled. 'Maybe a kid. I'm maybe mature and ready enough!'

He opened his patio doors and puffed smoke into the garden.

'But I still don't feel like a grown up,' he insisted. 'I have the emotional intelligence of an eighty-year-old man on his deathbed, but the everything else of a twenty-five-year-old. Let's see who takes that on.'

Sixteen years on from a mumbling near-mute and Steve Mason was now fearlessly opinionated. Engaging him on politics unearthed a powerhouse of profound scepticism – 'Question everything,' he urged, 'on all sides.' He rejected both party politics and the vote – 'I don't agree with democracy' – viewed capitalism as the most destructive force on Earth – 'it's catastrophic; love and compassion are not valued in capitalism, they're worthless' – and deemed all powerful politicians 'psychopaths, by nature'. He believed work should be abolished – 'people give all their time, the most valuable thing, to work, because jobs are so badly paid now' – and saw the planet's principal problem as 'the establishment'. fuelled by the fear-generating news media.

'This never-ending fantastical Muslim threat,' he snorted of widespread Islamophobia, 'we've been harassing the Islamic world since the fucking Crusades. If you wanna find out where the problem lies, look at who's providing you with an enemy.'

What was his best alternative?

'It's not my job to provide an alternative,' he retorted. 'Read some Kropotkin [late-nineteenth/early-twentieth-century Russian anarchist]. *Find* alternatives. Get off your fucking arse. Change comes through small conversations. No one's gonna roll up, like *The Young Ones*, with a truck full of money and food. Change *yourself* first.'

His contribution to change was his art, his music an elevational search for human connection.

'In the darkest of times, art is at its most valuable,' he declared. 'I would never prize love and compassion more highly than I do right now.'

Disastrously for us all, then, he continued, music as a driver of cultural change now barely existed.

'Now, it's the entertainment industry,' he withered. 'Which encourages you to buy perfume. Musicians want money and fame. The sort of person willing to be a pop star is the sort of person willing to hand over power of attorney to the management company, the label, they're zipped up from day one, saying nothing, so fucking dull.'

He despaired some more, over 'not even middle, *upper-class* musicians' for whom music is 'like a gap year'. Much like Noel Gallagher on one of his state-of-the-nation addresses, he was soon vibrating with indignation.

'They're essentially little businesspeople and I don't want those *fuckers* making music!' he roared. 'I'd put them all in a fucking trash compactor. The whole system is set up against anything real coming through. Venues are being systematically closed down. Through noise complaint bullshit. There's no stepping stone venues for bands. In ten, twenty years, this is gonna seem like some weird void. *Assuming* it gets better. But I can't see it. In ten years' time there'll be one venue in town, owned by Vodafone, and on the outskirts the O2 Arena. That little venue, that'll be used for a press launch for an indie band and you'll get a load of fucking journalists down there, and their mates, and pretend it's a real fucking gig before they're scooted out to the O2 having been on Saturday night TV for the last five months on the Egg Factor. This is what's happening to the thing that we're involved in. People like me and Jason [Williamson, of Sleaford Mods] are the last generation of real people making music.'

He puffed some more.

'I want art, based on reality!' he foamed. 'Not fake emotion written by songwriters, by committee, for incredibly handsome men and women, beautifully coiffured, I don't give a fuck about *them*. I've just watched the *Johnny Moped* DVD [documentary of chaotic proto-punk band], a bunch of scuzz balls, that's what I want, and I want them to be successful! Privileged people go through stage school and learn how to do an interview and I *hate* it, I don't want them to . . . exist! They should be fucking *banned*. Their instruments taken off them and sent on youth opportunities work schemes to learn about sweeping the fucking streets. And give their opportunities to people with *real* passion.'

He clattered his mug on the table.

'I think we drink the Kool-Aid now,' he announced, with a bellow of rueful laughter.

Steve Mason's spectacular indignation was balanced, equally, with spectacular romanticism. We pondered a recurring theme throughout his musical life, his preoccupation with the most staggering reality we know: our existence in the universe.

'Look up, what *is* all that?' marvelled the man who'd lived alone for years, under the stars, with zero light pollution, in a forest. 'We don't know what's out there. It might be teeming with life out there! Scientists, it's all just fucking guesswork. And society sometimes feels like it's designed to drum all that romance and beauty and imagination out of you.'

It was surely one of humanity's greatest disappointments, then, that we'd never get to meet the aliens.

'Well, me and Martin Duffy have been working on that!' he grinned, hunting out a large, black, meticulously hand-written notebook detailing an on-going side-project, the *Alien Stadium* E.P. One song, 'The Judgement', featured an alien's derisive speech on Earthlings, who'd ruined their own planet, while 'Titanic Dance' ruminated on society's continuing, metaphorical dance on the Titanic. 'We're all fucked, we may as well go out dancing,' he chirped. 'So we all get melted on drugs and have a big party and go "Bollocks to it". Which is basically what's happening anyway.'

Inside a pub in central Hove, near the sea, which bathes the planet, suspended in the unknowable universe, all was teeming with life. Steve's band were here, alongside Martin Duffy, as Steve DJ'd from his large-screened laptop, now playing a mid-nineties song from fellow revolutionary outlaw Johnny Cash. Back in London in '99, he'd told me his greatest lifelong ambition was to 'make beautiful music and have some fun'. Tonight, it looked like he was finally doing both. 'Definitely,' he affirmed. 'See? Everything I said was right. And that album *was* rubbish!' It's hard to believe, now, he was once a traumatised recluse, the Howard Hughes of transcendental art-pop.

'Redemption does exist,' he reasoned, over a red wine. 'I spent ten years battling manic depression, anxiety and agoraphobia. Suicidal. And I reached an epiphany: you haven't actually killed me. I'm not dead. I thought, "D'you know what? *Fuck you*. Let's fucking have it!" I came off anti-depressants and knew I'd kind of beaten it, y'know? It tried to get me so many times and never succeeded. So, I *won*.'

He wandered outside for a roll-up on a crowded pavement, a laughing man in a badass hat, meeting the humans. Who probably wouldn't have minded, finally, if some of those humans believed in him.

Three years after our Brighton summit, in 2018, still living in the seaside haven, the fully societally integrated Steve Mason was now married with a one-year-old daughter, not a turnip in sight. He'd turned out, too, to be something of a visionary. Since 2015 grassroots music venues in the UK alone had been increasingly, brutally decimated: between 2023 and 2024, 125 of those once-vital stepping stones had been shut down, the equivalent of at least two every week. The mega-venues, like the O2 (partnered by Giffgaff, Virgin Mobile, Sky Mobile, and Tesco Mobile) continue to sell out the megastars at increasingly exorbitant cost and in 2024 Co-op Live opened in Manchester, now the UK's biggest arena, a mammoth black box with a capacity of 23,500, a venue hosting that year the pop and heritage giants: Olivia Rodrigo, Take That, Eric Clapton, the Eagles, Pet Shop Boys, The Killers, Stevie Nicks, Justin Timberlake, Niall Horan, Slipknot, Simply Red and, er, Hits Radio Live.

In 2024, meanwhile, the Beta Band astonishingly announced their reformation, with the original line-up and tours through 2024/25 of the UK and North America. The official statement on their unexpected new chapter was typically wry: 'The Beta Band, as everyone knows, is an institution, like Bedlam, or the RSPCA, and as such has its own indelible stain on the bedsheet of Western culture. It was the great John Noakes who said, "You have to shake it out at least once every couple of decades, if you want to know what the moths did".'

17

KNIVES OUT

2000, *Radiohead release* Kid A *and confound millions*

Throughout 2000 twinklesome pop continued, led by an infinite landscape of boybands and girlbands flourishing as if doused in Miracle Gro pop potassium. Westlife were now even *more* enormous, as were the Backstreet Boys, *NSYNC and the newly dominant Destiny's Child, the UK permanently bouncing to Steps, S Club 7 and winningly aloof trio Sugababes. Simultaneously, a new term began embedding itself with the ferocious reach of a global pandemic: Celebrity Culture. This was the year of the UK's inaugural *Big Brother* TV series and its exploitation by struggling new magazine *Heat*, soon turbocharging its fortunes to an era-defining extent as reality TV and talent shows began their deathless reign. Beyond this shimmering horizon, with the music industry now morphed even further into the Entertainment Industry, Radiohead loomed like a planetary gas giant blocking out the sun, their third album *OK Computer* back in '97 now acknowledged as a prophetic vision of the all-surface, consumerist twenty-first century. A haunting, beautiful, conceptual atmospheric, it reflected both a generational dread over the incoming, dehumanising digital era and the horrors of hypercapitalism.

When *OK Computer* emerged in '97 I was no Radiohead geek, significantly more absorbed by the transcendental romance of the Verve's *Urban Hymns*. To me, Radiohead were defined by a single word, *serious*, a band who stuck it to the Man by banning corporate logos at their shows and going on about, like, 'mazin' acoustics and American jazz-cat 'Mingus'. In Thom Yorke they had a singer so disturbingly serious that when he sang, he not only looked like a man in tortuous psychic agony, but a man doing an impersonation of that screamy-mouth-on-a-really-long-neck beast so horrifyingly painted by Francis Bacon in his 1944 triptych 'Three Studies for Figures at the Base of a Crucifixion'. *Brrrrr.* No one, I imagined, would ever send the likes of me to interview the mythologically venerated Thom Yorke.

Three years later...

December 2000 in Oxford, and I was waiting for Thom Yorke, who loathed interviews, who was travelling here by bike, in the relentlessly pelting rain. We weren't off to a corking start. Since Radiohead fully emerged in '92 with the soaring, crunchy, irresistible outsider's anthem 'Creep', Thom Yorke had been spectral angst-rock's least garrulous social butterfly, a media-loathing man of advanced suspicion who'd long adopted a 'no interviews' policy and refused to read anything about either himself *or* Radiohead, who were now a *religiously* revered band. My perception of his little-known persona was one of a gravely sombre, expensively educated, politically engaged and possibly conspiracy-level theorist, a vocal environmental campaigner and supporter in the 2000 American election of then-Green Party candidate Ralph Nader. The Radiohead website, radiohead.com (in those online infancy days), featured a page of politicised links, from climate change activism to Drop the Debt, to Indymedia to CorpWatch. Thom Yorke was now, officially, glum-rock's foremost heavily active agitator, a righteous character clearly not big on the larks.

We'd never met – few journalists had *ever* met Thom Yorke – but now, in this drizzly millennium winter, he had acquiesced. Just this once. There was a solitary publication he approved of, the charity-based *Big Issue*, the none-more-worthy magazine which rarely intruded into personal lives and invited interviewees to talk instead about, er, the big issues of the day. He also had a new album to promote, Radiohead's fourth, *Kid A*, a seemingly contrary, electro-art-rock curiosity dimensions away from *OK Computer*, though hardly any bigger on lyrical larks.

The sarcastic cynics over at his most despised music paper, *NME*, he hadn't talked to in five long years, denying them any interviews throughout the lifespan of *OK Computer*. Radiohead had been routinely dismissed by the lily-livered, intellectual misfits of the *NME* as lily-livered, intellectual misfits, whose photos the cackling scribes would caption with the words 'ugly ugly ugly'. Worse, and not lost on Thom Yorke, *OK Computer* was deemed the Greatest Album Ever Made by exactly the types who bought and indeed wrote for *NME*, and this year he was denying them again. The album had also seen Radiohead crowned the Best Band in the World, seen them further anointed the Most Important Band in the World, all officially augmented by their stunning Glastonbury '97 headline show, sanctified by Michael Eavis himself as the greatest Glastonbury performance *of all time*. This *Big Issue* interview would be the single interview he granted for this stage of the *Kid A* promotional campaign, an actual old-school World Exclusive.

No pressure, then.

*

Thom Yorke had cycled, emission-free, through the storm, squelching into a large, airy café in central Oxford, unzipping his sturdy orange cagoul and settling onto a bench at a wooden table, hair dripping into his neck.

To some, sending me to interview Thom Yorke was like sending someone to interview John Lennon who had only heard *Sgt Pepper* once and was far more interested in the Liverpudlian gags. There was logic, though, in the commission: sending hyperventilating fanboys (and they were usually boys) risked the kind of overawed reverence which trapped Thom Yorke forever in, say, the fun-free vortex of the lyrical subtext of a flexi-disc B-side from before they were even signed. So, my task was to find some human levity, if any existed, in the most serious frontman in the most serious band in serious musical history. To some astonishment, then, he opened the conversation with a reasonable punt at a rain-related joke.

'What gets me is the people in this country are just accepting it,' he announced, of our also rainy summers, which he blamed on the serious subject of climate change. 'Accepting their lot. Accepting their *moat*.'

Blimey! Thom Yorke turned out to be, occasionally, seriously funny. Not stand-up rib-cracking, granted, but more comedy indignant than righteously glum. Radiohead watchers in the US that year were blaming him for the election of George W. Bush after he'd held up a Green Party-supporting placard on *Saturday Night Live* saying, 'Let Ralph [Nader] Debate'. 'There were fucking sacks of post saying I'd destroyed the [Democrat nominee] Gore Campaign,' he fumed, stabbing at his chest. 'Me? *Me!?*'

We had a reasonably relaxed conversation, musing on a series of serious subjects: his meltdown post-*OK Computer* because he couldn't handle the relentless, global reverence which left him emotionally pummelled to 'a complete fucking mess'; how he beat the resulting writer's block by skulking through local woodlands drawing hawthorn hedges because they reminded him of a human brain; how chuffed he was over the mixed response to *Kid A's* sonic sorcery because it 'burst the bubble – I'm not and we're not . . . *the thing*, so it's far less intense.' He'd spent '99 in a state of 'apocalyptic thought' on society, humanity, politicians, capitalism, climate change, the future, his own demons and the searing self-consciousness which tortures 'people like me'. He'd been traumatised by 'guilt' his whole life over his privileged upbringing (an Exeter public schoolboy). 'I've had a very expensive education,' he reminded me, 'and it took me years to come to terms with that.' He'd learned to physically fight as a way of combating the tormenting bullies who mocked his wonky eye. As a young man he was 'very ambitious'. At thirty-two that day in Oxford, not so anymore.

'Ambitious for what?' he wrestled out loud, over a single cup of tea. 'What for? I thought when I got to where I wanted to be everything would be different. I'd be somewhere else. And then I got here.'

He thought he'd be . . . in the light? 'Yeah,' he laughed. 'I did! I thought it'd be all white fluffy clouds.'

And instead it was, 'Oh no, I'm still here'?

'Still here,' he nodded. *'Still here.'*

Why, in the end, had he done what he'd done with his life?

'It's filling the hole,' he replied. 'It's just filling the hole. That's all anyone does.'

Enormous pause.

'And it's still there.'

But maybe it changed shape?

'Yeah. And now it's . . . heheh! A triangle.'

Was he a hippie or a punk rocker?

'Oh, I'm a hippie. Definitely a hippie. I haven't got the balls to be a punk.'

Soon, he was back on his bicycle while myself and his PR Caffy St Luce (who'd been sat at a nearby table) readied ourselves for the train journey back to London. I picked up my swish new Sony Recording Walkman, a glittering neon-blue number with fancy buttons, briefly rewound the tape and pressed play, just to check the voice was clear, like I always did.

Silence.

A stab of fear in the heart.

Don't panic, it'll be in there somewhere ...

Rewind, play.

Silence.

A tsunami of tingling fear crashed throughout my torso, blood flooding into a fizzing brain.

Oh God. Where the fuck is the interview!? It must be here, it must be here ...

I took the tape out, replaced it, pressed play again.

Silence.

I took it out again, turned it over, pressed play.

Silence.

Three minutes of repeated manoeuvres later, with shaking hands and a metaphorical volley of punches to one's own stupid bastard head, I had to face it: there was nothing whatsoever anywhere on the tape. I'd simply done what every print mag interviewer feared above all: I'd pressed the wrong button. *And this was a World Exclusive.*

Caffy and I thundered towards Oxford train station, purchased a bottle of wine, opened it on contact with our seats and spent the journey back to London trying to remember every single syllable Thom Yorke had said (I wouldn't normally welcome a PR listening in, but this time I kissed her face), scribbling,

scribbling, scribbling in haste lest the memory suddenly evaporate. And so I was able to send the *Big Issue* their world exclusive interview with Thom Yorke in late 2000. A colossal professional clanger that I, naturally, told them nothing about.

Sorry about that, lovely *Big Issue*.

Four months later...

April 2001, and something had given way in the holey heart of Thom Yorke, who'd finally agreed to an interview with the *NME*. I was duly dispatched to his Oxford management office (possibly vetted from the previous year) to take whatever was coming to me from a five-year grudge match I had nothing to do with. No pressure here either, then.

Drinking tea together at a wrought-iron table in a springtime sun-cooked courtyard, Thom Yorke was so edgy he was practically disappearing side-on. Outsize shades dominated his intense face, huge, angular, frame-less, burgundy-tint numbers almost as weirdly shaped as his fawn, parallelogram shoes. In a plain grey T-shirt and jeans, he scratched at several days' beard growth and attempted to explain this seismic communication climbdown.

So ... why now?

'Hmm,' he replied and there followed the first of several enormous pauses while he stared at the courtyard underfoot, thinking, as birds tweeted overhead.

'I just got sick of holding grudges basically,' he eventually managed. 'Enough's enough. Erm. [Tweet, tweet.] Not least because the people involved have all left. Anyway, I'm doing the *NME* a favour. Fattening themselves up for floating themselves on the international money market and no doubt this will help, because I'm a name. [Monumental derision] *NME-dot-com.*'

The sun, suddenly, went in. Immediately, his shades came off.

Why was he 'party' to any of this, then?

'Because otherwise they just make loads of shit up. So, enough shit. That's all. It's like talking to CNN, innit? Neheheh! Generally, though, I just got pissed off a little bit with what happened on *Kid A* and thought, OK, let's try and set the record straight. Slightly.'

Opening explanation over, he relaxed, slightly, soon bewilderingly swinging from profound amusement to profound offence in the space of the same sentence. He had a loud, nasal, sarcastic laugh: 'Neheheh!' The world's adverse reaction to the apparent anti-media, anti-fame, anti-success, anti-fan, anti-rock'n'roll volte-face of *Kid A* (and now parts of the speedily forthcoming fifth album, *Amnesiac*) was something Thom Yorke did not understand. It made him, frankly, furious. After *OK Computer* (and its unofficial title the Era-Defining Album of the Decade) Radiohead merely, he maintained, wanted to do things 'differently', on every level, including not playing the media game. And so the games masters doled out the punishment. Nonetheless, it was Number One across planet Earth.

'*All* it was,' he stressed, 'was claiming the ability to go off in whatever direction we chose. Instead of repeating the formula endlessly and making loads of wonga.'

The mythology remained that it was a reaction to oppressive reverence. It was the rock'n'roll lexicon, the reverence arrives and . . .

'The Reverend. Reverend, will you stop coming?'

So, there he was, the Reverend, standing at the Best Band in the World crossroads, and he took the fork marked 'Avant-Garde' . . .

'Oh yeah, get in the Range Rover and down the off-road,' he withered. 'I don't think it's avant-garde *at all*.'

It was his own fault, anyway. He articulated big things with

OK Computer and therefore was seen to shun his 'responsibility' by then not saying anything at all.

'Well, from my point of view these two records say far more of relevance and importance than *OK Computer* did. *OK Computer* was like flicking channels on the TV and this is ... um ... that's a shame. I think that's *a real shame* people would think that. And who the fuck is going to want to sit down and write a bunch of words that that's gonna happen to? Nobody. You'd end up having some sort of bizarre critical house party going on in your head! But I absolutely don't think that's true at all. I absolutely think the exact *opposite* is true.'

So, what exactly was he saying with these records?

And here, being halfway through our conversation, the tape-recorder switched itself off: *click*. (I'd learned to use it properly by then.)

'Neheheh!' guffawed Thom Yorke, delighted. 'Tape's run out! Thank fuck!'

And he literally ran away, for a drink of water, returning with a delighted 'Next!'

We talked about what some fans said about *Kid A*. There was a hoo-ha in the *NME* letters page.

'Oh goody.'

There were things about cop-out, about selling his art short.

'Mmm. Hmm.'

Things about being reluctant to commit himself emotionally.

And here, like a man being shot in the chest, Thom Yorke threw his head back in a flip-top of genuine hysteria. 'Ahahahahargh!' he bellowed, snorting everywhere. 'Ahahahahargh! [Furious clapping.] Hurghurghurgh! Fuck you, you silly cow, person, whoever you are. Fuck you entirely! Get out of my face and stay there forever. I'm not even gonna commit myself emotionally to a response. Next!'

*

Thom Yorke was a weirdo, alright (though very far from a creep). You could have touched a live, raw nerve standing in a different country. He was the most contrary, unfathomable human being I'd ever met and was unquestionably, in this respect, A Proper Rock Star. His very DNA was sculpted from indignation, contempt and attitude, like the punk he claimed he didn't have the balls to be. Much of *Amnesiac*, he felt, concerned the death of everything: the planet, culture, humankind, whichever came first (and we think the Gen Zedders today are apocalyptic).

'The reason you create music or art or write is in order to put things in a way you can possibly deal with it,' he surmised, emphatically, 'and death is one of those areas. [Becoming annoyed] But we don't seem to spend much time with it, do we? If you're accused of being morbid or bleak, then you're onto a good thing, I'd say. Cos our culture is the most fucking desperate, desperately trying to avoid anything vaguely depressing, which is alarming because what's the result? Well, we all know what that is, don't we? We're at a time when we are being presented with undeniable changes in the global climate and fundamental issues that affect every single one of us, and it's the time we're listening to the most hokey shite on the radio and watching vacuous bullshit celebrities being vacuous bullshit celebrities and desperately trying to forget about everything. Which is fine, you know, but personally speaking, I can't do that. It's not even to do with necessarily taking yourself seriously, it's just to do with, "Well, no, I think we use music as a way of turning bad energy into good energy."' He half laughed. 'Or making something out of inexpressible emotion, which could be useful.'

'Knives Out', from *Amnesiac*, with its melodic chorus and lyrics of not coming back, was seen as a veiled 'goodbye' to the music industry.

'Not at all,' replied Thom, naturally. 'It's partly the idea of the businessman walking out on his wife and kids and never coming back. It's also the thousand-yard stare when you look at someone close to you and you know they're gonna die. It's like a shadow over them, or the way they look straight through you. The shine goes out of their eyes.'

Who had he seen that in the eyes of?

(Huge pause, penetrating stare straight into my soul.) 'A few people.'

Fame, the Machine, worldwide success, and the Reverend, he carried on, had all brought him to the brink of insanity, 'in ways that fucked me up for years afterwards and nobody is coming close to me with that shit again.' *Kid A* and *Amnesiac*, you could say, saved his soul (he'd never say it himself).

'I just needed to sort myself out, really,' he noted, plainly, before a panoramic pause. 'Insanity is something different. This was more . . . I just absorb things very quickly.'

Could he describe what Fame Madness felt like?

'Well, there was lots of bullshit involved, that ends up feeling eventually like it's real and then you have to go away and tell the difference,' he mused. 'You actually start believing your own bullshit. Like John Cleese said on *Parkinson*, "I can only do about three weeks promo because after a while I start to feel less like I'm really human, just a little bit . . . false". You talk for so long it gets a bit . . . funny. And people were throwing things like that *NME* letter at me, a lot. Things started to get pretty unpleasant. And pretty personal. And I'm not . . . particularly tough. And not particularly adept at dealing with personal attacks. Which is my own fault for choosing such a stupid thing to do. *It is*. It's true.'

Did he lack a second skin? That's what the Manic Street Preachers used to say about Richey (Edwards, the Manics' talismanic 'guitarist' who disappeared, presumed to have taken his own life, in 1994).

'Hmm, I dunno. Most things are fine, but things do get through still. If someone came up to me in a pub and said what that letter said, I would be really upset.'

It really bothered him that much?

'I would be really *really* upset.'

It sounded like he needed a psychic shield. Everyone needs a psychic shield, I told him. Otherwise too much of the world gets in and you're fucked. (It seemed he, too, wasn't so very different from Evan Dando with the hole in the ozone layer of his soul.)

'Everyone needs a psychic shield?' he pondered, without laughing me off my seat. 'That's true, actually. I think that *is* true. Well, I'm lucky because my friends do look out for me. But it's weird when, by definition, your motives are doubted. And if you're not very tough, it can sort of . . . do your head in.'

Why did he still do what he did, when so much that surrounds it did his head in?

Nineteen seconds passed. Three generations of tweetsome birds overhead were born, set their children free, and died.

'Personally speaking, I have to use music to sort things out. Because that's what I *do*.'

Thom Yorke, beyond music as existential puzzle, was equally compelled to activism, an advocate for Drop the Debt (slogan of the late nineties campaign for international debt cancellation) and Reclaim the Streets (a movement critiquing polluting car culture, corporate dominance and globalisation), seriously important subjects he saw the media sensationalise with what he called 'hokey shite', like 'a chintzy photo of Bono shaking hands with Blair and Bob Geldof and not one motherfucker among them talking about the issue of debt, not *one motherfucker, not one*.' He fumed some more. 'I know some stuff about MI5 that would shit your . . . brain. Mmm.

But I can't tell you. Cos they'll do it to me, too. Seriously. And I'm not winding you up, either.' His Generational Spokesman mantle he naturally deplored though did not care 'how stupid I look', a man merely appalled that the world is run by 'a bunch of old miserable motherfucking economists'.

Where did his compulsion come from, to Make a Difference?

'Oh, definitely guilt,' he replied immediately. 'It's all just guilt, basically.'

I really didn't understand that.

'What?'

Why guilt was such a driver in his life.

'I was joking.' (He rolled his eyes heavenwards.)

I told him he'd talked about guilt in all seriousness before.

'When?'

Four months ago. With me!

'Oh really!? Bugger. Neheheh!'

That year, Thom had become a family man, with a house in Dorset and a son called, biblically enough, Noah, which gave added urgency to his world-changing ways. His was the kind of cynicism which got stuff done, as opposed to the other, powerless kind.

'The sad thing is,' he contemplated, 'if an issue is laughed at and patronised by mainstream media, then it's up against it big time. I read some journalist recently lecturing the anti-globalisation lobby, saying, "This is the way capitalism works, all capitalism is exploitation and to make it try and do something else, it's never gonna happen." And it's like, yeah, but where does that leave us? This is somehow God's will, all this? It's God's will that we sit in traffic? It's God's will that millions of people are gonna die this year, millions of . . . beautiful children!' Here, he seemed very close to tears. 'Because of some outmoded economic policies? No, it's not! It's like some deranged sacrificial altar, the high priests of the global economy holding up these millions of children each year, like [arms aloft], "We wish to please you, oh Gods of free trade!" It's like . . . give us all a fucking break!'

The devil at work?

'If there is a devil at work,' he observed, coolly, 'then he rests in institutions and not in individuals. An individual can abdicate responsibility. The assumption that we're all utterly powerless, *that's* the devil at work.'

He eyed the tape-recorder, uncannily detecting when one hour to the second was up.

'One last question! A little one.'

Fatherhood: best thing that had ever happened to him?

'All those corny things,' he smiled. 'Put it this way, I'm not taking things quite so seriously as before. Especially myself.'

Pthrthrt!

'I'm not! Because I don't have the time. I'm not throwing my toys out of the cot anymore, he's doing it for me. There'll be lots of corny songs about children now. Or maybe I've already sung 'em, you never know, in all those hidden lyrics. Neheheh!'

Some weeks later, after his first *NME* cover story in five years had been published, I was at a gig in central London when Thom Yorke stepped towards me, out of the shadows. He reached out a hand, vigorously shook mine, briefly, and disappeared back into the shadows. Not one word spoken.

Weirdo.

18

AIN'T NOTHIN TA F'WIT

2000, *Wu-Tang Clan release* The W *album in the year hip-hop dominates everything*

In the year 2000, alongside the promenade of pop contenders, hip-hop reached its own significant peak-years milestone: for the first time ever it outsold country music in America. Hip-hop was now the nation's biggest-selling genre, its sounds, styles and attitudes infiltrating every aspect of culture worldwide, from film to fashion to gaming to the way business deals were done. The hip-hop giants were also our pop stars now, their often-brutal, lawless backgrounds part of pop's ever-evolving folklore. In 2000 I became a sort of hip-hop correspondent despite being no hip-hop scholar, dispatched by *NME* to seek some cheer in these mostly American, often formidably hardcore characters. West coast hobos Cypress Hill, whose irresistibizzle '93 single 'Insane in the Brain' made reluctant superstars of the stern-faced trio, proved both media suspicious and winningly tolerant of jokes about weed and Phil Collins. Detroit's Eminem, meanwhile, still on his stratospheric rise that year with the world-class 'Stan', would prove both media suspicious and given to 'comedy' rape threats under cartoon Slim Shady cover.

Of all the genre's formidable characters, however, the most fearsomely mythologised were New York's Wu-Tang Clan. Hard-raised hustlers on the streets of Staten Island, the ten-strong, existential hip-hop colossus numbered several ex-drug dealers (weed, crack), some serving sizeable jail terms, living life in an episode of *The Wire*, f'real. They'd even been known, on occasion, to respond to the wrong journalistic probe by beating reporters up, to the point of hospitalisation.

They were no mere crew, they were a *Federation*, gifted lyricists all, who'd invented their own language and pioneered the concept of the portfolio hip-hop entrepreneur in the 1990s, no doubt inspiring the young Jay-Z and every multi-zwillionaire hip-hop mogul thereafter. My assignment, then – to interview *all ten* in New York in autumn 2000 – was tough enough and made tougher still given my openly scant knowledge: so much so, a sympathetic colleague took me pubwards beforehand with a selection of promo photos for an education in who was who. The following day, I boarded a flight to New York, the trepidation mounting ...

Five days later ...

For three full days in New York the Wu-Tang Clan had been missing in action, a scenario known back then as 'hip-hop time', referencing the rapper's historically loose relationship with the clock – even if three days late for our scheduled interview *was* excessive. Still waiting on day four, I was seated inside the vast, multi-roomed, $2,500-a-night Presidential Suite of New York's Portland Hotel, when the suite door stealthily opened with a portentous creak.

'BOOOO!' exploded Method Man as I jumped fifteen feet

into the ceiling, a physical reaction which made Method Man fulsomely cackle, beam expansively and vigorously shake my hand. 'I like you British!' he boomed, all silver teeth and pretty-girl's almond eyes. He knew, as all the Clan knew, how intimidating a prospect they could be (whether they actually were or not), soon sauntering over to a gilded occasional table and picking up a silver-plated tray bearing a Perspex trinket boxes containing individual portions of finest, mintiest 'erb. 'Hors d'oeuvres?' he announced, proffering the trinkets as a welcome gift, on an actual silver salver. So much for beating journalists up: the Wu-Tang Clan were *giving me free drugs instead*.

Mind you, he wasn't U-God, the one best known for beating journalists up, who was currently outside the hotel having been refused entry four times by a suspicious staff member complaining of 'some guy running around cursing downstairs'. 'He a loose cannon nigga when he drunk!' cautioned Method Man as U-God eventually stormed through the door, a discernibly aggrieved man whose doom-laden pronouncements would verge on comedy gold. 'I don' keep it in!' he yelped, by way of cursing justification. 'I ain't gonna get ill. That's why my mental is so fucking clear.'

Now GZA (aka Genius, Maxi Million, Justice, real name Gary) turned up, a vision in a silken purple tracksuit who was up for being interviewed *now*, opining elegantly on how 'music is an art form, a science, expression, music be the link between y'all,' a bright, philosophical, sensitive soul who loathed the effects of consumer culture. 'You got kids stealing stuff in stores cos of rhymes on records, can't spell the shit but wanna wear it, a limited mentality,' he intoned. Soon, Method Man and U-God were seated at a hefty wooden table wolfing restorative meals of burgers and fries while, simultaneously, smoking outsize blunts. Method Man (aka Johnny Blaze,

Shaquan, Methical, MZA, The Riddler, real name Clifford) considered how their mid-nineties solo albums almost broke the Clan up.

'We felt like a buncha solo artists trying to come together as a group, and we were all generals . . .' he pondered, before he abruptly stopped, forkful of fries in mid-air. 'Oh shit, I gone lost it already,' he chuckled, snapping a lengthy finger.

U-God (aka Lucky Hands, Golden Arms, real name Lamont) was unimpressed.

'He's burnt out, this guy here. Cranium crunches.'

'I was gonna make a good ass point, too!' beamed Method Man. '*Damn*. I hate when I do that shit, it come from smoking too much marijuana, man! *Word*.'

Here, he correctly identified my Caledonian whinny. 'And y'all smoke a looootta marijuana in Scahtland! We smoke more marijuana in the United States than we eat wheat!'

The Wu-Tang Clan, like all the best pop stars, winningly bestrode the cultural pillars between artistes of import and animation superheroes, between fearless belligerence and birds-from-trees charisma, whose debut album in '93, *Enter the Wu-Tang (36 Chambers)*, changed the sound of hip-hop forever. They were radicals alright, young black men who'd tunnelled themselves out of multi-fold urban trauma to revolutionise not only their own lives but contemporary music itself, creating the most menacing, bewildering, dense, paranoid, funny and intelligent hip-hop soundscapes the world had ever known.

The Clan ran an autonomous operation, overseeing their own management, label, recording studio, video production company, publishing house and solo careers, created their own clothing label (Wu Wear, sold in major department stores) and a PlayStation game, *Wu-Tang: Shaolin Style*. They'd built their dominion from the crime-bedevilled streets upwards, a pioneering juggernaut with a vision to live, and prosper, outside the self-serving sewers of the Music Industry. All this they did with stealth and determination, affording them Wu Mansions, their five-acre country pile in New Jersey where they sporadically lived and worked, a business turning over, by '97, $180 million. That year their central force, RZA, appeared on the cover of the *New York Times* business section as Entrepreneur of the Year. Ol' Dirty Bastard, meanwhile (ODB, aka Osiris, Dirt McGirt, Unique Ason, The Specialist, Joe Bananas, Panty Raider, Big Baby Jesus, Young Dirty, real name Russell), on the day I met the Clan, was in jail, or rather a drug rehabilitation penal facility in Staten Island. Twenty-one days from then he would spring himself out, a bona fide fugitive on the run from the entire US judicial system.

Back in the Presidential Suite, Method Man and U-God were musing over a society gone rogue, corrupted by money and drugs, seeing a dysfunction forged through the eighties they grew up in, now entrenched in a new generation.

'In the seventies everybody was getting married, wasn't too much divorce,' said Meth. 'When I was growing up in the eighties? You got fifteen-year-old girls with babies youknowhatImean? Ain't no marriage, no bonds, no nothing. A lotta kids now don't even know their mother, they stay with their grandparents, shit like that, y'knowhumsayin'? Moral values!'

U-God: 'I used to have to be in the house at eight o'clock before the sun go down.'

Meth: 'I didn't get no pussy till I was fifteen! Now? You got thirteen, twelve-year-old girls. I seen a girl pregnant, sixteen, by a thirteen-year-old boy. It's not the lack of education man, the education's out there, it's just who wants it? I'm talking about America, this whole society is hypocritical, you can't be anything unless you go to school, and you got basketball players can't even spell their own fucking name making millions-a dollars. That's the American Dream right there, taking short-cuts.'

Drugs remained, as ever, a central problem.

'Crack was big in the eighties,' noted Meth. 'In the nineties it was smack, now it's ecstasy.'

It was hip-hop's new drug, so I'd heard.

Meth: 'Any drug is hip-hop's drug! For real, babe. I been in parties, man, where I walk in the front door, I smell weed, by the time I get to the back I can smell dust, cocaine, crack, knowhumsayin'? And this ain't just hip-hop clubs, cos we tour rockers, too. *Every* drug, don't give a fuck.'

U-God: 'Trying to escape this miserable fuckin' wretched life.'

Meth: 'When I was a shorty, we was taking mescalin and drinking forty shots. We the products of our parents, Woodstock, all that shit, they had babies and all that shit was already in the babies [he battered his chest] who was us! And look at us! Smoking and *aaaaall kindsa shit.*'

So, the Wu-Tang Clan blamed the parents?

Meth: 'Yeah I blame the parents, man! It's *all* on the parents.'

So where did they think we were headed with all this?

U-God: 'Into a shit hole. But I'm gonna die one day so I'm not worried about nothing. I been through so much fucking shit, *piles-a* shit done fell on me. I'm a marine though, I'm a fucking marine.'

Growing up in the Staten Island of the seventies and eighties, the young men of the Clan lived, as U-God had it, 'inside our heads'. Outside their heads was dope, crack, guns, crowds, stinking elevators, and No Hope in the local projects named Killer Hills. Childhood friends, they immersed themselves in kung-fu culture, nine-hour marathons inside flea-pit movie theatres while, by '88, crack was an everyday inner-city reality. Method Man, U-God and RZA were dealers, some in weed, some in crack. Business boomed, they had money, girls, clothes, even introduced the Staten Island hip-hop scenesters to Tommy Hilfiger, Polo and underground hip-hop sounds. Inevitably, much like the UK's post-Madchester comedown period, things turned shady: Deck and U-God went to prison, RZA was on mescaline and addicted to PCP (angel dust), once offering out fifty Puerto Ricans, alone and unarmed. In '92 he was involved in a shoot-out over a woman and charged with attempted murder. Already a signed artist under the name Prince Rakeem, his then-label Tommy Boy refused to bail him out this time, and dropped him. Acquitted from the charge, the epiphany happened: enough hustling, they'd transcend instead through creativity. The Wu-Tang Clan was born.

Raekwon (The Chef, Lex Diamonds, real name Corey) was lying sideways, horizontally, across a plush armchair with his hands behind his head, beaming, all the better to see his diamond-studded, gold-plated teeth. From one highly relaxed hand dangled a pouch of pungent weed.

'Sit down,' he glimmered, 'what's vibing? Where you from? Scahtland? Scahtland Yard?'

Not me, honest guv!

'Heheh! D'you think I'd look fly in a green skirt?'

He contemplated the Clan's mission.

'What we say describes the ghetto,' he began, 'where we come from. We teach about when you living rough, how you go about handling living rough. Reality shit. Don't let nothing supersede the truth. The truth is the shit. *Word.*'

He contemplated their formidable reputation.

'We came from a beastful way of life,' he reflected. 'But as you get older, you get wiser, we have families, brothers is fathers, we look at this business as a business now. All my friends done been to jail before. All my friends done did whatever they do. I'm not gonna neglect them, if they're my friends forever, that makes me a part of them. Wu-Tang is a basic hip-hop foundation that started from the urban communities, and we believed in ourselves, we said we're gonna come out together and make it happen and that's what we did.'

No Clan member ever forgot where they came from. Method Man, especially, despaired over the Absent Father syndrome which dug deep into the soul of Black America, a family reality for many hip-hop artists throughout history. He believed in Individual Responsibility, had children himself and without his fiscal position doubted he'd ever have had them at all.

'I'd be all stressed in some fucking job,' he was certain, still perched at the wooden table with U-God, blunt still on the go. 'Probably wouldn't have no babies. Cos I'd be scared to have any kids I couldn't take care of. I know how it was for my mom. *F'real*. I never understood it, but my mom used to have us just sitting in a huddle like this [he folded his arms around his chest] and she used to just rock back and forth and cry in front of my sisters. I used to look at them like "Y'all punks! What they crying about?" I never understood why. D'you know how it feels to come home and know you can't feed your fucking kids? And the man that you gave the greatest fucking gift he ain't no place to be fuckin' found. And then when he come in, he fresh [he clutched his jacket], got brand new shit on, and his babies is fucking starving. Y'know? More times we sat down and we eating our little dinner and my momma ain't even eating. I remember going to sleep, went back in the goddam kitchen and our momma sitting there eating our food, what we left over. That shit there? I don't never want no child to have to go through that shit, you can't be a child like that, what kinda childhood is that, man? When reality's smacking you in the face like that.'

So that's what they were about: breaking the cycle?

'You really have to go into the matrix, man, I'm telling you,' he nodded. 'Start with yourself and then look at everything around you. Cos if you're not happy with you, all a negative person gonna do is draw negative attention. Y'all, this is a unconventional interview right here, matter of fact it ain't even a interview, it's a *inner* view.'

Here Method Man stuck up for then-President Clinton (the year before the arrival of President George W. Bush and 9/11), 'one of the greatest presidents man, I tell you a lotta black-owned businesses came out with Clinton in office, whereas under that Reaganomics shit, a lotta drug dealers got rich.' They were, then, pioneers for societal change with a clear-sighted vision. Did they, too, think their reputation was unfair?

Method Mad (adopting a comedy demonic voice): 'Wooooo Taaaaang, right? Hee hee!'

U-God: 'See!? Everybody that come amongst us be like "Damn! Y'all ain't as terrible as they fucking say you be!"'

Method Mad: 'Basically, "Y'all not as bad as your *record label* had us thinking y'all was gonna be."'

U-God: 'But in a way? It gives us room. Makes motherfuckers move out our way. Makes the job a little easier. Y'all scared? Get the fuck outta here. A lotta people got misconceptions. We do wreck shit though. We might run with a little . . . recreation.'

Did U-God really beat journalists up, if they annoyed him enough?

'Yeah. I do. Sometimes you be nice to journalists, they say they're gonna print certain situations and they print something different.'

Suddenly, his phone rang. 'Whassup, punk?' he hollered. Naturally, it was his girlfriend.

*

The following day, an unprecedented seven members of the Wu-Tang Clan turned up at Chelsea Pier for photographic purposes, a vast complex of cavernous empty studios, under two hours late (positively early). Other than the incarcerated ODB, only the studio-bound RZA and Cappadonna (aka Cappachino, real name Darryl, the Clan's unofficial tenth member) were missing. Here was comedy-grump U-God, his mood 'middling', charming Method Man booming 'Hiii baby!', Raekwon blaming a bulging trouser pocket on 'a gun, heheh!' while Masta Killa (aka Noodles, Jamel, real name Elgin) asserted that the Wu-Tang Clan were, in fact, exactly the same as 'the Jackson Five!'

It was becoming preposterous: the Wu-Tang Clan were less menacing mobsters, more stoned comedian gentlemen whose hard-won wisdoms would've seen them employed as teachers, social workers and government consultants fixing the problems of poverty, drugs, violence and inequality everywhere across the planet. I quipped to the supposedly terrifyingly titled Masta Killa that he must be an impostor: where was his bulletproof vest? A quip that would no doubt have me cancelled today for negative racial stereotyping, this was meant, in fact, to illustrate just how negatively racially stereotyped these men had always been.

'Killa' burst out laughing. 'Bulletproof vest?' he cackled. 'I'm a family man! Is Robert De Niro a Godfather? Robert De Niro, Al Pacino, all them cats, do they be robbing and shooting and murdering? Is the Incredible Hulk a giant green man? It's our job!'

Ghostface Killah (aka Iron Man, Sun Dog, Tony Starks, real name Dennis) arrived. A solitary, heavily hooded presence, he was, unlike all the others, palpably suspicious, hood permanently up, underneath which stared one huge eye and one smaller one firmly trained on what he clearly assessed was someone not to be trusted. In '98 he served three months in prison for armed robbery, his personal reputation remaining, of a volatile, edgy figure.

'Trouble don't come to us, it's sent to us,' he told me in a deep, intense burr. 'America sends it to the African man, be it drugs, jail, guns. Plus, a lotta times the media blows this shit up. It's what they wanna be true. I ain't got no gun, there ain't no guns, the cops don't find no gun on me. Every day the black man go to jail. We put there by the Devil. Whitey knows what whitey's done.' Here, his smaller eye pierced outwards like an industrial laser. 'I ain't from America. I'm from Africa. The Devil kidnapped the black man and brought him here. And what's here, knowhumsayin'? There ain't nothing here. The Devil know who he is. The black man's struggle is every day, in hip-hop, on the streets.'

He was still, clearly, an angry young man.

'I ain't angry,' he countered. 'I'm happy. No one knows the good we do. We give computers to schools, give clothes to kids, feed the babies, no one knows. We [contemptuously] "the bad niggas". We the African American man. This is our struggle, every day. God knows the truth though. We about the positive, about faith, about wisdom, the babies, the heart, the peoples.' Both his eyes studied my recorder, possibly the lone member of the Wu-Tang Clan to correctly identify a Wu-Tang novice in his midst. 'My name,' he reminded me, 'is Ghostface. Don't be printing that wrong in your magazine.'

As he said his last few words my recorder, unfathomably, reset itself to the radio setting, picking up a random US hip-hop station and so, when playing it back on return to the UK, Ghostface Killah's voice suddenly segued into the unmistakeable sound of Grandmaster Flash and Melle Mel's 'White Lines', at exactly this point: ' …a free kid gets arrested …' As serendipitous surrealism goes, this was as

Wu-Tang Clan as it gets. For people like me, 'White Lines' was a clever, important song about racist US drug laws; for Ghostface Killah it was a life, and indeed a truth.

Meeting Inspectah Deck (aka Rebel, INS, Rollie Fingers, real name Jason), meanwhile, I asked just what it was these none-more-perpetually tardy hip-hop dudes were actually *doing* when they were always late? 'We the Wu-Tang!' he roared, with an almighty guffaw. 'We just gotta *lotta stuff to do.*'

Three weeks later back in London, RZA (aka Chief Abbot, Rzarecta, Bobby Steels, real name Robert) finally appeared on the transatlantic blower with the opening words: 'Hey wassup? What's the word?' The word, that very day, was that Ol' Dirty Bastard had fled his confinement, which the studio-immersed RZA knew nothing about. 'That's on the news?' he replied, startled. 'I gotta sit down and watch the motherfucking news.' He contemplated how the contemporary hip-hop heroes were always being threatened with prison, even as their music was now folded into the mainstream. That year, it was happening to its latest million-selling upstart, Eminem, who faced up to five years' incarceration for pulling a gun on Insane Clown Posse associate Douglas Dail. (The following year he was sentenced to one year probation and community service.)

'Put away our heroes?' snorted RZA. 'Listen, man, I don't think they're gonna do that, cos first of all we American and we represent America all over the world. We all better than ambassadors! The youth love and appreciate the culture of America. So even when he [Eminem] complains about a lotta shit, what the fuck, there's a lot to complain about, but he still grew up here, he's a product of America. How the fuck you gonna front with your own product? That's like saying let's go and spray paint the Statue of Liberty, y'knowhumsayin'?'

He contemplated how the Wu-Tang Clan had, in fact,

as their reputation never told you, made the world a better place.

'To be honest with you, I do think we contributed to that,' he nodded. 'I think Ol' Dirty contributed a lot to that too because he expresses so much freedom in life. I feel real good when I go to our concerts and I see human families all together with their hands in the air. I feel like yo, peace be right there. Some of our words are harsh too. But if your father was to tell you that shit for real, you'd be better off. Our generation was a fatherless generation. And the white suburban youth had fathers who worked so much they just like having no fathers. So, we're giving it to 'em raw. And not raw like, "guns, shooting, this that", we also give 'em feedback and advance knowledge. Experience they say is the best teacher but some things you don't have to experience. The knowledge we give becomes just as good as the experience. You have to feed kids' imagination. We give you words you supposed to go research and it'll help you out later on, just by understanding different things in this society. You know what time it is though. So, I gotta go head now ...'

He had, of course, a lotta stuff to do.

'Yeah, I'm always doing something!' he chortled. 'We just like American Superheroes, it's like "Spiderman's busy, you gotta lotta supervillains out there!" So, thank you for listening. Must assess. Peace.'

*

I never got the chance to talk to the freedom-representing Ol' Dirty Bastard that month, and I never would. On 13 November 2004 ODB collapsed and died from an accidental drugs overdose at RZA's studio in New York. He was thirty-six years old.

19

WHAT A WASTER

2002, *The Libertines* release Up the Bracket *and* Pete Doherty *becomes both outlaw and celebrity drug fiend*

2002 would be the last year I worked for *NME*, the paper given a younger, glossier, consumerist 'relaunch' while positioning itself as champ of a 'New Rock Revolution' in the era of the Strokes, White Stripes and the newly ascending Libertines. An old timer like me, therefore, would be dispatched on the road, bewildered, with the 'revolutionary' also-rans outside the Big Three, trundling on buses along rock's ever-lost highway with the likes of monochrome-clad Swedish herberts the Hives and grease-rock Kiwis the Datsuns. The wider culture, meanwhile, had now fully capitulated to reality TV, the year almost fourteen million people watched Will Young supposedly rob Gareth Gates of his *Pop Idol* crown, Girls Aloud glimmer gamely on *Pop Stars: The Rivals* and *I'm a Celebrity Get Me Out of Here!* make its jubilant jungle debut. It was a mainstream realignment brutally summed up that year by Noel Gallagher back in the tartan-tweedy hotel foyer in Aberdeen. The era of the rock'n'roll nutter, he balked, *his* era, had now been overthrown by 'ordinary, fookin' talentless idiots from Tesco with a lisp or celebrity cunts in the jungle.'

NME's 2002 reality, however, would soon be bullseye centred on the Libertines, the wayward rapscallions permanently on the cover (it was, already, like the 2001-adored Americans, the Strokes and White Stripes, had never happened), the staff thrilled at the reappearance of the homegrown, reckless spirit. Their coverlines spelled it out: 'Come on England! Why London's finest will rock your summer!'; 'Scrapping, screwing & getting trashed with Britain's most f***ed up band'; 'England's Screaming: On the road and on the run with the 21st Century Sex Pistols'. Sometime in 2002 I went to see the Libertines in a tiny, crammed London boozer and, by the end, was cackling uncontrollably, yelping out loud 'Really? Is that it!?', hearing little more than a threadbare, ramshackle skiffle band, short on tunage and abundant in self-belief. They had, however, in Pete Doherty, an enigmatic, deftly romantic lyricist, even if he permanently threatened to evaporate into a tapering narcotic wisp.

By 2003, the Libertines had fallen apart already. In January, Pete burgled his co-frontman and compadre Carl Barât's flat and was punted off to prison; a restraining order was issued preventing Pete contacting Carl, effectively forcing him out, a position reinforced by Carl. The band toured without Pete, reunited and recorded music – albeit precariously – in 2004, and in January 2005 finally split up. By then the rambunctious, brawling, 'indie heroes' were barely mentioned in public. Instead, Celebrity Culture was now so entrenched in the UK that Pete Doherty was a household name as the nation's foremost Celebrity Drug Addict. His partner in narcotic crime was now his girlfriend, the newly dubbed Cocaine Kate, after photos appeared of supermodel Kate Moss *on the bugle* on the cover of the *Daily Mirror*. Shortly afterwards, Kate Moss entered Arizona's Meadows rehab clinic, stayed a month, emerged fully clean and her career, if anything, was significantly rebooted. Not so, it would turn out, for the permanently erratic Pete Doherty . . .

One year later . . .

Pete Doherty's own drug-related notoriety was now dimensions more famous than his music ever was, so tabloid friendly by 2006 he was the subject of the daytime *Trisha* show. 'My teenager ran off with Pete Doherty!' shrieked the TV caption as goth-pale, black-clothed, sixteen-year-old Natasha – who was 'desperate to get into the modelling industry' – revealed how 'the bad-boy rocker' had said, 'come with us and you'll be famous by Wednesday.' To the then-merciless tabloids, in the early days of the Amy Winehouse-hounding era, Pete Doherty was the gift that kept on going to prison.

In 2006 I was invited round his 'lovely' home in Hackney, its plywood boarded-up front door more befitting of a derelict squat, as was the living room/kitchen inside. A fair-sized L-shape, this was Student Hell on a supernova three-year bender, bestrewn with a huge, second-hand amp, microphones, tripods, guitars, banjos, drums, laptops, flight cases, cans, bottles, mugs, ashtrays and empty mobile phone boxes, the kitchen worktop littered with spoons, saucers, empty cigarette packets and empty drug-wraps. No light penetrated the only window, obscured by a yellowing cloth drape. In the bathroom, an empty bottle of Jack Daniels lay discarded under the sink while a used hypodermic needle perched on the lid of a sanitary bin.

The twenty-seven-year-old Pete Doherty was a gentle character, unexpectedly tall, six feet two, his flimsy frame draped in a fawn Burberry raincoat, wearing his signature pork pie hat, a white V-necked T-shirt, black patent shoes and grey drainpipes, legs no thicker than fireside pokers. His huge, chocolate-drop eyes were baleful, his blistered mouth permanently open, his fingers Dickensian sooty. He was talking to the press, he told me, to 'keep the idea of Babyshambles alive', the band which fell, like a car door finally busting off its hinge, from the burnt-out vehicle of the Libertines. He was without a manager, record label or record deal and supposedly clean from heroin, adhering to a methadone programme, which accounted for his dreamy, will-o'-the-wisp demeanour. Throughout the flat, Pete's drawings were daubed on the grubby, off-white walls, many in his own blood, gleaned from a syringe after heroin use. His dominant etching theme was a long, thin, dripping love-heart, now faded into rusty-brown. Elsewhere were canvas paintings, like the one in the hall where a scratchy match-stick couple sat together on a bench. 'This is the only thing I'm gonna say about *her*,' sighed Pete and pointed to the words in the top left-hand corner. 'It's the nicest text message she ever sent me. I think that's really romantic.' The message from Kate Moss read, exactly: 'YOUR IN MY BLOOD, YOU FUCK.'

Relocating to his bedroom, he swayed alarmingly between the door, a tall, Victorian, orange-tasselled standard lamp and his acoustic guitar, attempting a conversation in between bursts of song and disappearances out the door.

What did he hope to do next, with his life?

'Next … just what's happening really, melody and debauchery,' he decided, evenly. 'For a little while things were too dark to fucking even begin to get my head around. Spending all my time dropping my trousers to the police. Sat in cells. So, a little bit of self-control combined with a continuation of the full-on Arcadian dream.'

Is this what he wanted? To continue on as this mythological drug taker which people now saw him as?

'Or is that just the people who come across me via ... the mythologising ... *news*. Bollocks.'

His face collapsed in a shadowy frown, he then disappeared, returned and climbed onto his wooden-framed bed, his duvet cover a silky deep purple. With no chairs available, I perched on the edge of the bed.

How did he feel these days about the tabloids?

'*So* annoying,' he frowned. 'It's all about her Majesty [Kate Moss]. She is the queen of England. It's not so bad when it's just about me. Y'know, I was nine days in Arizona [in the Meadows rehab clinic]. Nine days clean. Touching my toes. Up early. Eating well. And then I woke up and thought, "What the fuck am I doing here? I've gotta get back to London." I've got a rehab diary. I've never shown anyone, actually ...'

He rummaged around for a large, rectangular, maroon-red diary, flopped back on the bed and began reading: '7.11 a.m. The night was all bundled up like a recluse. Stone the crows. Like a pig grunting and snoring in the valley, the day began restless ...'

He threw his crack-pipe on the bed, a miniature bottle of Bailey's Irish Cream, sawn off at the bottom with a black filter inside the neck, the reason his fingers and bottom lip were black. From here I lost him, smoking his make-shift pipe for twenty minutes, eyes closed, eyeballs clearly moving from side-to-side under heavy lids, while we both sat on his bed in silence. After the wave passed he began singing, 'Fixing up! Fixing up to go!' while guitars pranged up in the living room. Members of Babyshambles had arrived – there'd been talk of an impromptu guerrilla gig that night in North London.

Did he learn anything in rehab?

'Yeah. That I'm a terrible judge of character. I'd just come out of a fucking serious situation, we know who did it and they're fucking cunts.'

He meant whoever sold the highly lucrative Cocaine Kate

mobile phone shots to the tabloids. I'd heard these people worked for him.

'No,' he responded, annoyed. 'They don't anymore. Fucking money, man. I've lost eight laptops now. Stolen. Music on there, everything. People steal a laptop and sell it for a twenty-pound rock.'

There were rumours that the wads of money he reportedly carried around were from Kate, who paid him to stay silent about their relationship and stop him selling stories to the papers.

'Bollocks. Y'know, I've done interviews with the tabloids where they didn't use one word of mine. I could sue. And I don't. Kate sues all the time and she always wins. She's got Prince Charles' lawyer, and I've got legal aid.'

If things had been very different, he could be sitting in a very big house in the country right now, a rich and successful rock star?

'I wouldn't mind a little place by the seaside. I never wanted to be a millionaire.'

He clutched his stomach, said 'I'm feeling gouge-y,' made undulating movements with his upper body and edged off the bed while a decision was made that he wouldn't, after all, play that night's Babyshambles show. He simply wouldn't turn up, like he usually didn't. He picked up his rehab diary, flicked through the pages of handwritten poetry until the writing stopped, replaced by several pages of dried brown blood in dense, kaleidoscopic swirls. 'London,' noted Pete, ruefully, and flicked on, until the swirling pages stopped and there was page after page after page of absolutely nothing at all.

Seven years later...

Thirty-four-year-old Pete Doherty was, so far, a manageable two hours late for a photo shoot in East London. By 2013 he was, reportedly, an improved character (if not exactly reformed), now living in Paris with a steady girlfriend, away from the destructive hangers-on. His Babyshambles bandmates were also waiting, cerebral bassist Drew McConnell, thirty-four, and world-weary guitarist Mick Whitnall, forty-four. With our window of photographic opportunity already dwindled to a porthole (Pete, in the midst of a solo acoustic tour, would have to leave in three hours for Swindon), the Shambles ruminated on the new, improved, Paris Pete. 'He's calmer, hassled less, there's less distractions,' noted Drew. 'From the jamboree of arseholes,' added Mick, rumly. Today, despite being banned from driving in Britain, Pete was driving himself and his manager Andy Boyd eight miles from Andy's flat in Kentish Town, a journey which began two hours previously. Even London traffic wasn't *this* bad.

Drew's phone rang. It was Andy (Pete didn't own a mobile phone). 'Hello, hello, is anyone there?' The line went dead. Mick was a candid man, confessing Pete recently told Andy he couldn't 'be arsed to tour the new album'. In Paris, Pete had found what he called 'the Holy Grail', pure China White heroin. 'He was saying a bit back,' elaborated Mick, '"I've hit the pinnacle in my fucked-up journey, I've got a China White heroin habit now, living in Paris, in Pigalle, it's all I've ever wanted to do."'

Two more hours evaporated. Pete and Andy were now, we heard, 'screaming at each other'. Pete was crying with acute toothache, he had 'a hole in his face'. Eventually, his car reached the end of our road and five minutes later he had suddenly, inexplicably, 'gone to Swindon'.

Nine days later . . .

Pete Doherty finally turned up at Andy's Kentish Town flat, confessing to 'a good old-fashioned panic attack' (leading to his photo shoot no show). He was dimensions more coherent than seven years previously, but the sometime pretty-boy dandy had rapidly aged: hair prematurely greying, teeth brown-stained with nicotine, a sore healing on his cheek, circular needle-stabbed pock marks scattering up arms unhidden in a short-sleeved nautical T-shirt. On a sofa in an artwork-littered living room he smoked Lucky Strikes and drank tea, those chocolate-drop eyes still baleful, full of the wide-open vulnerability which immediately disarmed anyone in Pete Doherty's company, no matter your inclination to boot his errant backside.

Initially, he was Comedy Pete, telling the rollicking tale of yesterday's 'opium adventure' on tour in Prague, a story starring rent boys, beggars and a seventy-year-old man with a 'No Future' tattoo, injecting into his big toe. Andy, who was perched protectively on the living-room window seat, was appalled already: 'Don't tell that story!'

Pete remained a chaotic conversationalist, mild-mannered, softly spoken and vague, yet volatile, conflicted, sensitive and emotional, prone to bewildering tangents, tears of torment and bursts of song, including Derek B's 1988 hip-hop caper 'Bad Young Brother'. We talked about the lost years Mick had suffered while Pete was never around (Mick's serious addictions had left him isolated and broke) and his assertion that Pete couldn't be arsed to tour. Suddenly, Pete crumbled.

'Oh *don't*,' he pleaded. 'Yes, it's fucked, yes it's a mess! Yes, alright, but that's what fuels it . . . but you're confusing a lack of punctuality with not caring about the band. When I'm thinking straight and rested, there's no question I'm gonna do it. It's just ... I need to grow up and get some self-discipline. I owe Mick and Drew that. I love them. Whoo ...'

He was sobbing now, chin quivering, oval tears splashing down his cheeks. 'Mick's done miracles, getting clean,' he managed. 'It's mad that Mick is still there for me. *Bloody hell.*'

Andy leapt down from the window seat and sat next to him, placed a reassuring hand on his back. We talked about the China White heroin/Pigalle statement, which considerably irked him.

'So I'm a pathetic cliché, is that what you're saying?' he recoiled. 'That just happened to be my life, but new songs are up there with China White, y'know? Crack and cocaine is really the fucking problem.'

He still wasn't interested in rehab. 'I lead,' he insisted, 'a fully functional life.' He was enraged by a society that encouraged 'deadly alcohol' and demonised addicts, kept drugs illegal and sent people like him to jail. 'It's 2013, y'know? Striving so hard to be free you end up in fucking *prison*.' Paris had become Pete's permanent sanctuary, from both police and paparazzi, the civilised city where 'there is no tabloid culture'. London life had become intolerable, the Kate Moss years and his friendship/romance with Amy Winehouse leaving 'a legacy', even after the paparazzi had disappeared.

'I'd ended up in a little flat in Camden with a fucking tag round my ankles and riots in the streets,' he sighed. 'I was using quite heavily at that time as well. There was literally nowhere left to run.'

This had been his life in summer 2011, the summer of both the London riots and Amy's death, Pete newly out of Pentonville prison (a cocaine bust) following the death in his Hackney flat in 2009 of his long-time friend Robyn Whitehead, something he was deemed complicit in, which he furiously refuted, deeming the media 'twisted bastards'. Amy's death left him 'reeling': they'd been lovers for a while.

'I was a little bit in awe of the girl, y'know?' he reflected. 'We'd jam and she'd take the piss, "Is that your best new riff?" And "You're not really a singer, are you?" I think I was bang in love with Amy from when I first saw her. And then, bang, the queen is dead. But Amy's music, that was glory, not tragedy.'

For years, the trouble with Pete Doherty had been too much tragedy, not enough glory, the youthful Libertines' fans seeing in him their generation's potential Morrissey, who threw it all away for drugs, who never made, unlike Amy, that immortal piece of work.

'So, what, I'm the failed Morrissey?' he balked. 'Well let *them* create an immortal piece of work. The one I didn't do.'

Andy: 'Don't put your life in the hands of a rock'n'roll band . . .'

Pete: 'I wish I'd written that line!'

I wondered if the Straight Life for some might simply be too dull to contemplate (catastrophically addictive personalities aside). Perhaps Pete was like his hero George Best, who used his new liver in 2002 for three more years on the booze.

'He was also an incredible footballer!' he replied, indignantly. 'Oh, you can't just *condemn* people. We all have our foibles. I live a fucking *very* straight life. It's not even real chaos, my chaos. I'm very certain of what works and what and who I need to avoid.'

It was, he said cryptically, 'the Rainman' (the authorities) he needed to avoid, 'this force, who wants to put me in a box [prison] for nothing.' His face crumpled once more, sobbing harder than ever.

'That last time was *frightening*, my friend Robyn fucking *died*,' he openly wept. 'I wasn't even invited to the funeral, portrayed in the papers as somehow having caused the death and sent to prison for possession of drugs that didn't even exist. It's *fucked up* when your whole life is so extravagantly fucked around with. So I have to just look out for myself and go and bury myself somewhere. Cos this fucking thing that's been created about me is *nasty* and I get squashed. *Bloody hell.*'

We repaired to a nearby pub, the Lord Stanley, where Pete, on Guinness and Sailor Jerry's rum (his favourite), became increasingly coherent, 'relieved' now the official interview was over. 'You had me right at it today, wasn't part of the plan, but it's good to let it out.' In Paris, his life was low-key, where he kept himself wilfully 'cut off from London, the madness and chaos'. He watched old black-and-white movies (Humphrey Bogart, war classics) and his French girlfriend Katia was 'completely straight, she doesn't use'. He played acoustic shows for cash – 'I have to be a working musician' – had long since spent the Libertines' reunion tour 2010 pay-out ('about £260,000 after tax and all that bollocks') but non-payment of other bills meant, 'I had to go bankrupt.' We talked about heroin addiction, which he coolly described as 'a selfish lifestyle choice', while also acknowledging the 'serious disease of addiction' and how addicts should be treated as sick people, in need of care.

'That's what people thought originally, when heroin was pharmaceutically created – but it's seen as a spiritual crime now, to be a junkie, the lowest thing.'

What did freedom mean to him now?

'The same for anyone. Not being forced into anything you don't wanna do.'

Did he feel free?

'Mostly.'

He remained breathtakingly honest, even as he remained, beyond his devoted fans, the most easily judged and reviled character in contemporary music, for the crimes of his own self-destruction. If he was an exasperating, unrepentant waster of other people's time, there was no trace here of a nasty piece of work. There were, no doubt, more sinister characters at the end of our streets, never mind in 'showbiz', and certainly lurking with intent across our increasingly beleaguered planet.

Three years later...

Exactly one year and three days since ninety music fans were slaughtered by rifle-toting ISIS terrorists in the Bataclan venue in Paris and Pete Doherty and his new band, the Puta Madres, were playing the freshly refurbished venue. It was November 2016 and Pete was in unusually robust voice, newly 'clean', not long back from the South American Libertines tour where he'd stayed on afterwards, alone, and finally kicked his heroin habit, even if his crack pipe was still never far away. That night, unannounced, Libertines compadre Carl Barât suddenly appeared on stage to explosive roars, the pair then hollering through the Libertines' best-loved songs, the Bataclan now a choppy sea of upturned, surfing legs as Pete proffered a V-sign and Carl saluted the crowd. By the encore, the old sparring pals were rolling around on top of each other, beaming, grinning, laughing. As the lights went up a few couples lingered on, dancing to imaginary music, waltzing across the floor. It had taken Pete Doherty, of all people, to turn the Bataclan from a funeral into a wedding.

Ten minutes later, upstairs in the Bataclan dressing room, there had been a curious development. There was another reporter there that night, whose scheduled post-show interview with Pete had apparently gone awry. Where he should've been in celebratory mood, he had a go at the woman from the *Sunday Times* for the crime of working for the *Sunday Times*, while having a simultaneous go at Carl Barât, who he erroneously called 'a racist'. Chaos had returned. (It never really went away.)

The following afternoon . . .

Thirty-seven-year-old Pete Doherty was yet to turn up, as ever, just two hours before stage time for his second Bataclan show. From early afternoon in the Bataclan dressing room we'd waited five hours – myself, a photographer, my ever-patient PR pal Tony Linkin and Pete's manager Jai (a stabilising childhood friend) – with no clue where the now long-fabled pimpernel might be. In 2016 he still owned no mobile phone and still lived in Paris, also sporadically living in his eighties campervan, having newly discovered UK road trips with Katia, now the Puta Madres keyboard player. As 8 p.m. arrived, with the show beginning at a stop-clocked 9 p.m., nerves were fizzing, with a photo session and interview not yet begun.

Finally, Pete ambled in, smiling, preoccupied, in a dishevelled, black pin-striped suit, brown fedora in position, grey-speckled hair wisping out in all directions.

'Alright?' he greeted me in his gentle tones, 'when did I last see you?'

Forty-five seconds later he left the room, returning ten full minutes later with a lengthy copper pipe attached to a jumble of chains and metal skulls, and headed straight into the bathroom. Emerging, he was now limping. 'Ur, I've stood on my toe!'

I asked him what his chains were all about. 'What are my dreams?' he misheard, which was a much better question anyway (his chains were trinkets from South America). We sat together on the dressing room sofa and I studied his eyes, which were clear, enormous and kind, and told him we hadn't much time. 'Really, what's happening, are they coming with guns again?' he replied, grimly. I told him last night's show was one of the most powerful of his life and he was instantly emotional.

'Ah don't, I know, I'm struggling now cos last night was awesome, proper, and now I'm in a head space where I don't know what to do,' he cringed. 'It's not that *usual*. Anyway ... you got a tipple?'

The dressing-room door opened and Jai presented him with a small pepperoni pizza in its box, which he tore a few strips from, cramming them into his mouth: 'Wanna bit?' After the Libertines' tour of South America that autumn – through Mexico, Chile and Argentina – Pete had found himself staying on in Buenos Aires for three weeks.

'I was maintaining myself and then it stopped in Buenos Aires and I just thought ... that's it,' he explained, of his coming off heroin process. 'You can't get gear there, y'know? They make it apparently and send it to the US. So I just sat in the hotel room, clucked out, listened to the La's constantly. Something switched. Normally I do detox, go to rehab, it's always on my mind. And I wasn't ... craving. It's like I finally saw the bad side of the girl that was never any good for me.'

Here, in his poetic way, he talked about the end of his love affair with the drug which had dogged him for decades via romantic metaphor.

'Just lost that feeling, that spark's gone,' he carried on. 'I thought about exactly what I'm doing it for. Basically, it's just a *mammoth sedative*. That saves you bothering. Y'know? It was always, "doesn't matter you've spent all your money, doesn't matter because we've always got each other." But she wasn't there for me in Buenos Aires.'

I wondered if he was now looking to a future where he'd finally get past crack, too?

'I can't carry on taking cocaine in Europe after visiting South America anyway,' he responded, obliquely. 'Cos I've realised, all these years I've never *really* been taking it, whatever the fuck they cut it with.'

When he said he was 'clean', he'd always just meant clean from heroin, hadn't he?

'Yeah,' he replied and said no more about the crack.

It was no joke, really, the life and times of 'Celebrity Crackhead' Pete Doherty, habitual prison dweller, who'd lost so many friends, all those arrests, the ankle tags, the tabloid glee. Today, certainly, was better than many days. And he was turning up – at last! – for shows. 'Yeah,' he suddenly smiled, proffering a handshake. I wondered what had happened the previous night, why he was so irked when he should've been celebrating?

'Oh fuck!' he yelped. 'Heavy drinks and I suddenly remembered some articles from the *Sunday Times* from years ago and I thought, "Actually, get out!" I *hate* the *Sunday Times*. I thought they must now be doing something good for the world [by being at this show]. Instead of just being part of a great big machine that's choking everybody culturally and probably destroying the planet.'

He looked aggrieved.

'I think I just fancied an argument,' he now decided. 'Provoking her. "You are representing the *Sunday Times*, justify everything you've written, justify your political view," and she was just like, "D'you miss Kate?" And you can quote me on that.'

And the argument with Carl?

'Oh shit!' he wobbled, head in his hands. 'OK, so I had a few drinks, was getting a bit lairy, Carl came all this way to play, he didn't deserve me bringing up ... why did I get kicked out the band again? It never gets discussed, y'see? Aw, I shouldn't have said it! I love him so much.'

He stood up, paced around the dressing room, head back in his hands.

'I offered him out as well!' he roared. '"Toe to toe on

the cobbles" was my expression. I took my jacket off! *Jesus Christ.*'

Where Pete Doherty was always preoccupied with his internal struggles, he was never oblivious to the struggles of the world, describing the Trump/Brexit-led geopolitics of 2016 as 'bonkers, disastrous, maybe we're just repeating cycles of taking a breather and then going absolutely spasmo again, letting out all this hatred and anger.' He remained, though, a romantic idealist, still believed in music and literature as balm to humanity's madness.

'I always thought that,' he nodded. 'When I was fourteen, fifteen, I had no wish to take part in society. Because it was rotting me from the inside out. It was only the *NME* letters page keeping me sane. And then when Jai, who I went to school with, gave me books and books and more books, and a tape with the Smiths and the Stone Roses on, I literally found songs that were giving me the same effect in three minutes. So I persevered. I was gonna die, I think. And this was something that was gonna lift me every day. It pulled me out of that *hell*, of reality. Until I was so hypnotised, by songs, by these idols, that *that* became my reality. And has been ever since. Because I can't return to that place, that thing my parents believed in: knuckle down, work, save, get your hair cut. Can't do that. I'd probably have become a psychopath. But in a subtle way.'

He'd chosen, wilfully, the financially precarious life, had declared himself bankrupt previously 'in order to get tax cancelled' but swore he'd 'never' missed a tax bill.

'But I have ... eternity things that automatically take six grand a month off me,' he confessed, alarmingly. 'And so many fines for parking tickets, you can't park a campervan anywhere these days, it's discrimination man! What am I, black!?'

I cheered him up by reminding him of our conversation

ten years previously, when he was on methadone and crack, when Babyshambles didn't have a record deal, when he lived in the needle-bestrewn dive in Hackney, about the perennial judgement of Pete Doherty as rock'n'roll's worst under-achiever, who'd never reached his full potential, who even called himself 'just a schmindie songwriter'. Seeing him last night on stage, the crowd singing all those beloved songs, he'd obviously done plenty. Maybe being a 'schmindie songwriter' was *enough*, after all.

'Oh. Fucking hell,' he now blinked, chin wobbling, on the verge of tears. 'Can we talk about this after the gig? I won't get lairy and throw you out!'

Backstage in the tiny, boxy, Bataclan dressing room, which the post-show Puta Madres had just bounded into, around ten people were crammed together, perched on the edges of seats, Pete reclining on the only sofa, where I now joined him. His shirt was off, his braces still on, hat off, hair askew, chains around his neck which bore an 'Astile' tattoo, the name of his now-twelve-year-old son. There were no 'dad' vibes here, though, his left hand fondling his latest favourite crack pipe, an ornate copper number in two sections. 'Don't think we quite matched the first night,' he lamented of the show (he was right, the energy was good but less euphoric). 'Looking out was glorious, looking inwards is the problem! Careful with that typewriter, man, it's an Olivetti!' he shouted over the assembled.

I looked around the room and saw an environment as druggy as the mythological 1990s. A nameless older man, maybe sixty, was starey-eyed and silent as his jaw visibly crunched to and fro; Pete dangled from a sooty finger an acorn-sized bag of crack cocaine; someone approached with an iPad, its black mirrored screen the perfect surface for a selection of ready-scored lines. 'Want one?' wondered Pete. I declined.

How *did* he maintain his newly productive, heroin-free life, with all this chemical carnage still involved?

'It's reliant on vast resources of energy, from different people,' he explained, curiously, before nodding to his PR, my heroic pal, the by now almost comically long-suffering Tony Linkin, also the former PR of Evan Dando, who was munching a few crisps. 'Look at this!' roared Pete. 'Are those Pringles any healthier than cocaine!? Once you pop, you can't shut up.'

Here, he manhandled my e-cig, wondering, 'Can you smoke crack through it?'

Wasn't this lifestyle unbelievably debilitating? Did he have the constitution of Keef Richards or what?

'No no no!' he recoiled, before a lengthy anecdote on meeting Keith Richards at the Isle of Wight festival in 2007, the year Pete was there with Amy Winehouse (who appeared on stage with the Stones). 'He said, "What, are you going in the veins? We only used to skin-pop in the sixties!" He said, "Come over 'ere, I'll show you how to make a vodka tonic." A big fuck-off vodka and tonic? That's a lot more debilitating; alcohol is a depressant!'

That night in 2007, he keeled over completely.

'I passed out in the Rolling Stones' dressing room and they had me dumped in the bins,' he cackled. 'They all had different coloured dressing rooms. Uncle Ronnie Wood, his room backstage was called the Detox Room, it was all white and then he dumped me in there, in the bins, with my legs in the air, on my back, like a dead cow. I heard Ronnie's voice in the midst of my dementia going [spot on impersonation], "Have him removed! He's a liability! And he doesn't get the blues!" *Now* I get it! Who's that singer, Blind Billie Barlow, no, Blind Bill Blake, the one who sings [he bawled] "When ah'm dead I be a long time gaaaaaawn!" Bargain on iTunes, man . . .'

I mentioned he was thirty-seven now.

'What are you saying!? You know what I'm gonna do? [voice of toff] "Going to get myself a good accountant! And invest in prop-er-taaay!" Sort it out with pounds! And pennies!'

He veered into comedy incoherence as a volley of impersonations of Spanish, Welsh and American voices arrived, before a selection of random songs, including the return of Derek B ('Derek B is very underrated!'), a blast of 'It's a long way to Tipperaraaaaay!' and American Civil Rights classic 'Michael Row the Boat Ashooooore, Halleilooooojah!', before inviting me to join him in a sustained duet of Scottish classics – 'Flower of Scotland', 'Loch Lomond' and the Proclaimers' 'I'm Gonna Be (500 Miles)'. 'Ya sassenach bastuuuurd!'

So how went the Arcadian Dream at the end of 2016?

'The Arcadian dream is alive and well,' he assured. 'Everyone's just pursuing their melodies and their dreams, getting their bargain frocks down the market. [He turned to Katia, who was wearing a tasselled Flapper girl frock.] Katia, make your frock shimmer! [She obliged, with a vigorous shimmy.] *That* is the Arcadian Dream, man! I've finally reached the vortex, cheers Boo-Boo, I luv ya!'

Was he happy?

'Right at this moment I am, yeah!' he yelped, happily, before another blast of song, the Chas & Dave legend 'Snooker Loopy'. I left him to it, hoped to see him again in three years' time, when he'd turn forty, at the mention of which he cringed. It's not so bad, I told him. It was a privilege to grow old. Become old, Pete. Get to forty, and well beyond. Don't do an Amy.

'Yeah, but what did she do, though?' he wondered, fairly.

She didn't eat enough, was my theory.

'She was frail,' he agreed. 'Well. I know I'm a bit messy, but I'm alright. I think *in myself* I'm alright. It's funny how it changes.'

*

As long as Pete kept at the pizzas, I thought that year, he'd surely be alright. Unexpectedly, then, by 2018, he was allowing himself to be photographed in the tabloids successfully tackling an 8,000-calorie breakfast 'challenge'. Turning forty in 2019, however, the drugs remained – that year he was arrested twice in Paris in forty-eight hours, where he pissed all over the reception counter of a police station, after which a conditional probation forced him to take the heroin-blocking injection Buvidal. In early 2020, the pandemic pretty much saved his life, his road to freedom from crack and heroin turning out to be a simple one: he couldn't access the dealers. Over the following few years he became, astonishingly, an overweight, heavily moustachioed man in his forties, sporting a flat cap, resembling more an avuncular Yorkshire dairy farmer than a maverick rock'n'roll madman. By then living in Normandy, Katia became his wife, soon with a baby daughter Billie-May. By 2022 he was telling several UK newspapers his newly sturdy self was buoyed by Comté on toast, creamy milk, bread, saucisson, champagne cocktails with rum and a new addiction: 'I've swapped crack for Camembert.'

Two years later ...

In the approach to Christmas 2024, now forty-six-year-old Pete Doherty was in a North London hotel restaurant tucking into pork belly, a spiced rum tinkling in his tumbler, his dog Gladys asleep at his feet, Katia nearby with the cartoon-beautiful toddler Billie-May in her arms.

'I'm glad things worked out this way, y'know?' he told me, in some understatement. 'This is how it should be.'

Now a reconstructed family man, he also toured regularly with the Libertines – their fourth studio album, *All Quiet on the Eastern Esplanade*, had been a UK No. 1 in 2024 – while his latest solo album, the joyously charming *Felt Better Alive*, was due in May 2025. It was an odd title. What did he mean?

'It's hard to put it into words,' he mused. 'It's connected to not being in an opiated state, maybe? It took me so long to give up drugs because it took me a long time to feel alright without it, y'know? It's an odd expression, *felt better alive*, because how does it feel to be dead? But in a strange way, I think I know how it feels, to be dead.'

But he wasn't. Against every imaginable odd, Pete Doherty had not only survived but thrived, despite now having type 2 diabetes and wearing orthopaedic shoes (a much better outcome, however, than the threatened loss of his toes).

'I think physically I've done a lot of damage, my lungs are pretty shattered, all my veins are pretty hammered,' he concluded that day, with a measured acceptance. 'But I feel alright. More adventures to come. And it doesn't have to be . . . illegal, anymore. It's trips to the park now. Billie-May getting on a swing by herself. That's happening soon. And that will be amazing.'

Funny how it changes, right enough.

20

I'M A FREE BITCH, BABY!

2008, *Lady Gaga releases* The Fame *and makes pop preposterous again*

In the year Amy Winehouse won five Grammy awards, watched her husband go to prison and herself to rehab, the year Adele emerged as new fodder for the ever-circling tabloids and 13.2 million viewers watched Alexandra Burke on the *X Factor* weep uncontrollably all the way through her triumph, I'd been mostly freelancing for two monthly magazines in the celeb- dominated noughties: the newly enormous women's magazine *Glamour* and the eighties-born, once-enormous contemporary music mag *Q* (still stoically clinging to a declining readership in the emerging digital era). The nature of interviews was changing, both the internet's reach and tabloid hysteria creating in our pop stars a newly acute suspicion which persists to this day (alongside strangling PR control), my encounters characterised by a palpable wariness. David and Victoria Beckham's 'people' vetted and vetoed any questions beyond the promotion of their latest fragrance, while Coldplay's Chris Martin, as we watched the Rolling Stones documentary *Shine a Light* together in an

IMAX cinema amid the general public, sank low in his seat in the pitch black with his hoodie still up, obliterating his face.

Lady Gaga emerged, fully formed, as the pop star for these times, suddenly ubiquitous in 2008 with her pointedly titled debut album *The Fame*, a dedicated scholar of celebrity who became pop's most dominant presence. That year her second single 'Poker Face' was No. 1 worldwide, the year's biggest selling single with fourteen million copies sold.

At first, I wasn't convinced: 'Poker Face' was a decent pop single, Gaga a winningly preposterous cartoon creation in her mirror shades, black latex catsuit and perpetual pants, but I wasn't hearing any immortal, world-class bangers. Then, overnight in October 2009, I *was* – with her bona fide masterpiece, the inarguably brilliant 'Bad Romance'.

It was her headline set at the UK's Royal Variety Performance that December, however, which proved to me this was true pop genius at work: on a none-more-public stage, the central act of the nation's perennially namby-pamby light entertainment carnival of the Straights, Lady Gaga gave us one of the most thrilling, audacious and unexpected moments of pop theatre spectacle *in history*. Suspended roof-wards on a swinging stool, playing her fantastical, surreal, sixteen-foot-high spindle-legged piano, witnessed by the Queen, perhaps even *more* audacious was the outfit she wore while playing it: the neon scarlet S&M Queen Elizabeth I latex number with chin-high ruff and comedy twenty-foot train, before meeting Queen Elizabeth II in person, who was, official photos confirmed, definitely amused. By the close of 2009 she'd become that rarest of cultural beasts: not only the biggest pop star on Earth but the most extreme. Much of this meant visually extreme, by the wearing of, variously, a coat of Kermit the Frogs, a lightbulb-festooned catsuit and a black, face-obliterating PVC gimp mask. She'd become, and increasingly so, *the real deal*.

Two months previously . . .

Before the Royal Variety spectacular, with Lady Gaga's best loved single still the lyrically risqué, Boney M-echoing 'Poker Face' (weeks before 'Bad Romance' detonated around the planet) and *Q* magazine was, with negligible enthusiasm, putting this curious American pop force on its cover. A magazine predominantly run by 'rock' blokes void of a solitary camp-pop bone, I was happy to take the assignment, with no idea what to expect when ushered by her 'people', in reverential silence, into the opulent penthouse suite of London's May Fair Hotel. Perched on a silvery-white L-shaped velvet sofa, she proved a pop-art provocateur from the off, announcing a not-so monarch-tickling idea for her increasingly subversive crusade.

'I want to wear a dick strapped to my vagina,' she declared, cheerfully, puffing on a Marlboro Light. 'We all know one of the biggest talking points of the year was that I have a dick, so why not give them what they want? I want to comment on that in a beautiful, artistic way [photographically], how *I* wanna show it. And I want to call this piece "Lady Gaga Dies Hard".'

This was the first time, in a now lengthy journalistic lifetime, I'd ever known any pop star have the artistic confidence to insist on both their own cover photo idea and the actual title of the story.

'I mean, you can take the credit for it,' she smiled, meaning *Q* itself. 'It'd be a real fucking story, right? Come on, come see me try to persuade everyone to let me wear a penis . . .'

In late 2009 Lady Gaga was pop's most controversial figure, a cartoon amalgam of a Tate Modern Madonna, Dame Elton John, Salvador Dali, David Bowie, Cher, Marilyn Manson, the Pet Shop Boys, Spinal Tap, Grace Jones, Freddie Mercury, Francis Bacon and the wardrobe and special effects department of *Doctor Who* on a hallucinogenic trip. 'Bad Romance' would reach No. 1 in twenty countries and sell twelve million copies worldwide, its fantastically futuristic kidnap video, as she put it herself (as the pop stars then never did), 'explores how the entertainment industry simulates human trafficking, the woman as commodity'. No wonder teenagers globally perched tinfoil on their heads, re-enacted the dance routine with bared teeth and 'ra ra!' wolf hands, before posting the results on YouTube in universal exhilaration.

Back at the May Fair, the Diva of Dada sat cross-legged on her silvery-white sofa, as serene as an alabaster sculpture. Today was our initial meeting before we travelled on the road with her Monster Ball tour and she wore nothing on her head but her wig (bouffant seventies disco meets Marilyn Monroe), staring straight at me with huge, steady brown eyes, bewitchingly younger and prettier in reality with a glorious Jewish nose. With the edges of her silk black dressing gown continually edging apart, blithely exposing her small, real, bare and undeniably female breasts, we discussed the 'Lady Gaga is a man/hermaphrodite' rumours (then vehemently believed by millions), an example, she decided, of an ancient story, the public savaging of the highly sexual woman, as Madonna was before her (particularly by straight men).

'When a guy says, "Oh I fucked all these chicks this week," there's a high five and a giggling,' noted Gaga, puffing away. 'But when a woman does it and it's publicised or she's open about her sexuality or she's liberated, there's a threat, it's "Oh, she must have a dick". I also carry myself on stage in a masculine way and sing in a low register. This is not out of nowhere, right?'

She was born a prodigious talent, a middle-class New York Italian-American named Stefani Joanne Angelina Germanotta who learnt piano by ear aged four, was highly educated at the

Catholic Convent of the Sacred Heart high school, a straight-A student who defied the nuns' strictures by wearing her skirts 'really high', who worshipped Judy Garland, David Bowie and Led Zeppelin. 'I wanted to be Boy George,' she added. 'I was a freak, a little bit insecure, my personality just didn't fit in – and I guess that's what I'm all about.'

By fifteen, she was already a paid nightclub singer/piano player and at seventeen was accepted into the prestigious Tisch School of the Arts, one of only twenty students in its forty-five-year history to be accepted early (alumni: Woody Allen, Angelina Jolie, Martin Scorsese). At nineteen, determined to make her own money (her dad Joseph, then fifty-three, a sometime long-haired rock'n'roll bar musician, was now a wealthy internet entrepreneur), she both waitressed and go-go danced in New York dive bars, had sexual relationships with women while only falling in love with men. She developed a cocaine habit, had 'bags and bags of cocaine' delivered to her apartment where she'd snort coke alone for hours and make herself up as classic David Bowie while continually blaring out the Cure. In 2006, now a twenty-year-old singer/songwriter/piano player, she supplemented her club-night earnings performing as one half of the burlesque cavalcade 'Lady Gaga and the Starlight Revue' with DJ/performance artist Lady Starlight, eleven years Gaga's senior, a philosophy graduate and metal-possessed DJ whose sets featured Metallica, Judas Priest and Rush. Gaga suggested the pair create a pop/metal hybrid, playing to bawdy metal crowds through simulated fog, dressed in $10 cheetah-print stripper bikinis and Indian headdresses, wielding a bow and arrow and a hatchet, while flailing to Iron Maiden's 'Run to the Hills'.

A year later she'd given up both go-go dancing and cocaine – 'I was able to stop [cocaine],' explained Gaga, 'because I was panicking more *on* the drugs than I was sober' – and decided, as the traditionally pop-dubious Americans never did, that her future lay in electronic pop: 'I thought, "If I wanna be *really* revolutionary, I'll make pop music."'

'Gaga was in the commercial pop world, which didn't encourage risk,' Lady Starlight told me on the blower, 'but she has absolutely a rock'n'roll mentality. So, I encouraged her: "If you have an idea, however ridiculous, do it. All the way." Rock'n'roll is supposed to stun. And appal. She wanted to shake up the industry, and I'd compare her to Bowie way before Madonna in terms of bringing alternative culture into the mainstream. She is *anarcho-punk*.'

At the 2009 MTV Music Video Awards, Lady Gaga sang 'Paparazzi' and 'hung' herself from the roof dripping in fake blood. She'd already worn a bird's-nest headpiece while sitting in the audience and then, picking up her 'Best New Artist' award (which she dedicated to 'God and the gays'), wore an all-over blood-red see-through lace gown, matching face-sock and spiky foot-high hell-crown (an Alexander McQueen spectacular). This unleashed a torrent of venomous mockery which exposed, overnight, just what Lady Gaga intended to expose through her shock-art provocation. One male host on an American entertainment website deemed Gaga 'an attention whore' with 'a busted face' who 'gains attention for her bullshit songs by putting bird's-nests on her face. I *hate* her!' 'It's the way she expresses herself,' countered his female co-host, 'and I know you're against that.' '*The way she expresses herself*,' he sneered. 'Oh, *please*.'

In an airy, white rectangular photo studio in North London, Lady Gaga had called for 'a creative meeting'. She was joined by six members of her Haus of Gaga team, the ten-strong collective who styled and physically built her visual extravaganzas, mostly big, older men, campy New York characters bearing elaborate tattoos. Alongside the four-strong, all-male *Q* visuals team, everyone was seated around an elongated sofa while Gaga stood barefoot at one end, still in her black silk dressing-gown, dangling from her daintily outstretched hand a silver studded harness bearing a medium-sized, inky-blue, strap-on dildo. For days, as approved by the Haus, *Q* Visuals had believed today's cover shoot was a death-related concept involving a hangman's noose. Discovering this earlier today, Gaga was unimpressed (communication with her Haus had evidently broken down), seeing a repeat of the recent MTV Awards.

'So, what I would like to do instead is make beautiful photography out of the most humorous rumour of my life thus far, that I have a penis,' she announced, exactly five foot zero and commanding the room like the mythological fifty-foot woman. 'So, we're gonna work this in: on my face, covering my eyes, folded into my hair. It's a statement about my femininity and makes fun of the hilarity of the media. And it's something that everybody will talk about, which I know is what you guys want too. I wanna do something memorable and ground-breaking and the whole world will say, "What the fuck is happening?"'

I was thrilled, seeing an unprecedented act of punk rock insurrection while *Q* Visuals was perplexed, not only blithely creatively undermined but now with an obscenity issue pending (while phone calls to publishers were hastily made). Twenty minutes of dildo placement discussion later, *Q* Visuals suggested wearing it inside her trousers, 'so the bulge is absolutely there, but it's not just you with a strap-on.' 'I am impressed,' beamed Gaga. 'And I am *rarely* impressed! I *love* it. Let's go!'

Everything Lady Gaga did was for a convention-boggling reason, the world's only female pop icon who deliberately presented herself as significantly less attractive than she really was, via comedy-ghoul make-up, or dressing up like a pile of Post-it notes, and less vocally astounding than she really was via demented foghorn singing. Fans were 'little monsters' because they were weirdos just like her, 'and they have a freak in me they can hang out with', describing herself as both 'a loser in love' and an emblem to the insecure, 'people who feel innately insecure, not just in adolescence, but always'.

Six years previously, as a teenage art student, she'd been obsessed with surrealism, Damien Hirst and New York installation artist Spencer Tunick, who specialised in huge groups of naked people in highly public spaces, and was repeatedly arrested for obscenity.

'I wrote about the death of God in relation to shock-art and analysed Tunick,' explained Gaga. 'Why are people so offended by the naked, organic person? And they're not offended by the evil that's surrounding them in Times Square? The commercialism, corporate America? And I talked about how money ruined this world and how the apocalypse has already happened. Racism, gay-bashing, wars, the presidents we've been through, [she whispered] *we're already in it*. So, now we must be joyful and rebuild.'

This was the twenty-first-century version of the eternal rock'n'roll blueprint, raging-against-the-Man, only this time wearing, say, a leather-studded golf course on its head. She was a life-long pop culture analyst – 'I used to read tabloids like textbooks, with a scholarly approach' – the first pop superstar to grow up through the decade of celebrity culture-led tabloid hysteria and come to embody the very thing she was satirising. A life-long feminist, she wore those high-waisted glittering pants, back in winter 2008, knowing the paparazzi would carry her image to the masses. 'I wore [them] so often and so frequently and so repetitively and consistently and diligently and punctually,' she explained, bizarrely, 'that it became a true statement about my freedom. I believe in the power of propaganda, of repetition.'

She eschewed the celebrity lifestyle, lived on the road, barely went out in public, worked to a self-imposed punishing work schedule and rarely gave interviews. 'I want,' she spelled out, 'to be detached from humanity, to create an escapist environment where my fans and myself are safe.'

Our literal-minded contemporary media, however, often failed to recognise even her most straightforward metaphorical intent, her MTV Awards fame-kills spectacle causing widespread consternation.

'Everybody was *freaking out*,' she recalled. 'MTV said, "What do you wanna do?", I said, "I wanna bleed to death for four minutes," and they're like [face of total confusion]. So I said, "The world is looking for a story about me being fallen. So maybe if I just show them what it looks like, they'll stop looking. Here's what I look like while I'm dying." And I bled to death surrounded by flashing lights and was hung like a martyr in all of my blonde glory. Like many others before. Princess Diana. Marilyn Monroe. Anna Nicole Smith.'

Even her label Interscope had been bewildered. Their initial reaction to her proposed artwork for *The Fame Monster* (in 2009's expanded reissue of *The Fame*), of a long, black-wigged Gaga crying black tears, was met with disbelief (a full nine years before Billie Eilish cried black tears in her 'When the Party's Over' video), insisting 'we need something beautiful'. Gaga denied them. 'Because the *last* thing any young person needs is another photograph of a woman rubbing her glistening tits, enjoying life, because that's not how we *fucking feel*.'

She pulled together her splayed silken dressing gown, suddenly self-conscious.

'If you're reading this article and think, "Lady Gaga is wildly pretentious and thinks she's the cat's miaow," that's not the case,' she wanted us to know. 'I just take what I do seriously. My art is liberation. Things confine us as human beings, as a society. And I want to *free you*.'

To the sounds of the Smiths, eighties goth tarts Gene Loves Jezebel and Rozalla's '91 rave-up anthem 'Everybody's Free (To Feel Good)', Lady Gaga, like a groin-possessed hip-hop dude, was persistently rearranging her crotch, tugging away and saying out loud, 'Gaahd, I'm glad I don't have a dick.' Standing in an expanse of white as the photo shoot began, she was *stunning*, soft pastel-pink make-up a winning contrast to the industrial strands of her chain-mail S&M 'vest', black liquid leggings holding the dildo in strategic position. With the two creative teams now gathered round the photographer's computer screen, the darkly comic caper became ever more surreal as ten men, both gay and straight, decided in some solemnity, 'There's not enough cock.' With the dildo too subtle under the black leggings, Gaga was also dismayed: 'I want it to be Mick Jagger.'

Over the next three hours, the shoot slowly disintegrated over lighting concerns, 'my eyes look dead', or it accentuated 'my weak chin'. The Haus of Gaga consoled her.

'But don't you like *this*, Gaga?' the make-up artist asked, circling his hand around his face. 'Face-wise? In this world? It's beautiful!'

'No,' she replied. 'It's yellow.'

Stubborn, single-minded, and determined to realise her vision, she offered some alternative lighting examples on her manager's PC, shots bathed in red lighting, where you could barely see her face. A Mexican standoff ensued.

'Listen to what I'm saying,' urged Gaga, more forthright and uncompromising than global pop entities twice her age, 'I just don't like the photo. I want this to feel beautiful, feminine and sexy but still be hard. And this is just *flat*.'

Soon, her invincible demeanour dissolved. 'I'm stressed,' she frowned, head down, arms tight around her chest. She retreated to her dressing room where a phone call from Interscope, about marketing, further upset her. Re-emerging, she was now in tears, wearing enormous shades, apologising and saying she'd have to leave and hoped to reschedule the shoot. 'I'm just not in a good place right now.'

Over the next month, negotiations to reschedule failed: Gaga's management would only use their own photographer, which *Q* rejected, and our mooted on-the-road adventure in America was cancelled. 'Bad Romance', meanwhile, stormed to No. 1 across the planet.

In December 2009, the month Lady Gaga was nominated for five Grammys, the wings of her ever-accelerating spacecraft began to show signs, perhaps not of falling off, but of flapping in distress. She broke down in tears on stage in LA on being told she'd now sold eight million albums (exactly one year previously, she'd supported Natasha Bedingfield at the same venue). By early January 2010, she was forced to upgrade her tour venues to accommodate the huge production (which she'd overspent on by £2 million), tweeting an apology to fans over 'a serious error by my production staff'. Delirious live reviews were now tempered by reports of on-stage exhaustion and further open weeping at the increasingly overwhelming adoration of her fans. On 14 January, she finally collapsed, passing out minutes before a show in Indiana, and was forced to cancel on doctors' orders (exhaustion, dehydration, dizziness, an irregular heartbeat). Lady Gaga was indeed, it seemed, dying hard.

In February 2010, *Q* magazine published its Lady Gaga story featuring the 'flat' photos, an arresting, semi-naked cover image causing a minor media hoo-ha in the UK, and an outright ban 'in some US outlets' (claimed *Q*) because a portion of her breast below the nipple could be seen – with no mention, staggeringly, of the dildo-shaped commotion in her liquid, spikey-sided leggings. With 'Bad Romance' still ricocheting out from every radio, we were still living in Lady Gaga's Moment, even as a senior *Q* staffer relived the photo shoot farrago in a talking head TV appearance as evidence of her supposedly appalling diva behaviour (to my mind a man unable to accept a young woman taking control of her own image). She had, he maintained, 'rocked up four hours late' to the shoot (he wasn't even there, and she was less than one hour late, early by industry standards), while a single comment from a Visuals team member, having now finally seen the 'Bad Romance' video, told me everything I needed to know.

'Unfortunately,' the quip went, 'she's good.'

Lady Gaga was far from your average pop star, a kind of disco Dalek with the brain of Vivienne Westwood, whirling in delirium on the edge of the twelfth dimension. Not everything she did back then succeeded, her creative ambitions too unfathomably berserk, but when it did, this truly *was* pop genius at work.

Exactly one month after *Q*'s shoot collapsed in November 2009, she performed on the *X Factor* in a giant bathtub dressed as a devil-horned industrial batwoman hollering 'I'm a free bitch baby!', weeks before captivating the Queen with her piano on stilts, and took 'Bad Romance' to No. 1 in the UK not once but twice. Not bad for a twenty-three-year-old five-foot goth with a complex over a weak chin.

Back on her silvery penthouse sofa in the May Fair Hotel she'd contemplated the world's other great Gaga misconception, that she wore her persona like a cloak, discarded in relief after an exhausting day of artifice.

'No, it's just me and I'm not exhausted,' she shimmered that day. 'Y'know, we always laugh when we get to some major magazines and they're like, [high-camp voice] "*So.* The art direction of the shoot *is*, we want the world to see *the real you.*" [She squeezed my thigh.] And I'm sitting there thinking, "These fucking people don't get it *at all.*" Because it's been gone for so long, I think, they've forgotten what it could be. It's mind-blowing to me. That's like saying [she whispered conspiratorially], "We know you're full of shit. But it's fine, *we* get it. So, let's just cut out the bullshit *for one shoot.*" But you don't really wanna get to know me or photograph my soul, you want to do some version of what you already think I am and then expose something that you believe is hidden. When the truth is, me and my big fucking *dick* are all out there for you. But I'm not angry, I'm laughing. The joke is not on *me*, it's on *you.*'

Lady Gaga would go on to become a global pop staple and Hollywood actor, seller of 170 million albums worldwide, winner of thirteen Grammys, eighteen MTV Video Awards and a Best Original Song Oscar in 2019 for 'Shallow', from *A Star Is Born*. Her contributions to the movie's soundtrack that year made her the first woman in history to win an Academy Award, BAFTA, Golden Globe Award and Grammy Award in a single year. She also has nineteen different species of fern named after her by researchers at Duke University in North Carolina, in recognition of her 'fervent defence of equality and individual expression'. She is surely, then, the most successful 'anarcho-punk' of all time.

No joke, indeed.

21

(NO) TYPICAL GIRL

2014, Viv Albertine's memoir Clothes Clothes Clothes, Music Music Music, Boys Boys Boys *transforms her into a reluctant legend*

The Slits, back in those searching days of my early adolescence, meant almost nothing to me. Their 1979 debut album, *Cut*, should've been a seismically pivotal life-changer but I just couldn't hear *the tunes*, man, found no rousing, sing-along melodies in their sparse, shouty, repetitive reggae-dub stylings. Not even in their No. 60 non-hit, the double A-side 'Typical Girls'/'I Heard It Through the Grapevine', the latter a dubby cover of the Marvin Gaye classic, their best-known song and to my ears a threadbare, moth-eaten flannelette duster compared to Marvin's sonically sumptuous Persian rug. The cover of *Cut*, too, perturbed me, the three Slits flagrantly loin-clothed, mud-caked and bare breasted, where in my righteously forming worldview – as a schoolgirl striding down corridors in a silver-grey men's raincoat pretending to be the Bunnymen's Ian McCulloch – androgyny was the only look in (revolutionary) town. But even so, I knew these young women were pioneers, art-punk iconoclasts having their DIY go in a post-punk world with a dearth of female voices.

By 2017, almost four decades later, Pharrell Williams' 'Happy' was the most played song on the planet, Ellie Goulding won Best British Female Solo Artist at the Brit Awards and a post-Brexit Nigel Farage was forever photographed in pubs celebrating the rise of UKIP with a pint of IPA. That year, I'd still never listened to the Slits' now revered *Cut* all the way through and found Viv Albertine far more interesting as an author in her early sixties, whose arresting first autobiography *Clothes Clothes Clothes, Music Music Music, Boys Boys Boys* in 2014 told the compelling story of unfeasible survival through constant, often catastrophic adversity. I'd newly had a book published myself, *I'm Not with the Band* (2016), a comi-tragic thirty-year tale of music, media and misadventure written in the mid-2010s, an increasingly financially perilous era for all music journalists as the music press faded ever further into obsolescence. Aside from *Q*, the only other magazine I occasionally worked for was the *Big Issue* and, as my lifelong pal and fellow journalist Tom 'Tommy the D' Doyle had it at the time, 'Could be worse, Sylv, you could be selling it.'

By 2017 *Clothes . . . Music . . . Boys* had become a best-selling book, which made Viv Albertine dimensions more accessible, known and acclaimed than the Slits ever had, winning *Q* magazine's coveted Maverick Award that year and agreeing to an accompanying interview. Sent on assignment, I felt thrilled to meet her literary self, our rendezvous scheduled in her favourite cake shop in Hackney, East London at 3 p.m. Five hours earlier that day, at 9.50 a.m., my mobile phone rang with an unknown number.

'It's Viv,' came the unexpected voice. 'I'm alright but . . . I just don't wanna do it!'

After several journalistic decades, this was a personal

first. For fifteen minutes Viv Albertine, sometime art-punk renegade turned fearless author, delivered a volley of rationale behind her refusal to either talk to me that day or attend the imminent ceremony.

'I'm not *in* music anymore,' she cringed. 'I only said I'd do it for my daughter, she was so excited, but you can't do things just to please other people, can you? Sorry! I should've said this weeks ago . . .'

The change-of-heart balance was tipped, it turned out, by *Q*'s photographic request, to bring her guitar and record sleeves from those distant, dissident Slits days with her. 'And I don't *care* about it anymore,' she persisted, 'I'd rather turn up with my *Dyson*.'

This was now hilarious to me – definitely an intriguing start should a feature somehow go ahead. She didn't, she added, care about *any* music anymore. 'It's all so fucking middle-class!' she blared and, despite my attempts at persuasion, would not budge. Would she at least *accept* the *Q* award? 'Pff, they won't give it to me now, will they?'

Five days later . . .

Late summer early evening and I was finally perched with Viv Albertine, then sixty-two, in the living room of her high-ceilinged Hackney apartment, her mind having been changed, indeed 'persuaded' by fellow seventies punk pioneer, the DJ/musician/director Don Letts, to accept her maverick mantle. Two nights previously she'd 'dragged' herself on a rare night out to an event where Don delivered the magic words: 'More women should be recognised.' Don was her lone true friend from the punk days. 'Only Don stuck around as a pal,' she noted, pointedly. 'When you're suddenly not in a band anymore, everyone just drops away.'

Her large, two-bedroomed flat was on the ground floor of a modern apartment block – live/work units purpose-built by the EU with an 'artists only' covenant – her living room sparsely furnished with two tables and two retro, green, low-slung armchairs, our voices echoing around mostly bare walls. She was moving soon, downsizing 'to pay off my debts' to a nearby one-bedroom flat after her eighteen-year-old daughter's move to university. The day she left, Viv wept 'non-stop' for two days.

Sipping a fizzy elderflower juice, she was genial, speedy, matter of fact, prone to expansive cursing and stinging, strident opinions – a tangibly heightened energy almost certainly the result of finding interviews 'a pain.' After sporadic solo singer-songwriter years from 2008 to 2014, she'd now abandoned music altogether.

'Music is not a radical artform anymore,' she declared. 'And I'm not interested in anything, any art, unless it makes you want to rebel.'

Since 2014 she'd been mostly known as a writer – 'but knowing me, how long will that last?' – the debut memoir which brought her to me the searing confessional of a uniquely dramatic life, detailing her visceral misfortunes through mid-to-late seventies London. Forensic and fearless, it's an odyssey through furious dissent, genital crabs and musical insurrection, her mates (and sometimes lovers) the mythologised main players of London's punk insurgence. She was a clothes-obsessed regular at Vivienne Westwood and Malcolm McLaren's SEX emporium; Sex Pistol, pal and sometime bandmate Sid Vicious was 'clever' despite being an adult bed-wetter; Johnny Rotten asked her for a blow-job, and she obliged, only to hear him whinge she was 'trying too hard'; Clash guitarist/songwriter Mick Jones was her boyfriend for eighteen months, resulting in an abortion she regretted twenty years later; Johnny Thunders persistently attempted to ply her with heroin. Throughout 2014–15 she relived it all again on a book tour and found the interviews a 'mortifying process'. After decades of no one talking about the Slits, Viv Albertine was suddenly a Legend.

'I thought, "What's this legend bollocks?"' she scoffed. 'I've been sweeping the floor for the last twenty years, picking my nose and going to Sainsbury's.'

She'd already written a second memoir, *To Throw Away Unopened* (later published in 2018), an exploration of 'the fuck up that I am' via her dysfunctional family's secrets, feminism and motherhood, a book she intended to be, unfeasibly, 'even more honest than the first'. Its premise began on the night of her book launch for *Clothes . . . Music . . . Boys*, surrounded by friends and paying audience, when an incoming call pulled her away – her mother had twenty minutes to live.

'I'd hired musicians, lights, was all dressed up, I thought, "I can't go, I can't let these people down",' she confessed. 'That *actually* crossed my mind.'

She left, joining her mum in a hospice for her final hours, all dramatically detailed in the book, including a violent confrontation with her sister as their mother lay dying before them. We weren't to be fooled, however, by her seemingly settled new literary life. Her insecurities remained – 'I don't know if it's any good,' she fretted of the latest book – her finances precarious, earning as a writer, she openly admitted, 'between five and ten [grand a year].'

We talked about the Slits, about their 'relentless battle' in a seventies music industry populated by 'sexist fucked-up twats, and this was the indie labels – and they're *still* like that, sexist old gits with their heads up their arses.'

Their lead singer was fifteen-year-old Ari Up (daughter of Nora Forster, eventual wife of John Lydon), natural-born provocateurs with 'hair sticking out, torn clothes', mixed sexual messages, 'bit of S&M, bit of Brownie uniform', who were banned from hotels and attacked in the street (Ari Up was stabbed, twice).

Prior to our meeting, I'd finally listened to *Cut* all the way through and still found it weird, chaotic reggae music, void of sing-along tunes. Perhaps inspired by Viv's honesty, I made the catastrophic blunder of telling her as much.

'Reggae?' she blinked. '*Oh*. And I wouldn't say it's chaos! Not at all, *no*. They're highly structured songs, with harmonies and considered lyrics.'

Learning nothing from this stinging riposte, I then blurted my teenage reaction to the loinclothed, mud-caked, naked-breasted artwork. Back then, I explained, to me anyway, it wasn't cool for girls to be topless: androgyny was everything.

'Well, we felt androgynous doing *that*,' she recoiled. Suddenly, she was outraged. 'It was totally feminist!' she scolded. 'In the seventies, naked female bodies were about porn, advertising, strewn across cars. Our stance was, "No mate, we're fucking taking our bodies back, fuck off, what the fuck are you looking at?" It was unheard of. And boys were terrified. Even if they were wanking over it. Hahaha! Oh God, Sylvia, you've disappointed me terribly. You didn't *get it*, did you?'

Viv Albertine was, then, someone who cared very deeply about the Slits after all, though this wasn't about sentimentality – she simply 'totally believed in the band'. She saw almost no one from the punk days and ascribed John Lydon's tendency to weep through interviews these days not to emotion but 'the beer'.

In 2016, when Vivienne Westwood and Malcolm McLaren's son Joe Corré burnt £5 million worth of punk memorabilia in protest at punk's commodification, she felt nothing.

'I couldn't have cared less, either way,' she assured. 'It was *forty years ago*. People go on and on about punk, it's like an old man going on about the *war* . . .'

Viv Albertine and her younger sister were brought up by their single mum in then threadbare-liberal Muswell Hill, North London, after their dad, 'a tyrant' who beat his daughters with a belt, disappeared overnight when Viv was eleven. As a kid she was so shy she'd soil herself in her classroom chair rather than put her hand up to use the bathroom. Music was everything – Bowie, John Lennon, soon Patti Smith – an adolescent boiling with 'the furies', expelled from school, an art-school drop-out entrenched in the violent London punk scene, a second-wave feminist fighting for the Revolution. She traced her uncompromising mindset back to her mother, who instilled in her a militant independence.

'My mother's generation missed out because of the war,' she said, fingers digging into her scalp, sweeping back lengthy hair. 'They felt so cheated, by life. They had independence during the war and then had to go back, into the home, to let the men come back. Then they were in the home in the Swinging Sixties, missing out again. And they poured their resentment into their daughters. Certainly, my mother did.'

She paused, as indignation burst through.

'When I started promoting the [first] book, all the male interviewers would be, "Ooh, Johnny Rotten, ooh Mick Jones, did he teach you how to play guitar?"' she remembered, with increasing disdain. 'All they wanted to know about was the guys. "Tell us about Sid Vicious." What, Sid Vicious, the spotty drug addict? Who didn't write an original song? Him? It dawned on me, "Shut the fuck up about the guys." The reason I am who I am is not because of Mick Jones, who I knew for eighteen months. My *mother* made me a punk.'

Beyond the Slits, who split up amicably in 1981 (Ari Up was pregnant), Viv zig-zagged along the wayward creative's pot-holed yellow-brick-road. For years already she'd been 'fiddling electricity meters, fiddling the dole', became an aerobics teacher in the eighties, a filmmaker in the nineties, eventually marrying a biker ten years her junior who once had Slits posters on his wall but was nonetheless conventional, an illustrator who believed in stability and making money ('Which I found attractive'). She became obsessed with having a child, almost died through an ectopic pregnancy, resulting in IVF necessity thereafter and 'seven years of hell', spent mostly drenched in her own miscarriage blood. Six weeks after the eventual birth of her daughter in 1999, an out-of-the-blue bloodbath saw her diagnosed with near-fatal cervical cancer. Unemployment, inertia, depression and divorce ensued, all agonisingly documented in her first book.

'But the thing is, I underplayed everything that happened to me in that book,' she insisted, astoundingly. 'Everything was ten times worse. Even my [ex]-husband, who I don't talk to that much, said "You totally underplayed what we went through." I had to, it was too much. I was on my knees, I left out huge operations, massive things that had gone wrong, traumas, constantly covered in blood, it was like [seventies Stephen King horror classic] *Carrie*. Guys fucked me over, the industry fucked me over. But it would've unbalanced the book.'

The couple moved to Hastings with their young child, where Viv – in recovery from cancer – found herself in domestic prison, unable to work, financially dependent on her husband. 'My mother always said, "Never rely on a man for money",' she noted, regretfully. 'And now I was no different to a woman in the fifties. I thought, "I'm *stuck*."' By 2008 she was edging back towards music, which her controlling husband then forbade her to pursue, telling her, 'You're not an artist, you're a wanker.'

The marriage inevitably collapsed, an inherited £17,000 from her grandmother allowing Viv, finally, to divorce.

'I've talked to a lot of [female] artists over the years, and they've all found it hard to find a partner,' she pointed out. 'Girls are happy to enable, while he makes his music, paints, whatever, but guys don't like it the other way around. Maybe they want the attention like their mothers gave them. They don't like it when you're away. My husband always thought I was fucking other people, at the age of forty-eight, with my kid. We didn't even do that in the Slits, let alone now! It's the male mentality, "Well, what would *I* do?" Because they don't have the imagination.'

The impact of her violent, abandoning late father had lasted 'forever', convinced she was blueprinted for doomed romance. 'Even if it's nothing to do with the men I choose and what total rubbish gits they are, it just *doesn't work*.' She was, in fact, done with relationships. 'I'm not able to compromise. I look around me [at women friends] and think, "How do they bear it?" People I dumped twenty years ago! I couldn't bear them *then*, never mind now.'

She felt no connection, whatsoever, to men.

'I just glimpse bits of oppression in them, bits of sexism, it's all too clear to me,' she reasoned. 'I don't look up to men. I don't want one in my home. It's all a bit of a con. I have absolutely *wrung that tea towel dry*. My daughter says, "Oh, but you just stay *in* all the time." Yeah, and that'd be sad if I hadn't been going out since age eleven, partying and travelling. If I hadn't been hassled, if I hadn't fucked a load of guys, married a guy. Honestly, I'm saying this from a position of extreme knowledge.'

Today, without their cumbersome burden, she was free.

'I can write books because of it,' she carried on. 'I've taken that whole waste of space out of my head. It is a *huge* relief. To be an artist you have to be a selfish cunt. Men can do it, they're channelled, don't mind who they hurt. We're brought up to nurture and enable and smile. And now, for the first time in my life, I can write what the fuck I want. You've got to do it alone.'

The last line in her first book, however, says this: 'I still believe in love.'

'It's the only lie in the book,' she now confessed. 'I had to give the reader *something*, to show I wasn't completely beaten. And I wasn't completely beaten. I'm more beaten *now*. But maybe everyone, after a certain age, is a bit broken.'

As she talked on she reclined, ever further, into the back of her armchair, becoming more reflective, more melancholy, as she finally slowed down. Her purpose today, it seemed, was to spell out, however brutally, what it takes to be a maverick, using her life as a cautionary tale, especially for young women. Last year she'd given a talk to school leavers at her daughter's comprehensive, introducing herself with the requisite positive resumé: she'd been in a band, was a solo artist, she'd written books.

'And then I said, "Now I'm going to give you my other CV,"' she recalled. 'Single parent mum, no money, council flat, dad fucked off, did shit at school, expelled, cancer, abortions, miscarriages, divorce, de-de-de. Remember that. Every time you read "This person's so great, oh, they made it when they were twenty-six," there will be an alternative CV in there *somewhere*. We've got all the slogans for young girls, "be who you are, take risks . . . be the maverick!" But if you aren't "pop" and middle-class and haven't got the bank of Mum and Dad, it's a struggle. You will be lonely. You will be poor, probably, for a very long time. If not forever.'

She contemplated her Maverick Award.

'Being outside means you have to be a bit of a loser,' she decided, in her matter-of-fact way. 'So, it's nice that's being rewarded, instead of people being rewarded for having loads of guitar lessons and going to university. I was a shy, useless, done-fuck-all-with-my-life, loser. And I still see myself as that, actually, inside.'

Really?

'I just can't pretend I'm hip, or not broken, or not sad. I *am*,' she replied. 'I can't be bothered to hide it anymore, Sylvia, or pretend. It doesn't mean I can't laugh or put all my energy into a book or fight for something I believe in. But I am broken, and I am sad. Even though it's uncool. I don't care anymore.'

She eyed the recorder.

'Are we done?'

Almost. Another book phrase came to my mind: as a young girl, she wrote, she'd felt 'left out of life'. And now?

'I feel the same now,' came the reply. 'Because I haven't played the game. But I have my home. And my daughter. Those two things redeemed me. And a certain amount of freedom. But there is a price. *This* is the price.'

Here, there came a lengthy pause.

'Can we *really* stop now? Can you switch that off!?'

She pondered the rest of her evening. 'I'll probably read,' she decided, literature being her favoured artform today, the one that's never let her down. Mostly dramatic, profound novels, by women. There would be no TV, definitely no music and no pleasing other people. Viv Albertine would be in peace, in silence, alone. Forever staying in, on the outside.

*

Eight years later, in 2025, the Slits version of 'I Heard It Through the Grapevine' soundtracked the debut UK TV ad for Primark, a youthfully exuberant denim campaign. Yet another example of where most of the revenue streams are for the majority of musicians today: anywhere but in music.

22

BOMB DISNEYLAND

2019, renegade cul-de-sac dwellers Fat White Family release Serfs Up! *and finally trouble the UK charts at No. 17*

In 2019, Fat White Family, the narcotically ravaged, squat-rock degenerates who emerged from the swamp in 2011 (Peckham, South London), were arguably the very last of their iconoclastic kind, a band defibrillating the spirit of offensive chaos to a flatlined contemporary culture. That year Ed Sheeran had been the UK's dominant musical force for years, Gen Z had never known a world where music was paid for, *The Crown* had been Netflix's greatest success since 2016 and Kardashian half-sibling Kylie Jenner's announcement of the birth of her daughter was outperformed by an egg – a stock photo of a real egg – for the planet's most-liked photo on Instagram after a viral social media campaign (fifty-two million likes). Pop culture to me was now a distant constellation teeming with unfathomable forms, as it would be, and surely should be, at my then fifty-something age, still working for the now equally middle-aged *Q* magazine in what would become the last year of its life, before Covid switched off its life support machine forever. President Donald Trump, meanwhile, who'd been legged up into power by an ever more 'disruptive' Facebook, was impeached to no impact whatsoever and the UK elected Boris Johnson as its comedy Prime Minister. The word 'maverick', now, was far more readily ascribed to the planet's wayward right-wing leaders than any element of antiquated rock'n'roll.

Fat White Family, my lone hope for carousing mischief, were giving it their best scattershot curveball anyway, led by Lias Saoudi, their provocateur frontman of Yorkshire/Algerian descent, whose life in music had been defined by itinerant destitution, obscene depravity and cock-out on-stage antics. Their original mission, Lias had said, was 'to upset people', to reignite lost seditionary values. Accordingly, they wrote songs called 'Bomb Disneyland', 'Is It Raining in Your Mouth?' and 'Cream of the Young', their signature woozy-grooved psyche-rock sounds buoyed by 'comedy' lyrical themes of Nazis, paedophilia, ejaculation, domestic violence and murder.

In 2019 I saw them play live for the first time and was bewitched, the shirtless Lias the kind of prowling, screaming, shock-art renegade blueprinted by Iggy Pop back in those far-off seventies (and for Lias, a guiding forefather). He had a brand-new scar, running five inches along his neckline, from his right ear around his throat, the result of a botched, then corrected, operation to remove a branchial cyst in late November 2018. A mere two months later he was shaking his shaggy-maned head so violently his face was a literal *blur* (definitely not what any doctor would've ordered). We were in the 200-capacity Lexington bar in North London, Lias moving like an undulating sex fiend but keeping his skinny jeans on – no early-years knob-out tomfoolery here – and where beer was once his on-stage staple (and a spiralling head full of E, acid and cocaine), he now wielded a bottle of water, a slight muscle definition to his skinny frame, as if – oh no! – he'd finally succumbed to the gym. Out in the crowd, the sixties-born old guard were here, Jarvis Cocker and Primal Scream's Bobby Gillespie, giving the nod to the kind of psychotic musical outlaws who'd informed their worldview forever, now an endangered species on the verge of full extinction.

Five days later...

Lias Saoudi slid into a booth in the Trinity pub, Brixton, a slight figure in a peach-striped vintage shirt, sipping a Guinness and puffing on a slim, discreet vape. This supposed terror-rock madman had unusually kind eyes, *pretty* eyes, as black as deep space. And he wasn't sober and drug-free at the Lexington, after all. Of course he wasn't.

'I've worked out the ideal amount to go on stage with,' he confided, cheerfully. 'Finally, after ten years of painstaking research. One to two Imodium, to stop you shitting yourself beforehand – I get the Fear bad, y'know? – two tequilas, two Guinness, two Red Bull and two to four drops of magic mushroom tincture. It was a revelation. I didn't even feel like doing any gak afterwards. Of course I did at about 6 a.m. So that's what I'm rolling with from now on. I need a system that works! That doesn't run you into the ground. You've got to be professional about your drug use in a group like this.'

No bands in 2019 talked this talk or walked this walk (and none have since), a band evangelically devoted to not only excess and its resultant psychological cluster-bomb, but who questioned masculinity and pursued a quest for artistic freedom at all acutely high costs. Lias had an accent which veered from South London to Irish, sounding unfeasibly Welsh at times, like Michael Sheen occupying the spirit of Richey Manic. We contemplated the scar he called 'wicked', the branchial cyst a birth defect, 'like your body trying to grow a gill, basically'. He looked like he'd had his throat slashed.

'Too late to lie about it now,' he smiled, sipping his Guinness. 'Could've said that was [combative founding member] Saul, couldn't I? "This is when I sacked him. It got bad, man. But we've still got the music."'

And he laughed, an infectious 'hyuck hyuck!' gurgle.

The Fat Whites had emerged with a mission: to rekindle the long-doused flames of prole art threat, incorporating comedy rock'n'roll shenanigans.

'It was, "Where's all the humour and the sex?"' he balked, of the early 2010s creative wilderness they formed in. 'No jokes. Never any jokes! I can't really sing, it wasn't like a career choice, but my favourite bands were always a bit kinky and funny and outrageous. And a bit sensual.'

The early years were, he marvelled, 'a carnival of booze and drugs', a band of merry men in their early twenties living in the Queens Head pub in Brixton, 'everyone in the kitchen, shirtless, dancing to Springsteen, innocent, no expectations'. His wingman, experimental sound-smith, co-songwriter, guitarist and Libertines obsessive Saul Adamczewski, was a considerably *more* wayward character even if he was, by 2019, no longer a heroin addict. The core musical duo of Lias and Saul modelled the Fat Whites on the Fall – 'an idea that other people came in and out of; when you get sick of 'em, sack 'em' – always the Fat Whites as long as himself and Saul remained, a symbiotic double-helix beholden to each other like the Ant 'n' Dec of provocative sleaze-rock. 'I'm Dec,' blurted Lias, 'he's *definitely* Ant!'

Saul had been seemingly born mentally askew (in ways that

Ant McPartlin surely wasn't), diagnosed as a kid with conduct disorder (official definition: a severe condition characterised by hostile and sometimes physically violent behaviour and a disregard for others), was expelled from school aged eleven for attacking a teacher, evolving into an adolescent prone to depression, agoraphobia and personality disorders. 'I've had periodic moments of insanity throughout my life,' Saul told me later that day, a physically striking man with a missing front tooth wearing an orange Kangol hat, an orange-and-green-checked lumber jacket, what appeared to be baggy beige woollen tights and a billowing black rubber overcoat. It was 5 p.m., he'd been up all night and day (cocaine and Valium were involved), his enormous pale blue eyes sunk into moats of surrounding grey. 'Music is the ultimate way of avoiding work,' he surmised. 'Without music, I'd just be a bum.'

Back in November 2015 Saul was sacked from the Fat Whites after a gig in Paris on the night of the Bataclan terror attacks. By then he was a long-entrenched heroin addict who persuaded the band the venue was the safest place to stay; in reality, he'd arranged to meet his dealer post-show. Next morning the horrified band took off in the tour bus without him. After their offensively titled 2013 debut album *Champagne Holocaust*, their already-recorded second album, *Songs for Our Mothers*, was mostly a threadbare musical void, most of the band at the time, noted Lias, 'hooked on smack, we were falling apart', his relationship with Saul 'terrible', the arguments 'barbaric'. Through 2015 they'd show up to gigs 'and there'd be people there waiting with heroin, we became *that* group'. Lias' addictions, meanwhile, were mostly cocaine and sundry 'uppers'.

'I'd started to use heroin towards the end, after Saul left,' he confessed, with a mischievous smile. 'He was the barrier between me and getting a toke. "No, go'n fuck yourself, I'm the junkie, I need it." So then I'd be, "gimme a tickle of that," from Nathan [his brother, the Fat Whites keyboard player], who was also on it. I dabbled but never really slipped in.'

Saul took to rehab in Mexico and Las Vegas, Lias firstly to a hut in Cambodia, alone, where he read literature, smoked weed and took magic mushrooms, then Sheffield, with Nathan, 'to get away from the drugs and the madness'. They built a make-shift studio, obsessed over Kanye West's *Yeezus* and the dubby B-side of Wham!'s 'Club Tropicana', 'Blue (Armed With Love)', Lias a life-long George Michael fan. 'Because he's the best, and that song is amazing, really sad.'

Now mercifully free from crack and smack, they took to ketamine with gusto. 'Me and Nathan were bustin' it the whole time,' beamed Lias, finding the horse tranquilliser an aid to creativity, 'taking just enough so you've still got motor function, but your mind is sideways'. *Serfs Up!* emerged, the most musically dynamic album of their lives – soaring, propulsive, featuring Gregorian chants and luscious strings, even if, as Lias indicated, 'the insidious aspects are tucked in'. The corking single 'Feet' was about anal sex with a man, lyrics loosely based on Jean Genet's *Prisoner of Love*. 'Non-stop all-round buggery,' savoured Lias. 'Sexual confusion is pretty much all I write about. I don't know what issues exactly I'm trying to get at, it's a compulsion. It's romantic.'

What he wasn't doing that year was directly addressing the political turmoil we'd all lived through since the Brexit/Trump-dominated 2016.

'If ever there was a time to look inside as opposed to outside it's now,' he pondered, those blackest eyes unblinking. 'Because we live in an age of . . . fundamentalist narcissism. *For all*. I don't know anything anymore, does anybody? Where are we, what's happening?'

During the Sheffield sessions, the newly heroin-clean Saul

returned to the Fat Whites, even if reconciliation turned to friction once more, ending in 'violent' arguments.

'As a group of people, you'd be hard pressed to cherry pick more dysfunctional individuals, myself included,' surmised Lias, evenly. 'I think it's because we found each other, y'know? When you find your kind it's like falling in love, it's unavoidable after that, you're just *in*. And then everything became fungal. Years later you realise not one of you has any remotely reasonable outlook on how you integrate with the rest of reality. It's . . . breakdowns galore.'

Lias Saoudi was a wry, comical, eloquent, charismatic, unique and profoundly smart character, with no trace of his on-stage exorcism anger. He was also, perhaps unfeasibly, a positive person, sweetly bewildered and grateful for the musical life he'd carved 'out of nothing, I can't believe my luck, that I've ended up doing this *at all*.' Nonetheless, he'd wilfully chosen an acutely precarious life and could've given a boggling TED Talk on the outsider art-rock existence, the 'perfect storm, all the clichés' of ego, insecurity, inter-band power struggles, drug abuse, loss of identity, confusion, ill health and arrested emotional development.

'Clichés are a key component to being in a band,' he carried on. 'The minute you say you're in a band, you're a cliché. You might as well go the whole hog and do it right, y'know? Most people don't have time to go off and become smack heads and recover in the desert and all that carry on. You can squeeze it in if you're a musician. It's a valuable service we're providing! How does it feel to have that big a hangover? We'll scout it out for you.'

He contemplated his impulse for on-stage nudity and excrement as body lotion.

'When you're completely naked and covered in your own shit, it's impossible to be embarrassed about performing the songs wrong anymore,' he explained. 'It can't get any more humiliating, it's liberating. What can they laugh at now? It just feels really good to be completely naked.'

Lias was born in Southampton to an Algerian immigrant dad, 'an Algerian mountain man with a penchant for the Eagles' and a Yorkshire coalmining mum (who was there in the days of the early eighties miners' strikes). At four, five years old he got his knob out in public for the first time, at primary school, when the teacher left the room.

'I got on the table and pulled my pants down, started wafting it about,' he recalled, merrily. 'Got in real shit with my parents.'

He constantly moved around, first to Ayrshire in Scotland, then Cookstown, Northern Ireland when his parents split up (he was twelve, Nathan nine). He was shy, non-confrontational, insecure, often silent and alone, in a house with no music, banned from watching TV. He was bullied and racially abused, called a 'paki' and loathed the sectarian politics, a pupil in a protestant school whose blazer featured the red hand of Ulster.

'You awake politically really early there, I couldn't stand it, didn't get on with the people. I was an oddball, a misfit, for sure. In an endless abyss of boredom.'

Soon he was a self-taught scholar of literature (Steinbeck, James Joyce, Jean Genet, Nabokov), of history and art, a painter and sketcher by aged twelve, obsessed with the nude works of Egon Schiele, painting photo-realist self-portraiture, half naked. A dream emerged, for art school in London. 'London became like this jewel on the horizon,' he reminisced. 'I had a plan worked out very young: I'm gonna go to this school and get my head down for six years, read books, do A-Levels, paint and draw.'

Three As at A-Level took him to London's prestigious Slade School of Art, aged eighteen, where he met privileged people for the first time, the wealthy and the public-school educated, alien beings built from entitlement and invincible self-belief.

'A wolf pit,' he described it. 'I didn't have the confidence necessary to project myself into this environment. I *shrank*. I got into drugs, parties. It was frustration. I thought everything was unfair. My class conscience really kicked in. I became an angry young man.'

He was kicked out, then reinstated, graduated, despite being at a huge financial disadvantage.

'I'd be doing a degree show with £400 and the girl next to me in the studio spent £10,000 on hers,' he scoffed. 'Well, the fucking playing field is just not level, this is horseshit. That was *the war*, for me. You're all connected to such and such a family and I'm *fucked*. I've got nothing. I don't have anywhere to go in London. I *hated* it. I wanted to make these people *sick*.'

Society then offered this bright, creative, ambitious young man no footholds to his dreams whatsoever. A punk rock spirit sparked into volcanic life. With no money, he existed in squats and on drug dealers' floors, met Saul and created ramshackle Libertines pretenders the Saoudis alongside brother Nathan, certain he was an impostor anyway.

'Music was abstract,' he felt. 'People who come from the *moon* do that, *you* don't, and no matter how much you wanna do that it's not possible and you're an idiot if you think it is.'

Soon came the bollock-naked, shit-smearing era, alongside shrieking incomprehensible lyrics from *Champagne Holocaust*.

'It had taken eight years to build up that level of resentment, for *everybody*,' he recalled. 'It was fear, I think. Slade was a big part of it. Because it gave me access to culture. I can pour scorn on middle-class people all I want but at the end of the day it's obviously a rejection thing. I know there's no nobility in poverty, I'm not an idiot. It's, "I want what *you* have." Nice conversation. Decent food.'

His lifestyle that day in 2019 had improved, even if 'everybody's still broke, living like dogs'. In his early thirties, he was now renting a room in a flat share in Streatham, South London, even if Nathan was currently living at the bottom of his bed. His expectations for their new album remained realistic, even low.

'Owning a flat in London is a pipe dream,' he knew for certain. 'But that's *the dream*. I'm just grateful I can afford a room. I can close the door.'

He knew what he'd like to do if and when the Fat Whites finally imploded.

'I'd like to write a book,' he decided. 'I was in Algeria last year, I tried to do Ramadan, I lasted four days. If you don't have Allah, it's just merciless introspection. But I kept a little diary for the first time. And had an idea of writing about ten years of serious hedonism through the prism of Ramadan. A sort of penance, for ten years of hideous decadence. The severe egotism of taking to the Atlas mountains to pen your experiences, it has a whiff of proper bastard about it, which I quite like.'

Until then, he'd carry on touring, in significantly improved conditions: the Fat Whites now had a proper tour bus.

'So you can lie down!' he serenaded. 'That's what kills you in a van, never lying straight, with a sixty-two-day hangover. I can't be at that carry-on anymore. I need my chunks of carrot backstage. Bagels. Hummus. Dips.'

He hadn't, he assured me, been down the gym. But he had been down the sauna.

'I do go in for a sauna and a steam,' he chuckled. 'Started in Sheffield, nothing to do, I'll try and get healthy. Sit there with your brethren, naked, sweat it out. I think the gym's years away but the manager says, "If you're gonna keep getting your shirt off, after this album you'll have to go down the gym." That was hard to hear. After all that . . . *spa*.'

His reputation, I ventured, was now *in tatters*.

'I know,' he chortled, imagining the jeers. '"It's all bullshit, man, they all went to Eton as well."'

*

Five years later, in 2023, following a profoundly troublesome lockdown, the Fat Whites had all but imploded: a lethal increase in fractious intra-band relationships meant Saul and Nathan were no longer in the group, and no friendship lingered for Lias and Saul, although Nathan would always remain Lias' little brother. Their December 2023 single, *Religion For One*, completed with the remaining Fats, arrived into my inbox with a promotional missive, a righteous analysis on the prevailing culture from an acutely withering Lias.

'Abject narcissism is our only real code of conduct anymore,' he decreed. 'Everything is thinly veiled self-interest. The postmodern post social media condition constitutes a complete death of outwardness. We are smothered by the infinite present. We have swapped art for the history of art. The game is up. The party's over ... NO SURRENDER!'

EPILOGUE

REQUIEM

I am now properly ancient. Newly stumbled into my sixties – *sixties!?!?* – with friends who are grandparents, now 'laughably' closer to death than I am to any youthquake uprising I've no right to be any part of. I'm still nosy, of course, and if there's anything 'happening' I want to know, even though I'm permanently convinced there's no shock-of-the-new to be found, musically at least, merely something quite good echoing something from the past, which I passionately loved, but never *quite* as good. Maybe something from forty-five years ago, which is the equivalent of someone in 1981 sounding a bit like Bing Crosby.

Some music fanatics, naturally, are having none of this. Some even find contemporary pop culture not only as vibrant as it ever was, but in some ways dynamically more so. Good on them, I'm saying, there's enough to be miserable about. In 2024 I spoke with Clara Amfo, then thirty-nine, the broadcaster, TV presenter and former host of Radio 1's new music flagship show *Future Sounds*, and proffered what's now, to me, a widespread theory: that music is no longer at the centre of youth culture, its once all-important tribal affiliations long gone – instead, the phone is, hosting its multiverse of entertainment.

'Wow, that is a hot take!' she exclaimed, an exuberant personality we've seen co-presenting the BBC's Glastonbury coverage since 2015. 'But I love how it's not as tribal anymore. I'm seeing a beautiful amalgamation. Especially at festivals or gigs, you see all different types of people, all enjoying it. I genuinely find that really exciting. I like the mushing. So, to answer your question, I disagree. I do think that music is still at the centre of youth culture. I *do*. I think other things coexist *alongside* it.'

So, the centre just got bigger?

'Exactly! I think it's still the nucleus.'

Which makes music, in official scientific dimensions, the size of a garden pea in the middle of Wembley Stadium.

Perhaps, though, this Great Mushing, alongside the relative ease of making new music (digitally at least), will provide opportunities for the return of the outsider and, crucially, the working-class voice. Back in 2018, at *Q* magazine's awards show, Jarvis Cocker presented that year's Maverick Award to idiosyncratic, not-so-much outsider as intergalactic boondocks dweller Lawrence (Felt, Denim, Go-Kart Mozart, Mozart Estate). Conditions, Jarvis felt, were now coalescing for the re-emergence of the maverick spirit.

'The one good thing about the collapse of the music industry is the only people making music are people who really wanna do it,' he decided. 'Because nobody's making any money out of it. So you're getting weirdos doing it again. What they get from it is what they get from playing it, not just holding their hands out waiting to get paid. People are making their own entertainment. That's how good things happen.'

In summer 2024, gothy alt-pop insurgent Cassyette, from Essex (real name Cassy Brooking) released her debut album, the frankly titled *This World Fucking Sucks* (No. 15 in the soaraway hit parade). A 'darkness'-fixated artist, she'd been deemed by online music platforms a 'nu-gen hero', by deathless horn-fingered *Kerrang!* magazine 'a modern alternative icon' and numbered fans in Debbie Harry and the Prodigy's Liam Howlett. That year she co-wrote the horror-pop thriller 'Doomsday Blue' for the Irish entry in the 2024 Eurovision Song Contest, performed by non-binary spook-pop spectre Bambie Thug (who came sixth). We had a Zoom conversation in 2023, the then-twenty-nine-year-old wearing a pink hairnet over peroxide hair, the word 'degenerate' and a barbed wire chain tattooed around her throat and, on her back, a tattoo of 'a massive, neo-goth-futuristic batwing situation'. We talked about the misfit mentality today (her fans were called the Degenerates) and the resurgence of the goth aesthetic across music, fashion and the arts: there were, and still are, kids wearing heavily ghoulish make-up, black PVC, with tattoos, piercings and cyber boots in every province in the land (and everywhere else in the Western world). Like so much alternative music today, she'd incorporated goth elements into both her look and sound, which veered from death metal to America's shouty-pop staple Pink. Outspokenly feminist, bipolar disordered and queer, she was a TikTok devotee.

'TikTok has facilitated loads of subcultures,' she enthused. 'Fashion TikTok, if that's on your algorithm, you have things like FairyCore, CottageCore, WhimsiGothCore, it's amazing.'

The difference for the spooky kids today, she pondered, was, 'You don't get bullied for it like you did before, there's definitely more acceptance,' which also meant, 'there's a whole culture that a lot of kids don't understand, they just wanna wear the clothes, but I don't believe in gatekeeping, it's about looking at the positives of that.'

In other words, like every other subculture forever, it's been comprehensively co-opted, mainstreamed and monetised. Throughout 2022, a Burberry couture campaign had been dramatically goth extreme, the Cure sold out three nights at Wembley Arena, the long elusive goth sphinx herself, Siouxsie Sioux, headlined Latitude Festival in 2023 and in 2025 the Tim Burton-directed Addams Family reboot *Wednesday* became the most-watched English-language series in Netflix history. The spirit endured, Cassyette mused, because the pain of being young will always endure, its radical look the outer representation of an inner existential pain.

'It's about your inner darkness,' she confirmed. 'And not conforming. And going as far away as you can from a society that makes you feel uncomfortable. And the patriarchy.'

The most obvious difference between then and now was in lifestyle: alt-pop/rock kids today are not living in drug-bedevilled chaos in threadbare squats, with no electricity, never mind no screens.

'They're very health conscious,' she agreed, adding their focus is on staying in control. 'It's access to fitness people online telling you that you have to do this, that,' she suggested. 'Fourteen-year-olds now look like they're twenty-four, it's mental, I looked awful when I was fourteen! Also, if they get fucked up, people can easily get their phone out and take a photograph, so people are more conscious and behave themselves.'

I wondered if she thought the resurgence could simply be the zeitgeist, Gen Z the apocalyptic thinking, horror-bombarded, digital natives who've grown up convinced the world is fucked, humanity is hideous and the world is run by idiots.

'You've nailed it with that!' she roared. 'And that's where being anti-society, anti-patriarchy comes in, because *fuck this*.'

Ultimately, she was not so very different to every previous rock'n'roll generation, her music, image and message defined by a single word: freedom.

'There came a point where I decided to just do what I want

and wear what I want and you give yourself that freedom,' she concluded. 'I've always believed in just being yourself unapologetically. It's armour in a way, protecting yourself from other people's judgements. Because it's all *so judgey*.'

Perhaps, I posited, not entirely convinced, TikTok could be the place to galvanise a truly revolutionary movement, one which could actually change the world. Did such an idea even exist anymore?

'It could a hundred per cent come from there!' she hollered. 'The subcategories, the algorithm feeds you what you're interested in, so the more you're automatically fed content which influences you, the more content you might start posting and you'll see the community grow. When I first went on TikTok I was the only person screaming on there. And doing death metal. I picked up a following really quickly and then duetting with people and cross-contaminating. It's tapping in, and the more drips into the bath the more it fills up and it's really fucking cool cos that's what's gonna create a revolution!'

So, it was still out there and us old gits who think it's all over could sling our hooks?

'It's not all over!' she guffawed. *'For sure.'*

The spirit of the weirdo, in the creative arts or otherwise, remains immortal. In music we just don't see them like we used to, have them define culture like they used to, have their songs ring throughout history like they used to. Instead, we have everything, everywhere, at exactly the same time and can hardly, simultaneously, see any of it, in an era not only of infinite new artists but an abundance of revivals. Here in the mid-2020s we've not only the return of Britpop thirty years later (reformed bands from the era now number Oasis, Blur, Pulp, Gene, Sleeper, Echobelly, Space, the Bluetones, Shed Seven, Cast and Super Furry Animals), but the return of nineties 'shoe gaze', a 'Gen Z-propelled jungle revival', a 'new wave of British jazz', a new wave of 'Brazil's baile funk scene', the rise of so-called micro trends ('dark plugg', 'evil plugg', 'murderdrill', 'sigilcore', 'sextrance', 'funk putaria'), the continuation of 'dark wave', a raft of 'goth adjacent' bands and ceaseless soundscapes 'capturing the anxiety of a generation'. The multi-hyphenate artist has long been standard, increasingly referred to as 'genre-fluid', 'genre-bending' or 'genre-defying' and arriving from every continent in a world where a 'breakout Los Angeles-based Icelandic-Chinese artist, composer and multi-instrumentalist' is announced in the same week as an Australian/Thai 'effervescent alt-pop artist and fashion curator', alongside a 'Bahrain-via-London' duo fusing 'the rich musical traditions of the SWANA region (South West Asia and North Africa) with 'Egyptian folk, Turkish psych, Algerian rai, Sudanese funk, Ethiopian jazz, and Khaleeji disco'. Everything is 'mosaic', the past glimmering through the prism of the present into a future where '3D audio and spatial sound' is emerging alongside music increasingly made, in its entirety, by AI and crafted uniquely for you.

Lyrical themes, meanwhile, turn ever more introspective, fixated on personal trauma: vulnerability, loss, death, suicide, regret, self-loathing, solitude, guilt, insecurity, obsession, revenge, body dysmorphia, anxiety, depression, gaslighting, loneliness, self-acceptance, self-care, healing, endless therapy (one indie pop outfit disclosed, in earnest, 'all of our therapists were a huge influence on this album'). No wonder, perhaps, we have the concept of the hitherto counterintuitive and increasingly well-attended Wellness Festival. Today's Glastonbury, sometime cradle of the counterculture populated by mystical druids literally on acid, can be an exercise in, er, exercise, where lockdown-famed fitness dude Joe Wicks leads the be-shorted masses in lunge-along aerobics.

Even Download Festival in Leicestershire, formerly Monsters of Rock at Donington Park, has 'pivoted', with artists and revellers now encouraged to live their best lives, decades after their forebears were determinedly living their *worst* lives. The Outpost stage at Download 2025 included live fire cooking demos, primitive skills workshops (Paddle Carving, Moccasin Making), chilli eating competitions and wellness mornings plus food and beverage offerings from the non-alcoholic LoNo Bar and vegan brand No Frickin' Chicken. Over in Cheshire every summer, Fearne Cotton's Happy Place Festival is an alcohol-free, vegetarian, bunting-bedecked jamboree where the japes on offer include: a 'Sound & Healing' teepee featuring gong bath meditations, a 'Yoga & Stretch' teepee featuring yin yoga, face yoga, laughter yoga, 'Untangling ADHD on the Mat: from Struggle to Strength' yoga, and workshops throughout including 'Crafting a Felt Flower Make Up Bag', 'Reiki Energy Healing', 'the Gut-Brain Connection', 'I Am Joy', 'An Adventure Through the Kingdom of Kindness', 'Discover the Power of Tapping', 'Men's Breathwork Experience', 'Baboo the Unusual Bee Storytelling and Craft Activity', 'Upbeat Handpan Set with the Handpan Gentlemen', 'Finding My Superpowers with Little Tweaks', 'Wand Making with Alice', 'Hormone House Party Panel', 'Affirmation Taper Candle Painting Workshop with Crouch End Candles', and (let yourself go people!) 'Live DJ Set with Denise Van Outen' . . .

It *is* all over. For me, at least. I belong to the Past, in lifestyle, worldview, values, attitude, interests, sense of humour and purpose upon the face of the Earth. Here in my dotage, I not only don't fit in, I can't possibly keep up, and no longer even want to. Today, besides forty years of artists across the permanent nostalgia circuit who will seemingly live forever (if not in reality, in holographic eternity), pop culture's infinite ocean comprises a handful of whale-sized megastars powering through prey-rich waters, above ten billion bottom feeders sustained on a mouthful of algae. Either way, none of this is meant for me anyway, which is absolutely as it should be. If anything, here on the old folks' pop bus on the coastline, clutching my bus pass, staring across said ocean at the young people enjoying themselves, it's a relief. My message to them is, in fact, enjoy yourselves *more*. If you think life is serious now, wait 'til you're in your fifties.

It's *always* later than you think.

In summer 2024 I met up with Lias Saoudi again, hoping a late-thirties millennial could help an old timer like me better understand today's alien landscape. By then he'd already been preparing his post-music 'exit strategy', now both Fat Whites frontman and searingly analytical writer, a columnist and author whose punishingly confessional 2023 memoir *Ten Thousand Apologies (Fat White Family and the Miracle of Failure)* was a *Sunday Times* bestseller.

He ambled into his reassuringly old-school local, the Joiner's Arms boozer in Camberwell, South London, still a slight figure, dressed in a graphic-illustrated white T-shirt and a khaki, multi-pocketed utility waistcoat, conjuring the ghost of Travis Bickle in *Taxi Driver*, pre-mohawk. Five years on and he was a notably more sober character in every way: I bought him a non-alcoholic beer which, alongside my soda water, cost a frankly criminal £7.20. He'd toured with the Fat Whites throughout Europe that year both alcohol and drug-free, a lifetime first, including the Glastonbury performance where he appeared naked other than heavy-duty flesh-coloured ladies' tights featuring alarming bulges either side of his hips, and one at his groin – smuggled-in sandwiches, which he then fished out of his tights, took a bite of, and threw into a clearly bewildered crowd.

Of this unexpected sobriety, he was resigned. 'The cracks were beginning to show. I'm thirty-eight now. The price [physically and mentally] just goes up and up and up.' Post-Glastonbury performance, though, he'd had 'a bit of a night' and then a month off partying in Berlin. 'That's where I go to do drugs and get all psychedelic, it still appeals to me.' Sipping his beer-flavoured water, he contemplated the 'dismantlement' of the rock'n'roll spirit, something he'd been witnessing since the late nineties – 'not that anything interesting hasn't happened since, but it's all derivative' – its corrosion then escalated by the incoming digital era and today's all-seeing surveillance culture.

'People are scared in the arts,' he lamented. 'Whether it's music, publishing, whatever, there's a general quiet terror that seeped in and never really left. This *plague* of self-censorship. This post-post-post-post-post-post-post-punk thing that we seem to be in forever, bands that *sound* post-punk but with the danger, menace and fucked-up-ness extracted so things are efficient. Provocation for provocation's sake, it just isn't worth it anymore. Every fucking statement has to be about gender, race. And it's your *art*. Your primary focus should be making something that actually engages with the human spirit, that helps you transcend the everyday.'

He was unimpressed with the identical nature of today's righteous, political flag-waving.

'I think it's riding to a certain extent a wave of post-colonial self-loathing, it's sanctioned, prescriptive rebelliousness,' he was certain. 'Because who the fuck would dare do otherwise? When you're forever exiled and there wasn't any money to begin with.'

He saw a perfect storm creating a dearth of working-class

creatives: zero money in the era of free music, no state support for the arts, small venues shutting down.

'I think in the future there'll be two types of bands,' he predicted. 'There'll be Taylor Swift. And Sleaford Mods. That's it! A mega type. And a bunch of guys travelling around with laptops, cos that's all you can fucking do anymore: make your shit at home, bring a laptop out, you don't need to pay for tech or sound or engineers or lighting rigs or a bus. The socio-economic specificities of the mid-twentieth century onward, that golden patch, that was *that*.'

Humans today, he carried on, were turning into machines, playing a social media-collated numbers game, 'people as streams of code, a pure mechanisation of our cultural sphere, just algorithmic liquid capital,' our lifestyles in thrall to health and monitored daily by wearable sensory technology and data-driven apps.

'There can be no chaos!' he spluttered. 'No room for error. No more "fool for a day". It's death by sheer reason. It's life by spreadsheet! It's what happens when you engage with everything at the level of materialism. Why would you wanna squander half of your week recovering from an acid experience in a field? Everything has to be maximised. Streamlined. We're all just part of this technological, post-human nightmare.'

We contemplated a Gen Z both obsessed with and traumatised by money, striving for extravagantly well-paid jobs, for whom the internet had created the most self-conscious and aggressively competitive generation in history.

'It's turned everybody into their own mad little venture capitalist,' he balked. 'It gives everybody the illusion of being their own captain of industry. This simulacrum of your *brand* and your *followers* and your *reach*, these little metrics, human life broken down into scores and numbers. It's truly dystopian, y'know? But not in a romantic, *Blade Runner* kind of dystopia, it's an incredibly banal dystopia, lame and disturbingly fucking servile.'

And causing all manner of mental health disasters . . .

'It's a mental health fucking apocalypse!' he exclaimed. 'And the remedy is always more therapy. More medication. It's never: maybe the underpinnings of this system are actually making people jump off cliffs, en masse. It's turning people into self-lobotomising automatons. I think this is where nationalism has a resurgence. Essentially, it's nostalgia, for a bygone era when the nation state actually had some influence. It doesn't. If you live in a corporate, globalised system, there isn't a party you can vote in that will actually change anything, because it's beyond the reach of any party. Power exists somewhere else. But people haven't fully accepted that. So ideas of nationhood and identity are seeing a resurgence *everywhere* in the West. But none of those fucking people [the far-right parties] can change anything either. It's just the absolutely out of control technological dystopic machine calling the shots. It's a complete runaway.'

His most alarming theory, however, on the erosion of youthful rebellion, was that it hadn't disappeared, it had been corrupted and diverted onto social media, where so many angry, abusive and outright violent voices are heard, ever more loudly, in acts of anonymous insurrection.

'Your garrulous, alienated teenager that's full of a will to extremity,' he suggested, 'all those countercultural energies which might have found their way down to the pub or into this band or a scene or a subculture or *something*, they're now soaked up into the digisphere. Into these personal, pocket propagandisation machines [phones] that are curated specifically to your personal whims, fears, desires and antagonisms. The internet births extremities, because people can find people on the other side of the world, in a bedroom, in Texas, and coagulate around truly mad, poisonous points of view, and build communities online. The alt-right, that's where the edge lords are now. That's where the edge lording goes down, whereas before it was something you associated with the left. As was freedom of expression. It's a dangerous and inevitable result of the social media landscape.'

Here in the mid-2020s Lias spent far more time reading than he ever did listening to music and was currently writing a new book, while the Fat Whites carried on, their notorious years behind them. Today he acknowledged his youthfully exuberant on-stage shit-smearing and protest-wanking (another of his 'art'-prank ruses) had been both a reaction to the early 2010s 'ultra banal fucking [indie] landfill zone' and a homage, 'an acknowledgement of our founding fathers, of Lou Reed and Iggy Pop – this was no new ground, why do we look back to the seventies and think, "Wow, things were crazy then, what happened to that?"'

We contemplated the recent tour and his sandwiches-down-tights malarkey.

'I had a baguette down there for a while, which kind of curled round the side,' he cackled, throatily. 'Again, we're supposed to be conscious of problematic masculinity now. Eyes down, for the *millennia* of patriarchy we must atone! And I just think, *not tonight*, d'youknowhatImean? You guys have got that covered, would you check the size of *this!?* Just take the opposite and run with it until you become a kind of cartoon. It's a tendency to play the villain, another thing that's really gone.'

He finished up his non-beery beer.

'Game's up,' he concluded, matter-of-factly. 'Young people envious of their parents' culture. Parents thinking their kids need to behave in a more chaotic way. Free expression being the preserve of the right. None of these things have any precedent. They're new and they're signifiers of real decline. It's like, everything we love about the world is dying.'

'Oh no!' I shrieked, unable to bear this devastating analysis, as truthful as it felt.

'But I still wanna have a family!' he reassured. 'And you've got to *try* and uphold the flame. Maybe if you live long enough, you'll be like a kind of high priest, that's the positive: I remember before the internet, when we had this thing called culture.'

Alexandra Palace, 28 May 2025

The seventy-eight-year-old Iggy Pop was stalking the stage like a leathery rock'n'roll shaman, shirt off, dirty blonde hair plunging onto lithesome shoulders, not so different to how he'd stalked the stage in his Stooges days back in the early seventies, and every decade thereafter. He now stalked, yes, with a wonky gait, the result of both the osteoarthritis in his right hip and the scoliosis of his spine, meaning one leg is an inch and a half shorter than the other, his weathered, tawny, crumple-skinned body like some tiny, 200-year-old willow tree, limbs bent-to-breaking but defiantly unbowed. He was still the Iggy Pop I fell in love with in 1979 and tonight he was singing a song from the *New Values* album which brought him to me, 'I'm Bored': I heard the same sandpaper vocal and euphorically lawless attitude which captivated a teenage soul like mine, searching for some kind of new value, for something more than a life which would leave me, as Iggy howled, 'chairman of the bored!'

I'd no idea back then of his already singular legacy, of how he not so much defined the very edge of rock'n'roll, but invented much of it, the freedom-fighting, drug-berserk, performance-art prankster, cock out (enormous), rolling around in broken glass, pioneer of the stage dive, held aloft on his feet by a fevered crowd, wearing white make-up, a bow tie and silver lamé gloves. As far back as '72, during his UK debut at London's King Cross Cinema, in silver pants, lipstick and panda-smudged eyeliner, clambering all over a bedazzled crowd, he inspired two audience members, John Lydon and Mick Jones, to either join or form a band, leading to the Sex Pistols and the Clash. Ever since he'd been the talismanic figure who chose art over commerce, remained penniless until middle age in the 1990s (discovered by millions through the 1996 *Trainspotting* soundtrack with 'Lust For Life' and 'Nightclubbing') and today, to survive in the hyper-capitalist twenty-first century, unapologetically appears in commercial ads, his latest campaign in 2025 for Dom Pérignon champagne named 'Creation Is an Eternal Journey'. To which I say a mighty 'Cheers!' and hope he's laughing even *harder* all the way to the bank than Billy Idol.

Out on the Great Hall floor of Alexandra Palace, I'd not long turned sixty, there with a lifelong buddy, Gilly B, my housemate back in the late eighties, both of us then in our early twenties, she a fellow escapee from the troublesome provinces (Belfast) and fellow teenage goth-haired, post-punk devotee, who remains a stylish art-rock vision today, without the bouffant fright-wig. She, too, would turn sixty this year and tonight was my birthday gift to her. The 10,000-capacity venue fizzed with Gen X Iggy devotees, alongside a significant turnout from the Young People, thrilled faces everywhere as Iggy played the hits, his muscular young band bouncing through the sing-along la la la's of 'The Passenger' (after which Iggy bellowed, 'fucking bless you!'), the rambunctious 'Lust For Life', the driving drone of 'I Wanna Be Your Dog', the propulsive groove of 'Nightclubbing' . . .

Suddenly, Iggy was inching open the lid of an upended

on-stage coffin lined in scarlet velvet, now blaring out 'Real Wild Child (Wild One)', as he hopped inside, leaving an arm outside supposedly waving us goodbye, before leaping out again, not yet ready for the box, to shrieks of cackling delight. We looked at each other, my old pal and me, beaming, tears spilling in our glistening, ancient eyes.

On nights like Iggy Pop at Ally Pally it doesn't seem to matter so much what's culturally ebbed away, when so much of it is still here. As Iggy so defiantly is: his unique back story and lifetime's work available to us all, at any time, forever, for anyone who cares in our infinitely atomised free-for-all. The young people I now encounter, meanwhile, through both work and daily life, continually tell me about their favourite bands: the Smiths, Oasis, the Cure, Fleetwood Mac, with the occasional nod to Ireland's contemporary post-punk herberts Fontaines DC. Primark today constantly sells all-our-yesterdays band and artist's T-shirts: Nirvana, Sex Pistols, Blur, Rolling Stones, Guns N' Roses, Green Day, Korn, Black Sabbath, Elvis, the Cure, Jimi Hendrix, Iron Maiden, Bruce Springsteen, Shania Twain, Nickelback (!), the Offspring, Imagine Dragons, Tupac, AC/DC, Johnny Cash, the Beatles, the Ramones, Blondie, Pink Floyd, Kurt Cobain, the Who, Slipknot, Ozzy Osbourne, Kiss, David Bowie, Ziggy Stardust and – the full roster flying a stamp-sized flag for the twenty-first century – Olivia Rodrigo, Ariana Grande, Burna Boy, Post Malone, Troye Sivan, Morgan Wallen, Sabrina Carpenter and Billie Eilish. It's a now permanent, inevitable, out-of-time development, a consequence of the everything-all-at-once digital era and simply how culture rolls today. And I can only hope, genuinely, that ver kids of today get as much out of my day as I did.

And for us old timers, who lived it all in thrilling real-time, as a lanky bass-playing Welshman in a feather boa once said: 'Fuck me we were lucky, to have that.' Like him, Johnny Marr and millions more, music gave me my life. It gave me the education which counted, a purpose, a belief system, a life-affirming adventure and a lifetime's work, with all the risk and repercussion that entails to this day. It spectacularly bolstered all of my friendships, underpinned a lifetime of thrills, sorrow and laughter, it even brought me the love of my life. So I say once again, like Abba, who changed my life even before Iggy, thank you for the music. It doesn't matter to me one scintilla that, at the time of writing in summer 2025, weedy Alex Warren has been blubbing away at No. 1 for *months*.

From where I'm sitting today, in fact, it looks like my generation, Generation X, turned out to be the most fortunate possibly in history. Who grew up in progressive times, in a liberal democracy, financially supported by a welfare state. In affordable times, when rents didn't cripple us, and home ownership dreams were realised. In creative times, when the arts not only took risks, but were valued and actually paid for. In independent times, when we pretty much brought ourselves up, outdoors, and only went home, under duress, for tea. In analogue adolescent times, spent constantly with friends who wrote amusing letters to each other when we moved away, and the word 'isolation' only applied to a Joy Division song. In DIY times, when we made our own luck through imagination, resilience and boundless belief. In socially transformative times, when protest and activism forced laws towards equality across race, gender and sexuality, with varying degrees of success, even if we did think sex could kill us through AIDS (with leaflets through our letter boxes, 'Don't Die of Ignorance', telling us all about it). In community-minded times, with a belief in collective consciousness, when 'we' took precedence over 'I'. In relatively stable geopolitical times, when we weren't threatened, daily, by the prospect of World War III even if we *were* threatened, daily, by the prospect of nuclear war (with more leaflets through our letter boxes, 'Protect and Survive', telling us all about it). In far less apocalyptically bombarded times, when the news didn't bring us every second of every day images of a world on fire, of ecosystems dying, of blown-up children, of mass starvation, of millions upon millions of people increasingly displaced by war, oppression and genocide. In technologically transformative times when personal computers were new and their impact overwhelmingly positive. In silly times, when daft jokes, absurdism and irreverence ruled, and no one was ever offended. And even if we were never truly free, we felt it.

For those, however, who are a product of these seemingly overwhelmingly stressful times, remember: there is always an alternative. And you're smart. Maybe the smartest of all time. Eras pass, cycles spin and the Man, occasionally, *can* be overthrown. And adversity, throughout history, tends to lead to creative brilliance. Meanwhile, you're welcome to all our old music, and everything else we've ever invented which might be any good. You have your infinitely boggling technology, a righteous political fury, an average lifespan of 109 and enviably excellent teeth. Everything else is your imagination. So use it well.

It's a wild world and a wild ride. And it's all yours, now, the Kids.

CREDITS

'Kings of the Wild Frontier' — Adam & the Ants
Words & Music by Adam Ant & Marco Pirroni; © 1980 CBS
Records

'ridicule is nothing to be scared of'
'Prince Charming' — Adam & the Ants
Words & Music by Adam Ant & Marco Pirroni; © 1981 CBS
Records

7.　　THERE IS A LIGHT - *Johnny Marr*

'you could meet somebody …'
'How Soon Is Now?' — The Smiths
Words by Morrissey; Music by Johnny Marr; © 1984 Rough
Trade Records

11.　　THEIR LAW - *The Prodigy*

'… fuck 'em all … an' their laaaw!'
'Their Law' — The Prodigy
Words & Music by Liam Howlett, Adam Mole, Graham Crabb,
Kerry Hammond, Clint Mansell, Richard March & Fuzz
Townshend; © 1994 XL

14.　　SHIZZLE MY NIZZLE - *Snoop Dogg*

'Da-da-da-da-dah … Daaaawg!'
'Who Am I (What's My Name)?' — Snoop Dogg
Words & Music by Calvin Broadus & Andre Young (plus
sample-writers George Clinton, Garry Shider & David
Spradley); © 1993 Death Row/Interscope Records

18.　　AIN'T NUTHIN TA F'WIT - *Wu-Tang Clan*

'… a free kid gets arrested …'
'White Lines (Don't Don't Do It)' — Grandmaster Flash &
Melle Mel

Words & Music by Melle Mel (Melvin Glover) & Sylvia
Robinson; © 1983 Sugar Hill Records

19.   WHAT A WASTER – *Pete Doherty*

'It's a long way to Tipperaraaaaay!'
'It's a Long Way to Tipperary'
Words & Music by Jack Judge & Harry Williams; published
1912; © (original publisher) John F. Warner & Sons

'Michael Row The Boat Ashooooore, Halleilooooojah!'
'Michael, Row the Boat Ashore'
Traditional African American spiritual; first published 1867 in
Slave Songs of the United States. 'Trad.'

ACKNOWLEDGEMENTS

Raging Within The Machine

Furtive handshakes from the infiltrator to The Team at Fleet (Little, Brown) for their belief, encouragement and guidance: Rhiannon Smith, Caitlin Landuyt, Matilda Singer and Stephanie Melrose.

Raging Against The Machine

Comrade salutes to all the eds, features eds, reviews eds and commissioning eds who sent me off into-the-field to roll with the loony-tune renegades featured in this book: at *NME*, *Q*, *The Word*, *Mojo*, *Big Issue* and the *Guardian*, with special appreciations to Ted Kessler and Mark Ellen. Further salutes to PR outlaws Tony Linkin, Ted Cummings, Steve Phillips and Susie Ember. Up the Revolution! to Kevin 'Agent P' Pocklington. And love forever (it's official) to my man on the inside, a true outsider, Simon Goddard.

RAISING READERS
Books Build Bright Futures

Dear Reader,

We'd love your attention for one more page to tell you about the crisis in children's reading, and what we can all do.

Studies have shown that reading for fun is the **single biggest predictor of a child's future life chances** – more than family circumstance, parents' educational background or income. It improves academic results, mental health, wealth, communication skills, ambition and happiness.[1]

The number of children reading for fun is in rapid decline. Young people have a lot of competition for their time. In 2024, 1 in 10 children and young people in the UK aged 5 to 18 did not own a single book at home.[2]

Hachette works extensively with schools, libraries and literacy charities, but here are some ways we can all raise more readers:

- Reading to children for just 10 minutes a day makes a difference
- Don't give up if children aren't regular readers – there will be books for them!
- Visit bookshops and libraries to get recommendations
- Encourage them to listen to audiobooks
- Support school libraries
- Give books as gifts

There's a lot more information about how to encourage children to read on our website: **www.RaisingReaders.co.uk**

Thank you for reading.

---

[1] OECD, '21st-Century Readers: Developing Literacy Skills in a Digital World', 2021, https://www.oecd.org/en/publications/21st-century-readers_a83d84cb-en.html

[2] National Literacy Trust, 'Book Ownership in 2024', November 2024, https://literacytrust.org.uk/research-services/research-reports/book-ownership-in-2024